Organization and Management Innovation

Series Editor: M. Sulzberger

Springer
Berlin
Heidelberg
New York
Hong Kong
London
Milan
Paris
Tokyo

Oskar Grün

Taming Giant Projects

Management
of Multi-Organization Enterprises

With 72 Figures and 31 Tables

 Springer

Professor Dr. Oskar Grün
Vienna University of Economics
and Business Administration
Augasse 2–6
A-1090 Wien
oskar.gruen@wu-wien.ac.at

Printed with support of *Bundesministerium für Bildung, Wissenschaft und Kultur* in Wien.

ISBN 3-540-21440-2 Springer-Verlag Berlin Heidelberg New York

Cataloging-in-Publication Data:
Library of Congress Control Number: 2004104222

Springer-Verlag is a part of Springer Science+Business Media

springeronline.com

© Springer-Verlag Berlin · Heidelberg 2004
Printed in Germany

Hardcover-Design: Erich Kirchner, Heidelberg

SPIN 10998366   43/3130-5 4 3 2 1 0 – Printed on acid-free paper

Foreword

Hardly any topic in today's management theory and practice is as important, complex and controversial and leads to heated discussions as project management. No company, public entity or non profit organization can refrain from realizing small, medium size or big projects in its quest for growth and development in an ever more rapidly changing corporate environment.

Tools how to do books about project management are legion. Consultants, dedicated schools and research institutes are a dime a dozen. These huge resources should easily guarantee success. Reality, however, looks quite different; the failure rate of small, medium and especially big projects is still enormous. Even when measured over a period of many years, the learning curve has been disappointingly flat. The resulting damage destroys stakeholder value, wastes time and money, crushes the motivation of the participants; and in many cases the tax payer is asked to pick up the bill. There is clearly a need to improve this situation in order to reduce the losses, to garner support and to foster trust and motivation for upcoming projects.

Multi-Organization Enterprises (MOE) are the most demanding of all project categories. Their size alone pits their expected enormous value creation against the risks of equally significant damage. The involvement of various constituencies, be it stakeholders representing a vast variety of interests, orders, mandates, political responsibilities and not least, personal pride, ensure high complexity. This is a haven for entrepreneurs, all vying to maximize their professional reputation and to benefit from the unique opportunity to invent at the bleeding edge of creation and be associated with new solutions. The long time horizon with its inherent silent power of time and the huge budgets at stake create the impression at the beginning of a project that anything is possible. Finally, public opinion, primarily represented by the media, plays a big role in creating positive or negative stories. One very specific aspect is the fact that most people involved have only a once-in-a-life-time opportunity to participate in a Multi-Organization Enterprise. This complicates the transfer of experience, hampers learning and makes the application of lessons learnt virtually impossible.

With his work, Oskar Grün presents a unique contribution to this key topic in today's societies. The sound theoretical foundation is followed by a detailed analysis of five real Multi-Organization Enterprises (Olympic Games, big hospitals, and a huge wind energy converter). Important data and material is presented for the first time, providing new insights. The comparison of strengths and weaknesses of these MOE creates a vast source of lessons learnt. With his work, Grün is contributing a significant piece of research to the state of the art theory of project management. The text contains a lot of facts, information and thoughts which can facilitate the realization of MOE. Finally, the book is easy to read, invites reflection and brings back memories of big events over the past years.

I am proud that the work of Oskar Grün is published in the series of the Swiss Association for Organization and Management. This unique piece of work fits very well into the series and represents a significant enhancement.

It is my wish that a lot of interested decision makers in project management and general management benefit from the important message of this work, enjoy the reading and arouse the attention for this key topic.

Markus Sulzberger

President of the Foundation of the
Swiss Association for Organization and Management

Preface: Message of this Book and for Whom it is Intended

What have the tower of Babel and a large wind energy converter like GROWIAN in common? Both are Multi-Organization Enterprises (MOEs) and both failed: The tower of Babel because of pure coordination problems (Babylonian language confusion), the GROWIAN because of its sophisticated technology.

Other giant building projects like the Panama Canal and revolutionary engineering projects such as the moon-landing could be successfully performed despite great challenges for management and technology. But the fate of the tower of Babel and of GROWIAN could repeat itself at any time. The taming of giant projects does not always succeed as the cases of the Concorde aircraft, the Transrapid train, the railway tunnel under the English Channel and the Millennium Dome in London demonstrate; they either failed because of substantial technical or commercial problems or they experienced serious crises.

The project owners of MOEs are still facing enormous technical, financial, and schedule risks. They are, therefore, the primary addressees of this book. It should help them to estimate the risks of giant projects more accurately and thus to limit them by adequate management measures.

Not only project owners but also project managers can gain from the expertise acquired in the case-study analyses of five large-scale projects and additional construction projects, transportation systems and mega events. Furthermore, we address the managers of contracting companies of large-scale projects, who can substantially contribute to the success of MOEs but also take enormous risks by participating in MOEs. The design of this book facilitates its use for academic teaching.

The author would like to thank the following people. Firstly those who opened their files knowing that our analysis would show not only successes and a high level of management performance but also failures and weaknesses in management. Jürgen Hauschildt und Jörn Pulczynski extended our empirical base by an additional case study. Susanne Riedler critically reviewed the first draft of this book, Marc Dressler and Alexander Koch were engaged in later versions. My colleague, Helmut Haschka, carefully reviewed the final draft. Markus Sulzberger and Robert Zaugg encouraged me to place the book in the series of publications of the Swiss Society for Organization (SGO). The Austrian Federal Ministry of Education, Science, and Culture promoted the printing by a considerable subsidy.

Vienna, March 2004   Oskar Grün

Table of Contents

Part One: A New Challenge for Project Management

A.   Big Projects – Big Problems

Multi-Organization Enterprises (MOEs) are commonly used to accomplish a mission either in technology, economy, culture, or politics. They are apt to meet challenges like developing space technology, improving public facilities (traffic, health services, and power supplies), hosting international events (like Olympic Games) or changing the social, economic, and ecological standards in developing and industrialized countries.

I.   MOEs: Giants Among Projects

Before addressing specific characteristics and problems of MOEs it may be helpful to remember the basic ideas and the evolution of projects and project management.

1. Basic Characteristics

The term "project" became common in the 1950s and 1960s to describe outstanding undertakings like the development of highly sophisticated weapons systems or the missiles and aerospace program "Mercury". As the idea of projects and project management was applied to R&D activities (including software-engineering), to internal development programs, e.g. organizational restructuring, to construction, and to the services industry (including non-profit services like social services), the variety of projects in terms of technical performance, size etc. increased enormously. Nevertheless, we can illustrate the basic characteristics as well as their variety in intensity in a simple scheme, as shown in Fig. 1 (the nature and the number of the project owners are discussed later on).

Singularity means that projects are unique. Singularity can refer to new goals, e.g. man on the moon, or to new dimensions of well known goals. An example of the latter case is the construction of a large university hospital by a construction company that has constructed only small hospitals so far. Singularity also means achieving well known goals under changed conditions like time pressure or other limited resources.

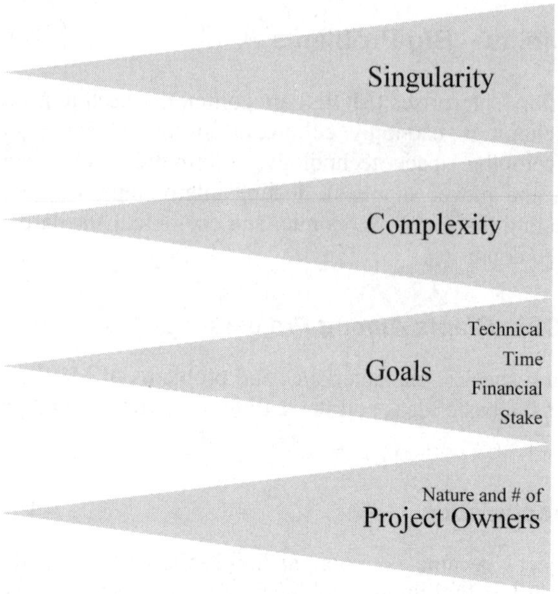

Fig. 1. Characteristics of Projects

Singularity ranges from undertakings which are nearly routine tasks to highly innovative undertakings. Accordingly, the project management faces low or high risk. As innovations include the unfamiliarity of individuals or institutions with a task or a situation, projects are always risky. Good project management can merely help to limit the risks.

Complexity is determined by the number of activities and milestones, and the number of participants who need to be coordinated to achieve the project goals. Complexity ranges from a few activities, dates and participants involved to hundreds of thousands of activities (many of them critical with respect to other activities and to the overall project schedule) and to thousands of internal and external participants of different industries representing a broad variety of professions and interests like suppliers, contractors, consultants, and legal authorities. In addition, complex projects (MOEs) often require know-how in different fields, such as engineering (construction, structural, electromechanic, electronic) and management (legal, financial, administrative).

Goal-orientation means the intention to achieve technical, time and financial goals which are formulated for a specific undertaking. Usually these goals are not readily available but the result of a separate goal-formulating process.

Technical goals determine the quality and quantity of the project output, e.g. a university hospital is required to provide a specific number of beds as well as to keep up with the latest medical and technological developments. Special tools such as space and functional requirements may help to specify the technical out-put.

Time goals either determine a fixed date or a time period within which the project is to be completed. This inherent time limit underlines the temporary and therefore "unique" nature of projects. The time goal for the entire project may be divided into sub-goals for parts, phases, or even single activities of the project.

Financial goals define the financial resources for the project. Therefore, both the budgeting of the project and the generation of sufficient funds are part of the goal formulation process. Unachieved financial goals, i.e. cost overruns, are – apart from schedule overruns – the most striking failures in project management.

Human resource aspects like leadership styles and interpersonal skills are not treated as a separate goal in this study but are taken into consideration as an important issue of management structure and management capacity in Chapter J.

Project management aims at achieving an *overall performance* which consequently requires a holistic view of technical, time, and financial goals (multiple goal-settings). Often, the relationship between the project goals is neither complementary nor neutral but rather conflicting, especially if the goals represent different stakeholders. The users of a facility may be interested in maximizing technical performance, whereas the project owners work towards minimizing constru-ction and operation & maintenance costs.

A special goal conflict refers to the *short-term vs. long-term orientation.* The short-term orientation with respect to completion costs of the project may differ substantially from the long-term orientation regarding costs of operation & main-tenance. The life-cycle concept requires the consideration of both perspectives.

The trade-off between conflicting goals is a crucial part of the goal formulation process, which often extends over the whole length of the project. We know about goal discussions and goal shifts even after project completion in order to justify the project (see the cases of Olympic Games Lake Placid and GROWIAN). Often the goals have to be reformulated when it becomes evident that their achievement is impossible.

The final aspect of the goal-orientation refers to the *stake* of the project owners in the outcome of the project. The question for judging the stake in a project is: "Would failure to complete the job on schedule or within the budget entail serious penalties for the company?" (Stewart 1965, p.59). The stake is high if the achievement of the project goals is immediately relevant for the success or even for the survival of the project owners, or if a repetition of the project is impossible for a long time once it has failed. The stake is low, if the failure of the project can be offset by the success of future undertakings, e.g. other R&D-projects.

2. MOEs as Challenge for Project Management

MOEs are *large-scale undertakings* ("giants") which may involve huge numbers of employees from different organizations (esp. different project owners, contrac-tors) and other participants. MOEs usually require the common effort, especially the funds of *more than one project owner* ("multi-organization"). The project owners may differ in the type of ownership (private, public), in size, in organizational characteristics, in management structure, and in their incentive system. They often differ in their stake concerning the outcome of the project. The project management of MOEs faces the problem of matching the interests of all project owners (not to mention the interests of other participants). Inherent goal-conflicts among the project owners usually rule out the possibility of performing the project as part of one project owner's organization. It requires a *project-specific company type of organization ("project company")*, shared by all project owners.[1]

Fig. 2 illustrates that the MOE characteristics (very high ratings for singularity, complexity, stake for at least one of the project owners, and goal conflict) can best be met by the project-specific company type. The project-specific company is the most powerful type of project organization and is totally separated from the parent organizations of the project owners.

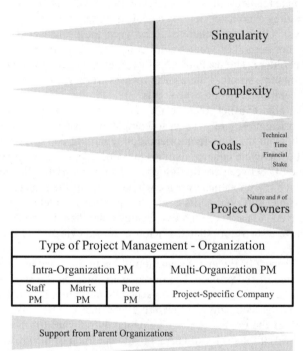

Fig. 2. Types of Project Organization and its Dependence upon the Project Task

Fig. 3 shows the Lake Placid Olympic Organizing Committee (LPOOC) for the Winter Games 1980 as an example of a project company.

---

[1] See also the characteristics of large-scale technological projects (McEachron/Teige 1977, p.III-3).

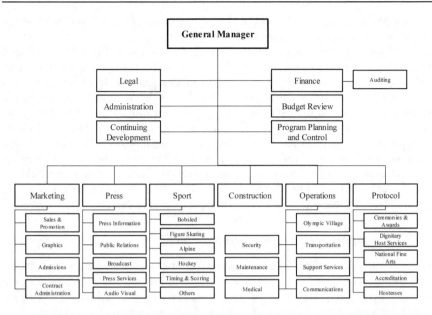

Fig. 3. Lake Placid Olympic Organizing Committee (LPOOC) for the Winter Games 1980

An important reason for establishing a project-specific company for MOEs is to separate the project risk from routine business of the parent organizations. The costs of setting up such a project company are offset by the advantages of a powerful organizational unit concentrating on the project task. The advantages are even more striking if the project company not only has the responsibility for the short-term completion (e.g. the construction of a building) but also for the long-term operation & maintenance.

Empirical findings on MOEs show great deviations in the *achievement of the technical, time, and financial goals*. There are projects with good or, at least, fair performance on all goal dimensions. Yet, MOEs are not only giants in size and level of aspiration but also in risk (Sykes 1982, p.142)[2] and have contributed a great deal to the history of project disasters. Both the successes and the fiascoes can serve as models for improving the project management performance of future undertakings. Improving the management performance of MOEs represents one of the most pressing challenges for today's theory and practice. It has to be seen as a "new dimension" of undertakings and their management.

Turning to the *fiascoes*, studies from the 1980s report excessive optimism in estimating costs and remarkable cost overruns in projects like London's third airport, the Anglo-French Concorde and Sydney's opera house (Perrson 1979, Hall

---

[2] Cost overruns are highly correlated with the size of projects and the difficulty in meeting technical specifications (see Murphy et al. 1974, p.84).

1980, Kharbanda/Stallworthy 1983). Our own case studies leave no doubt that little improvement has been made in managing big projects.[3]

Information concerning recent MOEs like the *Eurotunnel* between France and
Great Britain (delayed operation, doubled construction costs, and disappointing
ticket sales), the *Winter Olympics 1994 in Lillehammer* (a deficit of more than
$700m and insufficient post-Olympic utilization of the facilities)[4], as well as the
Olympic Summer Games 2000 in Sydney (cost explosion) and the *Millennium
Dome in London* indicate the ongoing mismanagement of MOEs. The lack of
transfer of learning from failure has been proven for projects with similar technical goals and socio-political environments. In some cases, the learning transfer
was not even achieved from very recent projects or from preceding undertakings
which had turned out to be obvious failures. Therefore, one of our key issues is to
find out how the learning transfer from one project to another could be achieved.

II.   Approaches to Research on MOEs

We will start with a critical note on the state of the relevant research. The discussion of major problems of research on MOEs will include a reference to our own
research approach. It should be helpful in encouraging and facilitating further research activities in this field and also allows for an evaluation of our findings.

1. Lack of Theory

The evolution of project management is rather recent compared to the history of
outstanding human efforts. We wonder how it was possible to perform outstanding
undertakings like the Egyptian pyramids and other wonders of the ancient world
as well as such remarkable construction works like the Brooklyn Bridge in New
York (1869, see McCullough 1982), and the Grossglockner Alpine Road in Austria (Wallack 1960). Obviously, large-scale projects are not an invention of the
present. The development of special management and organization techniques in
the 1950s, however, has increased the probability that projects can be managed
successfully.

Research on project management is also a "youngster" compared to the well established research on management that started with F.W. Taylor and H. Fayol at
the beginning of the 20th century. Even more immature is the research on MOEs as
a special type of projects. There exists a history of complaints about the inadequate theory on large-scale projects. Sykes (1982, p.141) states that the management of giant projects "...is still more art than science". Obviously, the strengths
and weaknesses of theory have not changed that much. The lack of theory may be
related to, but can not be sufficiently explained by, the only recent beginnings of

---

[3] Flyvberg et al. 2003, p.3, refer to a "performance paradox": "At the same time as many
more and much larger infrastructure projects are being proposed and built around the world,
it is becoming clear that many such projects have strikingly poor performance records in
terms of economy, environment and public support".
[4] Lillehammer Olympiske Organisationskomité 1994

systematic research and the lack of empirical data (see A.II.2). In this context, two additional factors should be noted. One has become known as the *"success-syndrome"*. The other factor is the dominance of descriptive and normative aspects especially in the early phases of the project management discussion (see e.g. Cleland 1964, Steiner/Ryan 1968, Baumgartner 1979).

The "success syndrome" addresses the fact that some very large and very challenging projects have experienced overwhelming success for a long time (see Fig. 4).

Topics	1950–1960	1960–1970	1970–1980	from 1980	Solutions (e.g.)
Planning and Control Techniques					network analysis work breakdown structure computer-based information systems
Structures and Procedures					types of PM multi-PM efficiency of PM contingency factors
Behavioral Aspects					role of project manager conflict in PM re-entry procedures
Managing the Socio-Political Environment					"be-aware" champion
Success Factors					goal formulation/change basic design socio-political environment management structure

Fig. 4. History of Project Management Application and Project Success/Failure

The first significant application of project management in the aerospace industry was based on government requirements for weapons and aerospace systems in the 1950s. It was the beginning of a long series of successful undertakings, such as the Mercury Program (see Swenson et al. 1966). The subsequent adoption of the project management idea in R&D activities and other internal programs like software engineering, restructuring of the organization, and to the construction and heavy equipment industry has not been difficult, as the participants were already familiar with the tasks. The new (project) management system improved the existing management methods, which so far had only met low standards.

The impact of the lasting success series on the development of theory was quite obvious: Project management became a popular management tool and a "modern" sometimes even fashionable topic in literature ("projectitis"). Like most new management methods, the basic ideas of project management were not always fully understood and its implications for the parent organization were often underestimated.

The series of successes ended in the late 1960s and early 1970s when a new dimension was added to MOEs. The conditions under which these projects had to be completed had changed significantly because of the growing skepticism about the benefits of technological progress – and nowadays – because of ecological concerns.

The *dominance of descriptive and normative aspects* has caused additional setbacks in the development of theory. The following Fig. 5 illustrates how different aspects of project management emerged.[5]

Topics	1950–1960	1960–1970	1970–1980	from 1980	Solutions (e.g.)
Planning and Control Techniques					network analysis work breakdown structure computer-based information systems
Structures and Procedures					types of PM multi-PM efficiency of PM contingency factors
Behavioral Aspects					role of project manager conflict in PM re-entry procedures
Managing the Socio-Political Environment					"be-aware" champion
Success Factors					goal formulation/change basic design socio-political environment management structure

Fig. 5. "Life Cycle" of Project Management Topics

The initial discussions concentrated on the basic ideas, the techniques, and the different types of project management. An incredible amount of resources was spent on developing and teaching techniques like network analysis, thus encouraging the misconception that the potential of network analysis alone guarantees project success. In the late 1960s, the discussion shifted to behavioral aspects for a better understanding and control of the human factor in project management, e.g. leadership styles, interpersonal skills, interpersonal conflicts, and re-entry problems. More recently, the management of the socio-political environment (as a response to the growing difficulties with external skeptics as well as outright opponents of MOEs, see Chapter I), and the integration of short-term and long-term aspects within the life cycle concept have become major topics.

Project management literature focused on the description of the contemporary standard of tools (like network analysis and work breakdown structure) usually

---

[5] See Baker/Wilemon 1977

combined with the normative recommendation to use them. The implicit message was: Project success is closely related to the use of the tools described. There was a marked deficit in the identification of the variables, the indication of their effects and the formulation of explicit hypotheses to be tested. Due to the lack and incompatibility of empirical studies, the theory of project management could not adequately respond to the practical requirements, especially to the problem of how to assess project success.

With the growing awareness of the socio-political environment and the occurrence of remarkable project failures the "naive" theoretical approach became obsolete. Literature took notice of context factors like the capacity or maturity of the parent organization and dealt with different methods of measuring the achievement of multiple goals. The emerging theoretical and empirical research on complex decision-making and innovations served as a driving force for intensified and more sophisticated research on MOEs. Projects (especially R&D projects) became a subject of decision-making and innovation theory. Their impact on project management research is obvious concerning the process of goal formulation and change, the role of promoters (see Witte et al. 1988), and the methods to measure the performance of projects. Pure descriptive and normative approaches are losing relevance in favor of statements formulated as hypotheses suitable for empirical tests.

2. Lack and Incompatibility of Empirical Studies

Due to the long-term character and complexity of MOEs, extraordinary efforts are required to meet the standards of sound empirical research. One reason for the shortage of empirical studies is the *remarkable workload* involved. Research on MOEs requires a significant amount of fieldwork. The idea of conducting MOE research from the "university desk" lacks realism. After having overcome the access barriers to data bases – per se a very time consuming task, often beyond the control of the researcher – a research strategy has to be formulated for every study on every single MOE. Hence, general rules on describing MOEs do not exist and the available data bases differ substantially. The relevant data bases and the methods of investigation which again depend on the substance of the data base, the research goals (specified by the hypotheses to be set up or tested) and, finally, the research capacity have to be considered.

Difficulties arise regardless of whether the data base is detailed or poor. In the case of detailed project information, a lot of research capacity is needed for reviewing and selecting the data base. In the case of poor project information, it is hard to find sufficient material for empirical verification. We also have to keep in mind that the lack of theory (see above) increases the workload. Well-defined variables and their connection to the hypotheses serve as guidelines when choosing the data bases; their absence will necessarily broaden the empirical research because the research team tends to maximize the volume of data to allow for a widespread retrieval process.

The most comprehensive empirical studies on MOEs deal with *public MOEs*.[6] As a rule, there is a greater availability of records when the fiasco is huge and the project is public; conversely, few records are available for unsuccessful private MOEs. Public projects are more likely to be addressed in political discussions, in hearings, and in audits, especially in the case of remarkable failures or even disasters. We have to keep this in mind when it comes to the question of how accurately our findings on five public MOEs represent the wide variety of MOEs.

Are public MOEs more likely to end in failures or even disasters? Is it justifiable to correlate success with the private and failures or fiascoes with the public sector? The fact is that project difficulties are not restricted to the public sector. One of a few empirical studies valid for comparing the success or failure of projects in the private sector with those in the public sector (conducted by Murphy et al. 1974), is based on a sample of about 650 responses. About one third of the projects covered by the study is public, about two thirds are private. Although the authors reveal specific features unique to private or to public projects, the study shows that there is no significant difference in the actual cost and schedule overruns in respect of private or public ownership.[7]

What are the implications for our study? First, when dealing with MOEs, it is not necessary to distinguish between their public or private nature. Second, we can analyze and illustrate the problems of MOEs using cases from the public sector. If we single out their success factors the management of both public and private projects will win.

Unfortunately, the lack of empirical data compounds the problem of the *incompatibility of data sources*.[8] The incompatibility of data basically results from the singularity of MOEs and correlates with the innovation rate of MOEs, their difference in size and variety of application, e.g. building a power plant in an industrialized country vs. starting a health program in a developing country. The problem of incompatibility can be reduced by sampling MOEs with identical or similar characteristics. We therefore compared various Olympic Games and university hospitals. But even then, different goal settings, e.g. the relationship between the short-

---

[6] See, e.g., the case studies published by the Harvard Business School, dealing with energy generation and the famous Supersonic Transport Program (SST, see Harvard 1977, Horwitch 1979a); the case studies of McEachron/Teige (1977) on the Parthenon, on energy generation, innovative transportation and housing systems, and on the Apollo Moon Landing; Baer et al. (1976a, 1976b) on federally founded demonstration projects; Horwitch (1979b) on large-scale, public-private technological enterprises; Morris/Hough (1993) on transportation systems, on energy generation, on computerization of public services, on a spacecraft system, and on a river barrier; Miller/Lessard (2000) with a benchmark study on 60 large engineering projects; Flyvberg et al. (2003) on the Channel tunnel, the Great Belt link, the Oeresund link, and a large number of MOEs in the public and private sector mainly in the field of transport infrastructure and energy generation.

[7] *"In general, the comparisons between private sector projects and public sector projects do not support many of our preconceptions.* Public sector projects certainly have their share of problems, but they have been maligned more than the evidence of this study warrants"* (Baker et al, 1983, p.928).

[8] Websites like Structurae (2003) offer only incomplete information for research purposes.

term goal of construction and the long-term goal of operation, different time periods of events, different socio-political environments, and different research methods have to be considered. As an illustration, think of the striking changes that have taken place in the socio-political environment within a few years (Horwitch/Prahalad 1982, p.19): "The traditional MOE protective cloak (under the name of national defense, national prestige, or absolute presidential commitment) that tended to help buffer former military- and space-oriented MOEs from criticism has lost much of its effectiveness. The opportunities for intervention from potential opponents or skeptics have grown significantly".

There is no pat solution for overcoming the barrier of incompatibility. The most advisable procedure seems to be that different research groups concentrate on different types of MOEs, using different research methods, and then exchange their findings.[9]

3. Our Research Approach

Our comments focus on the sampling of MOEs subject to our empirical analysis, the methods of data collection, and on data analysis.

The *Olympic Games* were the type of MOE we studied first. The case of the Summer Games 1972 in Munich was characterized by an extraordinarily easy access to files, including comprehensive reports to the board members and the minutes of their meetings, usually not released for external analysis. With some of the variables, even advanced statistical analyses could be performed.

On further investigation, the Olympic Games turned out to be a set of different sub-projects, most of them respectable in size and complexity and each of them worth a separate analysis. In particular, these sub-projects include the facilities for competitions and housing for the athletes. Analyzing these facilities as separate projects enlarged the sample significantly. From a methodological point of view, the chance to compare these sub-projects without the bias caused by different periods of performance, different socio-political environments, and different managerial frameworks was even more important. Fig. 6 shows the project structure of Olympic Games and their options for research.

After analyzing the Olympic Games in Munich 1972, it seemed reasonable to compare this project to similar undertakings. Therefore, we focused on other Olympic Games comparing the different projects as a whole as well as their respective sub-projects. Our research series of Olympic Games includes the Summer Games in Montreal 1976 (see Auf der Maur 1976 and Malouf et al. 1980), the Winter Games in Innsbruck 1964, as well as 1976, and the Winter Games in Lake Placid 1980. The Montreal and the Lake Placid Games allowed a comparison with the preceding Games in Munich and Innsbruck, respectively, as well as the possibility of observing any learning transfer from one project to the following one. Innsbruck offered the unique chance to compare two Games held in the same city

---

[9] Concerning the problems of research based on case studies see McClintock 1979 and Eisenhardt 1989.

within a period of 12 years (Organisationskomitee 1973-1976, Martinowsky 1987).

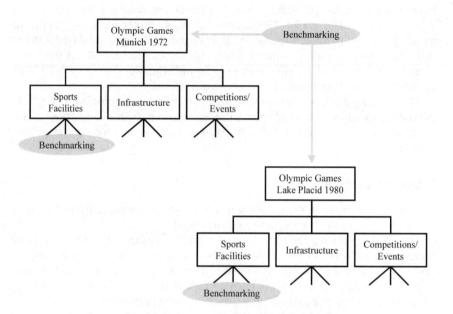

Fig. 6. Project Structure of Olympic Games and their Options for Research

Our research activities on MOEs were continued with the analysis of *university hospitals*. The Vienna Hospital (AKH) is a remarkable example of mismanagement. The auditing reports proved to be rich and reliable sources for our research on MOEs. As in the case of the Olympic Games it seemed reasonable to analyze similar undertakings. Fortunately, two German university hospitals comparable in size (Munich and Aachen) offered such an opportunity. Both projects were started at about the same time as the Vienna Hospital with similar problems, although not to the same extent as in Vienna.

Our list of research items representing the tradition of *ambitious engineering and construction projects* includes:
- the Brooklyn Bridge in New York, NY
- the Grossglockner Alpine Road in Austria
- the Tauernautobahn (Alpine Highway) in Austria and
- the Vienna International Center (see Hausner 1986)
- the Large Wind Energy Converter (GROWIAN).

The Brooklyn Bridge and the Grossglockner Alpine Road, both known as outstanding and successful constructions, were selected in order to gain insights into the management methods before project management was introduced. The Tauernautobahn (Alpine Highway) and the Vienna International Center were included to focus our attention on more common MOEs than Olympic Games and university hospitals. The Large Wind Energy Converter (Growian) has been analyzed from a somehow different perspective by a research team which was engaged in innovation theory (Hauschildt/Pulczynski, see Chapter P). Our survey on R&D projects was intended to bridge the gap between the MOEs and a sample of undertakings where project management had already become routine.

Five of the above mentioned MOEs are subject to our case studies in Part Four:
- The Olympic Summer Games in Munich (1972),
- the Olympic Winter Games in Lake Placid (1980),
- the Vienna Hospital,
- the Munich Hospital, and
- the Large Wind Energy Converter (GROWIAN)

The following table shows the characteristics and the crucial issues of the five cases.

- *Olympic Summer Games 1972 in Munich* (see Chapter L)

The case concentrates on the sports facilities, most of them new buildings. All facilities represent high technical standards for both the Olympic and post-Olympic (permanent) operations and were finished in time. The MOE suffered from an ambitious integrated design and enormous technical problems with the famous tent-shaped roof resulting in remarkable cost overruns. Driving forces (some of them external) to increase the level of the technical goals could not be sufficiently controlled by the project management.

- *Olympic Winter Games 1980 in Lake Placid* (see Chapter M)

The hosts of the Games focused on the permanent operation of facilities in order to avoid Olympic ruins. In contrast to the Olympic Games in Munich the functions of construction work and of organizing the Games were integrated in a single project company with a general contractor responsible for construction. Little attention was paid to the comfort of the spectators. World-class sports facilities contrasted with a collapsing transportation system during the Games provoking the press to recommend to the spectators: "Bring your own balloon". The project management suffered from preferences for local businessmen and dignitaries and from unprofessional decision-making procedures. The press commented: "The only real amateurs here are the ones who organized the Games". The management capacity was simply too small and, in our opinion, the crucial weakness of the Lake Placid Games. Finally, an external general manager was engaged as last-minute troubleshooter.

- *New Vienna University Hospital* (Allgemeines Krankenhaus, AKH, see Chapter N)

This case features a general hospital including all university clinics started in the middle of the 1950s and not completed until 1995. The cost explosion and the permanent schedule overruns combined with frauds committed by the project management and contractors led to protracted and often vitriolic discussions. This project has become known as the "AKH-scandal" and is considered to be the biggest scandal in Austria since the end of World War II. The genesis of the project was subject to various, intensive investigations by public auditing offices.

- *New Munich University Hospital* (see Chapter O)

Contrasting with the disastrous Vienna Hospital the project management of the Munich MOE, similar in size, was able to stabilize the goal formulation process and to ensure a balance between technical, financial and time goals. Based on a clear management structure and high recruitment standards for project managers, the Munich Hospital could be finished in time without substantial cost overruns, but the ambitious technical goals had to be redefined. The users had been integrated successfully in the early phases of planning thus paving the way for high performance in the operation phase of the MOE.

- *Large Wind Energy Converter GROWIAN* (see Chapter P)

GROWIAN, located in the German province of Schleswig Holstein, was intended to be the largest wind energy converter test plant and can be seen as a technological reaction to the energy crisis of 1973. GROWIAN aimed at testing the generation of electric energy by the natural movements of air on a large scale. Only five years after completion (1983) the converter was torn down (1988). The MOE suffered from the early fixation on a specific technical solution and from considerable problems in coordinating a public-private-partnership (PPP) with strong influences of the socio-political environment. Private industries refused to share in project ownership. This early warning signal was disregarded by the politicians and thus facilitated the dominance of technical over financial aspects.

Table 1. Characteristics of our Case Studies

Basically, all common *methods of data collecting* are suitable for analyzing MOEs. We used text analyses, interviews, and questionnaires (see Grün 1975b).

In all cases presented here, *text analysis* was the dominant method because it proved to be the most suitable for data recording. Our studies required the precise tracing of the "history" of the MOE, especially the emergence, change and achievement of the goals, the development of the project company and its management structure. Often, the people involved were not able to recall the project history as it spread over a time period of a decade or longer. Additionally, it should be mentioned that for various reasons the people who had worked on the project were no longer available. These are common problems when the research activity is started years after project completion. In some cases we faced an enormous amount of project files. For example, there were 25 files amounting to about 10,000 pages covering the discussions of the board of the project company for the Olympic Games in Munich. In other cases we had to cope with a rather poorly documented data base.

We used the *interview method* to confirm significant events in the development of MOEs and to compensate for deficits in the files. Furthermore, interviews provided the necessary information for evaluating the technical goals and their achievement. For example, we interviewed experts on sports buildings and representatives of sports associations to evaluate the functionality of the buildings for the Olympic Games in Munich 1972. The interviews were more efficient for gaining additional information on motivation and intentions than on specific project events and we were not surprised that the interviewees tried to justify failures when personally involved in the matter.

Questionnaires should only be used together with other recording methods such as the text analysis (we used them to examine the opinions of distinguished sports journalists and athletes on the functionality of the Olympic buildings in Munich 1972).

Most of our findings are not based on *statistical methods* as the data base was too small and too heterogeneous. Therefore, we often had to be content with *qualitative judgements*. Just think of questions like: Is the management capacity of an MOE sufficient in quantity and is its qualification adequate? Is the influence of the socio-political environment going to be strong or weak? To facilitate our qualitative judgements we derived them from quantitative information whenever possible. Most of the technical goals, duration and the cost of MOEs represent "hard facts" even though the result need not be a single number but rather a range. In this case, the achievement of the goals could be judged fairly well.

4. Design of the Book

The design of the book matches our intention to explain the achievement of the MOEs' technical, time, and financial goals as well as their overall performance (dependent variables) based on empirical evidence. Part Two opens with comments on the structure and achievement of the project goals. After discussing the technical, time, and financial goals of MOEs separately we turn to their overall performances.

Part Three presents the variables which are assumed to influence the achievement of the goals. We have singled out four independent variables ("success factors") featuring the most significant influence on MOEs:

- the process of the formulation and change of goals,
- the basic design,
- the socio-political environment, and
- the management structure and capacity.

After analyzing these independent variables and their interrelationship, their influence on goal achievement is summarized in a comprehensive survey. An overview is presented in Fig. 7.

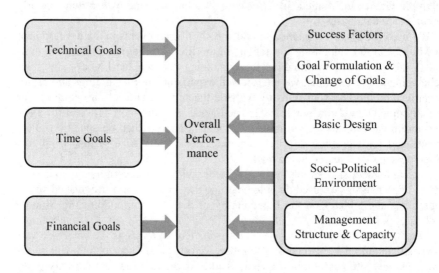

Fig. 7. Analysis of Dependent and Independent Variables

Our results are based on literature on MOEs and on conclusions drawn from the five case studies in Part Four of this book. The cases are presented not only for illustration but also for reasoning purposes. In order to make the reconstruction of our judgements transparent, the outline of the case studies in Part Four is consistent with Part Two and Part Three (see Fig. 8). This "matrix design" of the book offers two paths of access: The "horizontal access" focuses on goal achievement (Part Two) and on Success Factors (Part Three) based on and illustrated by our case studies (Part Four). The "vertical access" provides comprehensive "biographies" of the five MOEs, paying special attention to their goal achievement and success factors (Part Four). The results of our analysis are summarized in a conclusion: "Lessons for the Future" (Part Five).

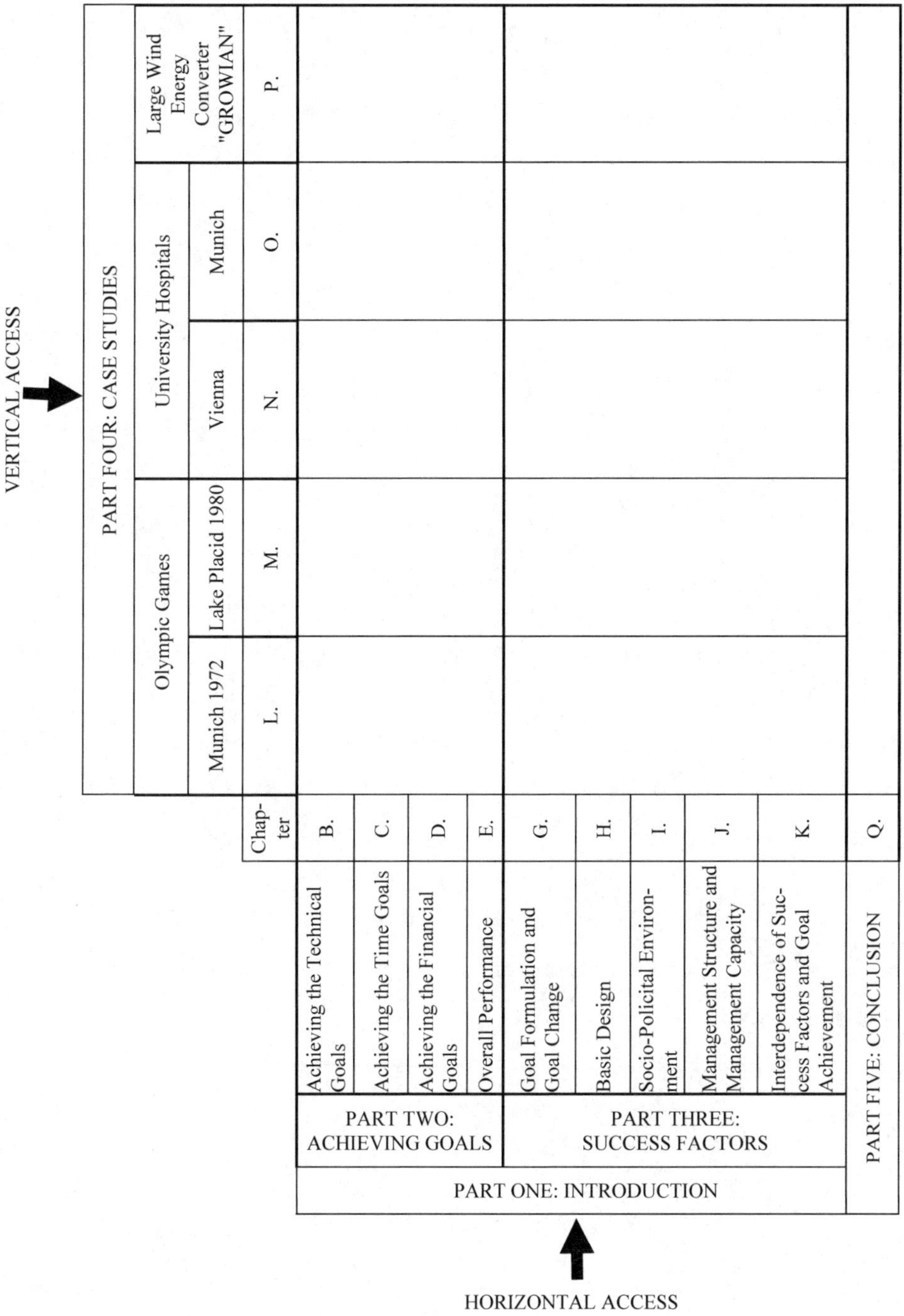

	Chap-ter	PART FOUR: CASE STUDIES				
		Olympic Games		University Hospitals		Large Wind Energy Converter "GROWIAN"
		Munich 1972	Lake Placid 1980	Vienna	Munich	
		L.	M.	N.	O.	P.
Achieving the Technical Goals	B.					
Achieving the Time Goals	C.					
Achieving the Financial Goals	D.					
Overall Performance	E.					
Goal Formulation and Goal Change	G.					
Basic Design	H.					
Socio-Policital Environ-ment	I.					
Management Structure and Management Capacity	J.					
Interdependence of Suc-cess Factors and Goal Achievement	K.					
PART TWO: ACHIEVING GOALS		PART THREE: SUCCESS FACTORS				
PART ONE: INTRODUCTION						
PART FIVE: CONCLUSION	Q.					

VERTICAL ACCESS

HORIZONTAL ACCESS

Fig. 8. Design of the Book

Part Two: Goal Achievement

Our studies on MOEs were motivated by the fact that a remarkable number of MOEs have been failures. In Part One we identified goal orientation and goal specification as important characteristics of MOEs. Therefore, evaluating the goal achievement appears to be an easy task by simply comparing the planned goals with what was actually achieved upon project completion.

This "simple" procedure often faces difficulties in practice because
- the initial goals are incompletely formulated,
- the achievement of the goals varies depending upon whether the short-term aspect of completion or the long-term aspect of operation & maintenance is considered (see Chapter B, C, and D),
- the rate of achievement is different for the technical, the time, and the financial goals and requires an overall performance evaluation (see Chapter E).

The background for the *incomplete formulation of the initial goals* is discussed in Chapter G. At this point, we merely consider the impact of incomplete goal formulation on the measurement of goal achievement. The goals may be formulated in a non-operational way by requiring "maximum" technical standards, "minimum" (i.e. shortest possible) completion time, or "optimum" costs without stating how to measure the maximum, the minimum, and the optimum. Sometimes the goals are incomplete because one of the dimensions (usually the time or the financial dimension) has not yet been considered at all, or the goal statement does not establish a point of achievement, like a specific date or specific costs, but rather indicates a range or an open scale, for example, completion within a time period or up to a limited amount of cost.

In general, the completeness of the goal formulation is a function of the project phase. The likelihood of an incomplete goal formulation is high at the beginning or in the early phases of projects. Therefore, the goal statement may not cover all phases of the project, or the statement itself may be ambiguous, for example, indicating different figures for possible cost overruns.

B. Technical Goals

I. Structure of Technical Goals

The technical goals of MOEs form a *goal-system* which consists of individual sub-goals. Not all sub-goals may be relevant to every MOE though. Olympic Games serve as an example to illustrate Fig. 9.

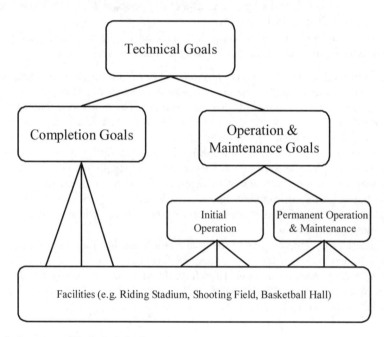

Fig. 9. Structure of Technical Goals

The *completion goals* refer not only to the planning and construction of Olympic facilities, such as a stadium or a ski jump facility, but also to the set-up of an organization to run competitions or art programs. The ultimate project goal is not the completion but the utilization of the facilities (operation & maintenance goals). A separate completion goal needs to be formulated though, because the time and the financial goals are generally stated in relation to the stage of completion.

In the case of Olympic Games, the project itself is a one-shot event but requires equipment which is intended for long-term use, e.g. buildings, transportation and communication systems. Therefore, we have to distinguish between initial and permanent operation & maintenance. *Initial operation* means the use of the project facilities for a limited period of time, which is usually only a fraction of the permanent operation & maintenance period. The initial Olympic operation period is measured in weeks or months and includes the Games themselves as well as pre-Olympic tests. The same holds true for MOEs like world fairs ("Expo"). The *permanent operation & maintenance* refer to the long-term utilization, e.g. the use of sports facilities for regular training and competition programs, or for special events like conventions and concerts.

Technical goals combine quantitative and qualitative aspects. Common *quantitative aspects* are the size of a facility or system (height, floors, usable floor space, area, number of rooms or user-units) and its capacity (number of users or spectators). *Qualitative aspects* may refer to the complexity or the innovation rate of a project, to economic aspects like the creation or preservation of jobs, as well as to securing a position of international supremacy ("No. One in Europe/in the world") for a company, a city, or a country.

It should be mentioned that the technical goals of MOEs may vary in their intended level of achievement. They are formulated as:

- a fixed point (specifying the number of beds in a university hospital or the number of seats for spectators in an Olympic building) or
- an absolute performance goal ("No. One in Europe") or
- a comparative performance goal ("better than").

The variety of technical goals of our cases is illustrated in the following table.

Technical goals → Type of MOE ↓	Completion Goals	Initial Operation	Permanent Operation & Maintenance
Olympic Games depending on sports (summer/winter), # of facilities new/adapted, # of athletes/spectators	• sports facilities (for various disciplines, e.g. stadium) • infrastructure - transportation - communication	• test events • Olympic competitions (various disciplines) • ceremonies - opening/closing - victory • art program	• (non-)professional sports • residential housing • public services • cultural events • tourism
University Hospitals depending on # of in-patients, out-patients, research requirements	• nursing units (beds) • surgery units • research units • infrastructure - transportation - catering - housing staff - administration	• stepwise operation mode possible	• hospital - medical services - nursing - accommodation • school of medicine - teaching - research
Large Energy Converter Depending on power output	• tower • power house • rotor blade • generator • control unit	• test (1-2 months)	• trial run (3 years) • feeding energy into the public grid • meteorological measurements • system evaluation

Table 2. Variety of Technical Goals

II.   Different Levels of Achievement

In general, the achievement of technical goals may be rated as follows:

(1) The achievement of the technical goals is high or at least adequate compared to the time and the financial goals.
(2) The achievement of the short-term goals of completion and initial operation is higher than the achievement of the long-term goals of permanent operation & maintenance.

(1) There are striking indications that project managers give priority to the achievement of technical goals. Three out of five MOE cases presented in this book show *remarkable overachievement* of the initial technical goals. In the case of the Olympic Games in Munich, the dominance of the technical goals already became apparent during the planning process: Technical aspects occurred three times as often in the records as financial aspects.

The reasons for higher achievement of the technical goals (compared to the other goals, see Murphy et al. 1974, p.134) are quite obvious. First of all, the technical goals are the ultimate purpose of an MOE. The motivation for starting an MOE is not to spend time or money but to create a facility or a program that serves present or future needs. Therefore, the motivation of the project owners, the project management and its staff, as well as the project participants is based on achieving the technical goals. Furthermore, technical goals are much more tangible than time or financial goals. Last but not least, the dominance of the technical goals is often due to the technical background of project staff members and project participants.

It has to be mentioned that the technical goals of university hospitals, compared to those of Olympic Games, represent high levels of singularity and complexity. Even if a city hosts the Olympic Games for the first time (which is the usual case), there is an Olympic protocol determining the number of events and specifying the necessary facilities. In addition, Olympic Games have an inherent tendency towards local decentralization with different sub-projects at different locations. These sub-projects are less complex than a single centralized facility like a university hospital. Planning and completing the different sub-projects can be done simultaneously with only minor interference. The limited time for completion (usually six years) also helps to prevent an upgrading of the technical standards.

(2) In general, *achieving the goals for completion and initial operation* are closely linked. This is understandable as both goals are short-term and strongly interdependent. Summarizing all case studies, the achievement of these short-term goals was greater than the achievement of the long-term goals (permanent operation & maintenance). Obviously, it was more challenging and motivating to organize an event which would attract world-wide attention rather than dealing with the day-to-day business of permanent operation. In addition, the incentives provided by the (expectedly positive) feed-back of the short-term achievement were higher than the incentives caused by the (at that point uncertain) success of the permanent operation.

MOEs	Completion/Initial Operation	Permanent Operation & Maintenance
Olympic Games Munich 1972	facilities ➤ high standard competitions ➤ satisfied athletes, many spectators, security problems housing ➤ comfortable for athletes transportation ➤ short distances, new subway	facilities ➤ good/mediocre ratings for technical standard/functionality, adequate capacity, infrastructural value tourism ➤ the image of Munich as the unofficial capital of Germany has been strengthened
Olympic Games Lake Placid 1980	facilities ➤ high ("world-class") standard competitions ➤ excellent organization, disappointing no. of spectators housing ➤ rather poor transportation ➤ for spectators: disastrous	facilities ➤ official training centers, international sports events, public services tourism ➤ significant development
Vienna Hospital	facilities ➤ oversized block-type building, equipment outdated because of delayed completion infrastructure ➤ central location, various transport facilities	hospital ➤ highly reputed school of medicine (teaching and research) ➤ outstanding international reputation
Munich Hospital	facilities ➤ block-type has proven satisfactory, old (downtown) hospital has to be operated simultaneously because of reduction of bed capacity, two- (instead of one-) tower block design would have been preferable infrastructure ➤ suburban location proved to be the right choice	hospital ➤ one of the leading hospitals in Germany, high bed capacity utilization, insufficient equipment for rehabilitation school of medicine (teaching and research) ➤ outstanding international reputation
Large Wind Energy Converter (GROWIAN)	rotor blades ➤ could not be constructed as planned and caused failure of the entire project	feeding in of energy ➤ only 420 hours instead of 3 years operating time; experience from GROWIAN made succeeding projects easier scientific goals ➤ mostly achieved

Table 3. Achievement of Technical Goals

The Games in Munich offered us the chance to analyze initial and permanent operation in detail.

Rating	Initial Operation		Permanent Operation & Maintenance
	Sports Experts	Hosts	
Average Rating	1.7	1.6	2.5
Standard Deviation	0.4	1.0	1.3
Scale: 1 (excellent) – 5 (poor)			

Table 4. Achievement of Goals for Initial and Permanent Operation & Maintenance at the Games in Munich

The ratings of the initial operation are based on the judgement of sports experts and the hosts of the Games. The ratings of the permanent operation & maintenance are based on judgements of the post-Olympic users. They refer to items such as the constructional condition of the facilities, the impact on infrastructure, and the variety and number of opportunities for permanent use. The evaluation of the permanent operation was quite positive, especially regarding the variety of permanent uses (on average, almost five different options for one facility were offered).

We assume that a trade-off process takes place between the short-term and the long-term goals. Our findings indicate that it is unlikely that high achievement levels for both the short-term and the long-term goals of MOEs can be gained. Usually, the short-term goals are the "winners" in this trade-off process as the permanent users either tend to be insufficiently represented in the planning process, or the initial users concentrate on the completion goals, sometimes assuming that they will not be involved in the operation & maintenance phase.

The Games in Lake Placid and the hospitals in Vienna and Munich are suitable for illustrating *different kinds of user representation*. In Lake Placid the hotels, tourist agencies, and other business firms strongly influenced the initial idea of hosting the Games and subsequently played an active part in the planning process. As permanent users, they were interested in facilities suitable for the post-Olympic operation & maintenance. Sometimes this interest even dominated the short-term goals. The result was not surprising. Lake Placid experienced a remarkable improvement in tourism; the summer tourism was enhanced especially and became a strong economic base aside from winter tourism. Lake Placid was also successful in marketing the Olympic facilities as landmarks. This quite remarkable learning process did not take place in other Olympic locations like Squaw Valley and Mexico City. They experienced post-Olympic ruins!

The Vienna Hospital also showed a marked influence by the permanent users (school of medicine). They concentrated on the completion goals, however, and enlarged them significantly. The problem was that the most influential faculty members were not likely to be involved in the permanent operation because they faced retirement before the delayed project completion. Therefore, the Vienna Hospital experienced enormous difficulties after going into full operation.

The strategy for the Munich Hospital was quite different. The project owners insisted on involving those faculty members who would undoubtedly have to live with the requirements they submitted during the planning process. The performance of the operation in Munich is correspondingly high. The hospital has become known as one of the leading hospitals in Germany.

III.   Summary and Conclusion

Literature on project management and MOEs pays much attention to the conflict between technical, time, and financial goals (see Kerzner 2001, p.875ff.). Our findings show a *clear dominance of the technical goals*. This indicates that in practice the time and the financial goals tend to be neglected, except in the case of MOEs with fixed dates of initial operation like Olympic Games. Another aspect – commonly ignored in current discussions – is the *conflict between the short-term and long-term technical goals*. The life-cycle concept has turned some attention to long-term aspects, predominantly to the costs of the permanent operation & maintenance.

In general, conflicts between the different technical goals increase with the *incompatibility of the technical sub-goals* and the *number of participants* representing these sub-goals. If an Olympic facility is dedicated to the same Olympic and post-Olympic use, e.g. to host popular mass sports, and if the hosts of the Olympic Games are identical with the post-Olympic owners or users of the facility, only minor problems are to be expected. Serious conflicts are likely if a facility is oversized for the post-Olympic use or, even worse, is dedicated to an Olympic discipline which is unknown or unpopular in that area. In the latter case, it may be hard to find an owner or user for the permanent operation & maintenance at all, and the frightening vision of post-Olympic ruins arises.

The conflict between the completion goals and the goals of operation & maintenance reflects the inherent contradiction of short-term and long-term aspects, as discussed above. It also reflects the *different priorities of project owners and project users*. For example, the user of a university hospital will insist on the best medical and technical standards, whereas the project owners are interested in restricting the technical goals for budgetary reasons. Even in the case of only one project owner being responsible for operation & maintenance, conflicts in achieving the technical goals may arise. Just think of MOEs where national or local prestige is at stake or which are set up as a monument to individual ambitions of a mayor, an architect, or both of them. Some of these monuments have shown a poor performance in their permanent operation.

The question is, whether *suitable management tools* exist (1) to avoid the dominance of technical goals and (2) to ensure a balance of short-term and long-term aspects of technical goals.

(1) Our studies have shown that in the case of conflicting technical goals the project owners tend to maximize and not to compromise. In the case of the Olympic Games in Munich, one project owner managed to push through a facility serving his post-Olympic interests although the need for the facility for Olympic

events could not be proven. The deal worked out because other owners were able to make similar arrangements in their favor.

By selecting suitable methods of goal formulation and by creating time pressure the dominance of the technical goals can be restricted. There have to be lower and upper limits to the *initial technical goals* in order to avoid underachievement or overachievement. Ranges are most appropriate to determine a sufficient level of achievement and to prevent heavy schedule and cost overruns caused by the expansion of technical goals.

The formulation of limited goals may often be insufficient to counterbalance the strong driving forces which aim at expanding the technical goals. These forces are hard to oppose (especially if the expansion is supported by arguments such as national prestige, job creation, or public welfare). Therefore, it is essential to have or to *create time pressure* for the project. Current academic discussions still pay too much attention to the likelihood of an increase in costs caused by time pressure (see Wildemann 1982, p.86). We believe, though, that the (negative) cost aspect is less effective than the (positive) influence that time pressure has on the formulation of the initial technical goals. The time pressure is likely to reduce the initial level of aspiration as well as the tendency to enlarge goals during the project planning process.

(2) As *long*-term *goals are inherently at a disadvantage,* close attention has to be paid to the permanent operation & maintenance from the very beginning (Flyvberg et al. 2003, p.137). This also includes the full involvement of the prospective users. The project owners themselves tend to ignore these aspects. A former chancellor of the Austrian Republic decided to start the construction of the Vienna International Center without having any idea or figures concerning the requirements and the costs of its permanent operation & maintenance. Serious discussions with the United Nations only started in 1974 when the shell construction was already finished!

Full involvement of the permanent users right from the beginning may help to clarify what the permanent use will be, which in turn is essential for estimating the permanent costs. Therefore, it is not sufficient to simply nominate some representatives and to give them a vote without engaging them in developing detailed operating procedures. Only the development of these operating procedures can ensure that the requirements of the permanent operation & maintenance phase will be considered as an essential element of the planning and completion phase. The worst case would be if no permanent users are nominated in the planning phase. The project may still be completed and the initial operation might work well, but the satisfactory permanent operation & maintenance would be left to chance.

C. Time Goals

MOEs are defined as temporary undertakings. Time goals should ensure project completion by a predetermined date or within a predetermined period. In some cases, the time goals are even crucial. For Olympic Games, the year of the event, the opening date, and the duration are fixed several years in advance. The failure to achieve time goals may have substantial consequences for the project, such as awarding the Games to another host city and therefore making the project obsolete. We will first deal with the structure of time goals and then turn to their achievement in MOEs.

I. Structure of Time Goals

Just as technical goals, time goals are formulated for the completion, the initial operation, and the permanent operation & maintenance of projects (see Fig. 9).

The completion goal may refer to the various project facilities (e.g. buildings). If there is only one complex facility, the time goal usually determines the completion of the sub-projects (e.g. central buildings, annexed buildings, and the infrastructure like transportation systems). The time goals for the facilities themselves can be divided into phases.

If there is only a permanent and no initial operation (e.g. university hospitals), the time goals for completion often coincide with the goals for operation & maintenance and sometimes even overlap. The permanent operation in one building of a university hospital may start, for example, while the completion of other buildings is still under way. In the case of initial *and* permanent operation the time goals (for completion and initial operation) are almost identical. Again, there may be an overlapping period if tests (such as pre-Olympic trials) are conducted in the final completion phase to improve the facility for the initial operation.

As with technical goals, time goals often suffer from *incomplete formulation*. The formulation is incomplete if the time goals for important project phases are omitted. The plans for Olympic Games may include scheduled dates for completion and for initial operation, but not for the beginning of the permanent operation & maintenance period.

Another aspect of incomplete formulation of time goals is the tendency to "forget" important project activities. The project owners of the Games as well as those of the university hospitals underestimated the time for setting up a project management structure and a project company. Often the time necessary for adapting facilities for permanent operation is underestimated. Other problems are reported from nuclear power plants where the procedure of obtaining the official approval was much more time-consuming than expected (see Hoyte 1982, pp.46-49).

Finally, the goal formulation is incomplete unless the project owner declares explicitly whether the time goals are indispensable or whether they can be extended in order to improve the chance of achieving the other goals (especially a better cost performance). Obviously, the latter is no option when dealing with in-variable dates of completion, as in the case of Olympic Games.

II.   Different Levels of Achievement

Our findings on the achievement of the time goals are summarized in the follow-ing table:

MOEs	Completion/Initial Operation	Permanent Operation & Maintenance
Olympic Games Munich 1972	most facilities were finished in time, allowing for extensive pre-Olympic tests	some facilities were handed over with delays to the permanent users
Olympic Games Lake Placid 1980	facilities finished in time de-spite some technical problems, unfavorable weather condi-tions, and delivery problems	delays because of problems with the setup of an adequate manage-ment structure and with funding
Vienna Hospital	completion delayed for dec-ades because of continuous enlargement of the technical goals and insufficient man-agement structure	start of operation in annexed build-ings of the hospital in 1974/75, full operation in 1994
Munich Hospital	the first and second completion phases (1974 and 1980, resp.) were finished in time	the two-phase completion mode enabled the early operation of ma-jor parts of the new hospital
Large Wind En-ergy Converter (GROWIAN)	the schedule (32 months for the construction and test pe-riod) was constantly missed (total delay: 55 months)	start of operation delayed (by 13.5 months) because of various prob-lems during the test phase

Table 5. Achievement of Time Goals

The analyzed Olympic Games were exemplary in achieving the time goals as far as completion and initial operation are concerned. This level of achievement was remarkable and justified the pride of the hosts (see, for example, the slogan used by the Lake Placid hosts: "Welcome World, We're Ready"). In some cases, the early completion even allowed for an intermediary use of the facilities. The time goals were achieved despite time pressures (often aggravated by unfavorable weather conditions and conflicts with unions and suppliers), despite substantial technical problems (many Games had at least one outstanding facility, such as the tent-shaped roof in Munich), ambitious project owners, and interventions from the socio-political environment (like the imposition of requirements which gave preference to local businesses). The good performance was due to the project owners' awareness that the achievement of the time goals represented a key success factor.

The Vienna Hospital is a glaring example of an MOE with a poor level of on-time goal achievement. In the 1950s, the discussion to replace the old university hospital (founded by Emperor Franz Josef in the 19th century) began. The original plan of 1955 aimed at replacing only one clinic in the 1960s. The revised plan of 1957 decided to replace the entire university hospital. The first estimates suggested that the completion date would be in the early 1970s. As the years passed, the gap between the date the estimates were made and the estimated dates of completion did not narrow, not even in 1972 when the construction of the main facility had begun. The following figure illustrates the repeated extension of the time goals over a period of more than 20 years:

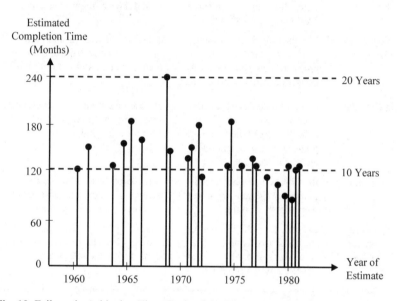

Fig. 10. Failures in Achieving Time Goals of the Vienna Hospital

The reason for this extraordinary delay in completion is an open secret: The basic design of the project was oversized, the project management capacity was insufficient, the technical goals were unlimited, and – after the disaster had become public – strong socio-political influences caused additional difficulties and schedule overruns. Other reasons, such as the annual budget period of the public project owners, sometimes quoted as justification for delays of MOEs, lack relevance. The costs of these schedule overruns can partially be quantified: about €30m had to be spent on indispensable repair work on the old buildings until 1980!

Schedule overruns are not the inevitable fate of university hospitals, as the Munich Hospital has demonstrated. In 1966, the project management fixed the dates for its first completion phase (1974) and for the final completion (1980). The management succeeded in meeting all time goals over a construction period of 13 years and about 25 years including the planning phase! The reasons for this successful time management were: The users' pressure to gain early access to the new university hospital, an experienced project management team, adequate management techniques (including substantial planning before starting construction), a reasonable breakdown of the total facility into sub-projects, and the employment of state-of-the-art construction methods, e.g. extensive use of prefabricated parts.

If a project is intended for both an initial and a permanent operation, the initial operation is usually favored by the project management. In this situation the beginning of the permanent operation may be delayed, as for example, the post-Olympic operation often was. In particular, three factors are crucial for handing over from the initial to the permanent operator in time: Setting up a user-management system, splitting the project facilities, and their adaptation. *Setting up a user-management system* is easy if the permanent users and the project owners are identical. If they are different, the permanent users need to be nominated at an early stage of the planning and completion process. Even the search for institutions with sufficient know-how, financial resources, and an interest in running the permanent operation may be very time consuming. *Splitting the project facilities* may be necessary to meet the specific requirements of different permanent users. The *adaptation of the facilities* includes repairs and alterations as well as the construction of additional facilities or equipment.

In the case of the Games in Munich, some of the owners were also the permanent users (City of Munich, State of Bavaria). Other permanent users were selected during the planning and completion process, including the "Olympia Park Gesellschaft" (responsible for managing the core facilities), a sports association, a non-profit housing company, and an exhibition organizer. The adaptation of the facilities caused only moderate delays.

In Lake Placid the set up of the permanent user-management system was impeded by high operation & maintenance costs. The potential sponsors required that all Olympic facilities be run by one institution (Olympic Regional Development Authority, ORDA), in order to avoid splitting the project design. Adaptations had to be made as well, e.g. repairing and reinstalling equipment like refrigeration. In addition, the Olympic Village had to be prepared for its final use as a prison.

One important aspect deals with financial issues of the handover. The permanent users were eager to charge the "Olympic account" with the maximum, thus enlarging the deficit of the Games but lowering the costs of the permanent operation. This entailed tough and time-consuming negotiations both in Munich and in Lake Placid.

III.   Summary and Conclusion

Our empirical findings show that the achievement of time goals is high when time represents a scarce resource from the very beginning. Projects have greatly missed their time goals when this pressure was absent. We also found strong evidence that an enlargement of the technical goals correlates with the duration of an MOE. Extended technical goals negatively affect the time goal, the cost goal, and the overall performance of the project. Therefore, *time pressure is a crucial variable for project success or, at least, for avoiding project disasters*. In this context, two important questions arise: How can the time goals be met without time pressure and how can time pressure be generated?

The use of various network techniques seemed to provide sufficient potential to ensure the achievement of the time goals. Indeed, the development of sophisticated network tools was an explicit topic of discussion at the Games in Munich and at the Vienna Hospital. When the hierarchical network tool, especially developed for the Munich Games by renowned experts, had completed its first run based on actual data, it indicated that it would be impossible to complete the project within the stated period. The project management had the choice of relying on the results of the network analysis, which would mean returning the Games to the International Olympic Committee, or simply to ignore the analysis. The management decided for the latter, relied on simple Gantt charts, and finished in time. In the case of the Vienna Hospital, several custom-made network tools were used and improved during the planning and completion period. The time goals, however, were missed completely.

Obviously, using network techniques is by no means sufficient for successful time management of MOEs. One may almost agree with the conclusions drawn by Kelley (1982a, p.11): "As projects get larger and more complex, we are beginning to back away from overquantified approaches and to look more at organizational factors." Looking for control systems to provide automatic management "... may be attributed to the fact most project managers and their immediate staffs have come up through technical or engineering professions, in which everything must be quantified." Similar results are reported by Murphy et al. (1974, p.8) and Sayles/Chandler 1971).

At this point, the question of how to perform successful time management and how to generate time pressure is left open. Kelley's comments, as well as our own findings draw attention to organizational factors. We will return to this question when discussing management capacity in Chapter J. Successful time management also involves aspects that refer to the basic design of the project. This will be discussed in Chapter H. (see also Chapter Q.II.1)

D. Financial Goals

One of the main arguments for setting up a project management system is its potential for limiting the financial consequences of large and risky undertakings. Experience has shown that the reasons for most of the outright disasters were the enormous cost "explosions". It is not surprising, therefore, that the literature on project management has focused on financial goals.[10] Flyvberg et al. (2003, pp.11), e.g., offer a "calamitous history of cost overrun". Consequently, they have also been a core topic of our research program.

The following sections deal with the structure and the level of achievement of the financial goals. They offer an explanation for different achievement levels. As financing problems are primarily based on budgeting problems, we will concentrate on the budgeting issues. Solving or at least reducing budgeting problems will reduce financing problems as well.

As a reminder: Our attention focuses on the project owners' position. We are not dealing with the capability of the contractors and their management methods which may often be very sophisticated and powerful.

I. Structure of Financial Goals

Meeting financial goals includes budgeting for the project properly and providing sufficient funds to meet this budget (see Wynant 1980, Fowler 1982). Budgeting, as well as financing, applies to all phases of the project, i.e. completion, initial operation, and permanent operation & maintenance. Usually the budgeting sub-goals refer to the different facilities or components and to the different project phases. Another item to be considered in the goal-system are the costs of the project management itself. The permanent operation creates one-off costs (like costs for the adaptation of the facilities after the initial operation) and current costs for operation & maintenance, including administration and marketing. A special aspect of financing public sector MOEs is the fact that the fiscal year – the common accounting period in the public sector budgeting procedure – does not adequately consider the long-term character of MOEs.

In general, the budgeting procedure involves project owners, users, experts, and contractors. The responsibility of the *owners* is twofold: They are authorized to specify the project requirements (especially the technical goals) which have an immediate influence on the budget. They are also responsible for raising the necessary funds. With some notable exceptions, the position of the *users* is basically the same as that of the owners. Sometimes the influence of the users on the process of formulating the technical goals is restricted due to their late nomination. More often, users have substantial influence in setting the technical goals but no or only limited responsibility for providing the funds necessary for completion and

---

[10] Morris (1982, p.158) cites studies of more than 1,000 projects with an average overrun of 60% and projects of $1 billion or more with an average overrun of 150%.

for permanent operation. This, for example, holds true for the school of medicine in a university hospital. *Experts*, such as architects, are another example of the frequent and often extreme imbalance between authority and responsibility. On the one hand, their influence on technical goals (especially regarding the design of buildings) is strong. On the other hand, they have no equivalent responsibility to observe the budget (for completion or operation) and its funding. Usually architects' payment is calculated as a percentage of the completion budget, thus encouraging them to enlarge the technical goals! *Contractors*, such as construction and installation companies and suppliers of equipment provide supplies and services which usually make up the major part of the completion budget.

The following table gives an overview of the structure of financial goals:

Criteria	Variants			
Aspect	financing		budgeting	
Source of Funds	project owners	users	spectators	advertising/sponsoring/ special collections
Components	facility A		facility X	project management structure
Phase	completion		initial operation	permanent operation & maintenance
Reliability	cost estimate		cost calculation	cost budget

Table 6. Structure of Financial Goals

Not only the technical and the time goals but also the financial goals may be *incompletely formulated* for the following reasons:

(1) essential components of the project were omitted,
(2) the project risk was not included in the calculations,
(3) the changes in the technical goals were not or only inadequately considered in the formulation of the financial goals
(4) the reliability of the financial projections has not been clarified,
(5) the inflation rate was not considered.

(1) Some project components are *likely to be omitted* in financial projections, even essential components such as the infrastructure of the project (systems of transportation, energy supply, and communications). Another example is the startling absence of explicit and quantified goals for the (permanent) operation & maintenance. This phase is either simply overlooked or dismissed as being unimportant. Obviously, such an attitude will bring about rather unfavorable evaluations of the actual operation & maintenance costs.

(2) MOE budgets ought to *consider the high risk nature* of MOEs including the risk to terminate the undertaking as experienced in the case of GROWIAN. Although the project owners are interested in defining an ultimate financial limit for the MOE, a single budget figure can neither be taken as a meaningful calculation of the risk nor as an adequate measure against the dominance of technical goals.

(3) Continuous *and significant changes* in the technical goals (for details see Chapter G) are not, or not immediately, reflected in the financial goals and therefore result in unreliable financial statements. As most of the changes lead to an enlargement of the technical goals the financial goals are likely to be missed. Admittedly, not all of the more than 30,000 changes made to the Vienna Hospital, for example, could have been seriously checked for their financial implications. But even changes in the basic design were not adequately considered in the formulation of the financial goals. When the one-block design was replaced by a two-block design the project management announced a cut in costs by about one million euros and an earlier completion date (by about one year), instead of calculating additional costs and a longer completion time. The following figure shows the erratic development of the cost estimates for the Vienna Hospital.

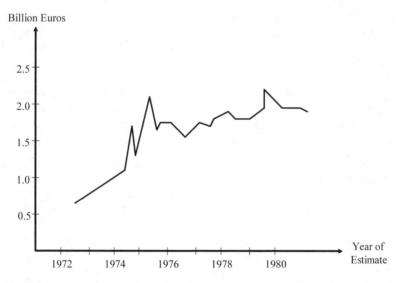

Fig. 11. Cost Estimates for the Vienna Hospital between 1972 and 1980 (Figures Adjusted for Inflation, basis 1981)

As the process of formulating the financial goals spreads over several years, the project owners may urge the project management to either gain experience in formulating realistic financial goals or to improve its skills in cost management. We have already mentioned that complex and centralized buildings (such as university hospitals) are usually broken down into components (such as core and annexed buildings). If relatively simple annexed buildings (e.g. buildings for housing employees or small buildings for a few clinics) have already caused remarkable cost and schedule overruns, the probability of the core building suffering the same fate is quite high. In the case of the Vienna Hospital, however, no learning transfer to the budget of the remaining core project parts could be detected.

(4) We have to realize that financial calculations differ with respect to their *reliability*. The *cost estimate* involves no real obligation. It merely reflects the initial cost assumption at the very beginning of an MOE. The *cost calculation* may be seen as an advanced cost estimate already including all the relevant project components and activities. The *cost budget* is the most reliable source of information in the planning process, especially when it is based on actual bids by the contractors (including experts' fees and charges) and when it is authorized by the project owners.

Unfortunately, the cost budget is not available until crucial decisions like the decision on the basic design of the project have been made. The dilemma of the project owners and the project management is obvious: Early decisions which are crucial to the development of the project have to be made on the basis of unreliable cost information; decisions in later project phases can rely on more serious cost information but are themselves predetermined by the decisions made earlier on. The dominant influence of early decisions may be illustrated by empirical findings. Thus, about 50% of the total project costs are fixed by the end of the first (initial) project phase and about 75% by the end of the second (conceptional) phase (see Wildemann 1982, pp.41, 44, 110 and Kerzner 2001, pp.779).

The project owners, responsible for financing, should always know whether their decisions are based on a cost estimate, a cost calculation, or a cost budget. This differentiation is also useful when releasing information to the general public. The project management has to make clear that information made public early in the process is based on estimates with only low reliability, thus avoiding misunderstandings among the project participants and the socio-political environment.

(5) The formulation of the financial goals of MOEs is prone to a special kind of shortcoming. Cost estimates usually do not indicate the adjusted costs upon completion, but rather the costs that would have to be incurred if the project was finished at present. This is done to avoid the difficulty of having to estimate the *inflation rate* during the completion period of the project. To evaluate the achievement of the financial goals properly the initial cost estimates have to be adjusted for inflation by forecasting the estimated values at the date of completion (see the following box)[11]. Furthermore, the capital costs have to be calculated.

---

[11] For details see Martinowsky 1987, pp.100

(1) The initial estimate is adjusted to the date of the start of construction using the national construction industry index: "adjusted estimate".

(2) The adjusted estimate is allocated over the construction period by using fictional proportions of construction. These fictional proportions are then multiplied with the relevant national construction industry index for every year of construction: "adjusted fictional proportions".

(3) The formula for calculating the cost overrun (absolute) is: actual costs minus total adjusted fictional proportions.

In summary, one can say that the incomplete formulation of financial goals is partly unavoidable due to the risks of MOEs in general, but it may also be just a sign of incompetent project owners and project management and/or the result of *overoptimism*. Overoptimism is the tendency to underestimate the difficulties of achieving the technical goals as well as to underestimate the completion and the operation & maintenance costs and the costs caused by the changing of technical goals. There are numerous empirical findings to prove this global phenomenon (see e.g. Murphy et al. 1974, p.78, Flyvberg et al. 2003, pp.16, 43, 44). Overoptimism is often employed to shield the MOEs from objections regarding their financial consequences. Proponents among the project owners, the project management, the contractors, and the planning experts have a fatal tendency to form an "overoptimism-coalition".

Of course, there may also be pessimistic cost estimates. If the MOE is subject to public discussion and political rivalry, the mere questioning of the cost estimates is likely to be denounced as pessimism. The cost estimates, therefore, always reflect the interests of the individuals or institutions making the estimate and can be used as a tool to promote their interests.

II.   *Different Levels of Achievement*

As with technical and time goals, the achievement of the financial goals greatly varied in our sample. The presentation of our findings and their discussion concentrate on the project costs with only a few additional comments on financing aspects.

1. Costs of Completion

The following table gives a comprehensive overview of the goal achievement of the MOEs we investigated.

MOEs	Completion/Initial Operation
Olympic Games Munich 1972	facilities: average cost overrun of 111% (maximum 722%, tent-shaped roof)
Olympic Games Lake Placid 1980	completion and initial operation: cost overrun of 76%
Vienna Hospital	cost overrun of 710%
Munich Hospital	achievement ranging from cost savings of 5% to cost overrun of 34% (depending on the calculation method)
Large Wind Energy Converter (GROWIAN)	cost overrun of 12%

Table 7. Achievement of Financial Goals (Completion Costs)

The MOEs investigated differ significantly in their level of achievement. They do not even show an internal consistency regarding their sub-projects or components. The facilities of the Games in Munich may serve as an example to illustrate this inconsistency.

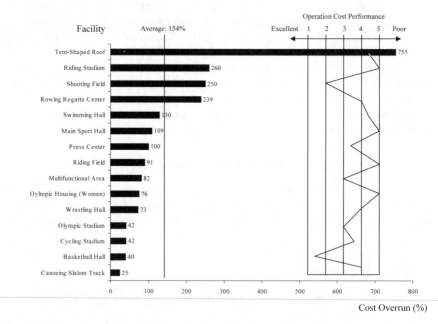

Fig. 12. Achievement of Financial Goals (Completion Costs) for Main Sports Facilities of the Munich Games (not Adjusted for Inflation)

The cost overruns of the above 15 facilities ranged from 25% to 755%. Without the tent-shaped roof the maximum cost overrun amounted to 260%. At first sight, the average cost overrun of 154% (111% without the tent-shaped roof) may seem to be very high. Compared to the cost overruns of other MOEs in our sample it is rather moderate.

Obviously, the level of achievement does not depend on the type of MOE. Olympic Games as well as university hospitals, and other MOEs have shown both high and low levels of achievement. A striking example of different achievement levels within the same category are the hospitals in Munich and Vienna.

At the very beginning in 1955, it was estimated that the Vienna Hospital would require less than €44m to complete. In 1963, experts came up with a revised cost estimate of as much as €254 m. In 1968, a €363m estimate was discussed. Our calculation starts in 1972 when the final basic design was already decided (total replacement of the "old" hospital, block-type building, two-block design; see Fig. 11).

Contrasting with Vienna, the Munich Hospital was finished without major cost overruns (34%) or even cost savings (5%). This difference in the achievement of the cost goal is not surprising. The technical goals of the Vienna Hospital were almost unlimited and continuously revised during the long planning and construction period, whereas the basic design of the Munich Hospital divided the facility into four sections which could be completed step by step. When the cost auditing indicated that the first of the four sections (which was more than 75% of the total facility) would absorb all available funds, the project owners cancelled the remaining three sections in order to avoid additional funding.

With regard to the Olympic Games it should be noted that the Innsbruck Games in 1976 achieved better results than the Games in 1964. Obviously, project owners and project management learned from previous Games. In addition, the European hosts were far more cautious at the beginning, not promising "cheap Games" as, for example, the mayor of Montreal did: "It's more likely that a male becomes pregnant than a single citizen of Montreal has to pay one penny for the Games," he announced (Süddeutsche Zeitung, Munich, 1976-08-01). The hosts of Lake Placid also promised to avoid a deficit, explicitly referring to the "financial disasters" of Sapporo and Innsbruck. Spurney, the general manager of the Lake Placid Games, announced: "We will pay our bill. We will not leave a deficit" (The Sporting News, 1980-02-16). Or: "But we made a commitment that we would bring the Games back into perspective. The whole history of the Olympic is losing money ... , and we simply do not have any way to absorb a loss" (Broadcasting, 1977-07-18).

The hosts of the Games in Lake Placid, however, were the first to successfully employ new *methods of financing*, especially for the initial operation. This may be seen as a milestone in the history of the Olympic Games. The traditional funding included ticket sales, public funds, and funding by special actions, such as stamp-editions and lottery-collections. The Lake Placid hosts initiated professional marketing methods like direct mailing, outdoor advertising, and posters. Not all marketing efforts showed the desired results, e.g. a direct mailing campaign turned out to be a flop. But they managed to engage about 200 official suppliers and sponsors for the Olympic Games (a car producer put about 500 cars at the hosts' disposal). Last but not least, the broadcasting rights were sold for more than $20 m. Public opinion was not very favorable and called the Games "... the most widely merchandized event ever held". But Lake Placid paved the way for the Los Angeles Games in 1984 which became the first in the history of the modern Olympic Games to avoid a deficit and to come up with a substantial profit (about $150 m).

2. Costs of Operation & Maintenance

The dominance of the technical goals affected not only the completion costs but also the costs of operation & maintenance. As there were no indicators available to quantify the operation & maintenance costs, we had to accept qualitative judgements based on comments by the permanent users (see Table 8). The judgements refer to the costs of comparable facilities, especially when an existing facility, e.g. an "old" university hospital, was replaced by a new one.

MOEs	Operation & Maintenance
Olympic Games Munich 1972	average rating for the cost of operation & maintenance by the permanent users 3.8 (scale running from 1=excellent to 5=poor)
Olympic Games Lake Placid 1980	besides revival of the local economy, state subsidies of up to $3.5m were reported
Vienna Hospital	costs per bed and costs per in-patient are far beyond comparable hospitals, e.g. Munich
Munich Hospital	costs increased because of higher nursing standards; additional costs caused by the simultaneous operation of the new and the old university hospitals
Large Wind Energy Converter (GROWIAN)	cost overrun of 19%

Table 8. Achievement of Financial Goals (Operation & Maintenance Costs)

Most of the Olympic Games as well as the university hospitals show insufficient levels of achievement of the cost goals of permanent operation. As Table 8 indicates, the costs of the Munich Hospital are considered to be quite reasonable. In Vienna they are rated to be very high and even affect the city's and the national hospital budgeting system.

Fig. 12 not only shows the completion costs but also the ratings for costs of operation & maintenance for fifteen facilities of the Games in Munich. The ratings are based on the judgements of the permanent users (see also Table 19). Only two out of fifteen facilities of the Munich Games received good ratings (< 2.0), six out of fourteen received rather poor ratings (> 4.0). These findings are confirmed by the Games in Lake Placid where some facilities were expected to gain a profit, e.g. the ski-jumps, others to cause high costs and only small revenues.

If the permanent operation is not dominated in importance by the initial operation, the costs of permanent operation & maintenance are expected to be more reasonable. But even with no initial operation at all, the permanent operation & maintenance costs may be enormous. A well known example is the "Concorde", the British-French supersonic aircraft. It became evident in the early phases of the project that the revenues would not cover the costs of R&D and of operation & maintenance. Quoting Herbert Culman, the former CEO of German Lufthansa: "If you tell me the number of Concordes I would have to buy for Lufthansa, I can tell you the date of my company's bankruptcy" (Süddeutsche Zeitung, Munich, 1976-06-04). Finally, in 2003 Concorde was withdrawn from service.

Unreasonable operation & maintenance costs are not only a characteristic of Olympic Games, university hospitals, or weapons and transportation systems. The warning of a former German Secretary of Commerce came too late for most of the cities which built gymnasiums and convention halls in the 1960s and 1970s: "Anybody who plans a convention hall today, should be imbedded in the walls of it."

In this context, the question arises whether the costs of permanent operation & maintenance correlate with the achievement of the financial goal for completion. The Olympic Games in Munich provided enough data to answer this question. Our analysis showed no correlation between operation & maintenance costs and the overrun of completion costs! We conclude that high completion costs cannot be justified by lower operation & maintenance costs. The question of how to ensure a reasonable financial burden for the project owners is still open.

III.   Approaches to Explain the Achievement of Financial Goals

Advanced methods to explain the costs are necessary in order to perform an effective cost management (see Chapter Q.III).

1. Overview

The approaches to explain the achievement of financial goals and to gain reliable cost estimates at the beginning of the project range from simple rules to sophisticated mathematical models. Three of them appear to be suitable for MOEs:

(1) the process-analytical approach,
(2) the life-cycle approach,
(3) the cost-accounting approach.

(1) The *process-analytical approach* is based on the assumption that technical goals can be broken down into distinctive small work packages and that reliable cost estimates for these packages can be made in the early phases of undertakings. As mentioned earlier, technical goals of MOEs suffer from incomplete formulation at the beginning and – once formulated – are likely to be changed during the planning and completion process. In addition, not only the goals are subject to

change but also the different ways of achieving them such as replanning and other workload caused by influences of the socio-political environment. Generally speaking, the process-analytical approach is vulnerable to the fact that the underlying uncertainty of MOEs prevents a clear definition of action from the very beginning. Therefore, reliable outcomes of this approach cannot be expected until non-reversible decisions concerning the project have been made.

(2) The *life-cycle approach* regards the total costs (including completion, operation & maintenance, and shut-down) to be the decisive criterion. Applying this criterion from the very beginning may require the modification of the project design in favor of reasonable operation & maintenance costs even by accepting higher completion costs. The life-cycle approach extends the design to cost concept – usually restricted to the completion goals – to cover the operation & maintenance costs as well. This approach was first introduced by the US Defense Department to fight the high operation costs of weapons systems and other equipment as they had become a crucial factor in the overall budget. The approach may be considered as a response to the dominance of the completion goals (see Wübbenhorst 1984).

Although some empirical proof is available to support this approach, its suitability for MOEs is rather questionable. The doubts refer especially to the complexity and long duration of MOEs. When serious estimates of the completion goals are already difficult, reliable estimates of the operation & maintenance costs seem to be almost impossible, especially when no figures drawn from past experience are available. The life-cycle approach clearly points out the importance of considering the costs of operation & maintenance in the adequate computation of MOE-costs, but cannot offer suitable methods to solve the problem.

(3) The *cost-accounting approach* explains the costs as a function of factor prices of the cost items, of the production equipment and the production program (cost determinants)[12]. Several authors have discussed the feasibility of the cost accounting approach for MOEs, in view of the dominance of technical goals, the overoptimism concerning the cost estimates, and socio-political influences (Wildemann 1982, pp.65). Therefore, with experience in the field of R&D projects and some adaptations to the specifics of MOEs, the cost-accounting approach may be a valuable tool for explaining their costs of completion.

It has to be taken into account that major or even all parts of MOEs are completed by contractors and that the project management and the project owners respectively, often have only limited control over the cost determinants. Therefore, project management authority and feedback time are important criteria to evaluate the cost determinants. The project management's authority is strong if it has close control over cost determinants, but weak in the case of poor ability to influence them. The project management's dispositions may be effective within a short period of time or may have only long-term effects.

The *factor prices of the cost items* depend on the market situation and the inflation rate during the long-lasting period of planning and completion of MOEs. Ob-

---

[12] For an overview see Heinen 1983, pp.449

viously, the control exercised by the project owners over the factor prices of cost items is rather weak and, therefore, this determinant is not of immediate relevance to the cost management of MOEs.

The *production equipment* (determined by the kind and number of facilities and by the characteristics of the production process) refers to the capacity of the contractors. This determinant is also of minor importance because the influence of the project management on quantitative and qualitative aspects of the contractors' production equipment is rather limited. The project management may be free to select from the contractors who have met certain prequalifications. After awarding the contract, though, its influence is restricted by the stipulations in the contractual agreement. In addition, its decisions regarding the contractors' equipment would suffer from remarkable time lags as changes in the capacity – or even the replacement of the contractors – require a long lead time.

The determinant *production program* (project task, determined by the kind and number of project parts and their allocation over time) can be controlled by project owners and project management but has to be specified by the following characteristics of MOEs:

- singularity (e.g. no or limited opportunity to gain experience from predecessors pioneering work),
- complexity (huge number of activities, participants, interdependent project components),
- stake (relevance of project success/failure to the project owners),
- time pressure (invariable time goals, unfavorable conditions for completion),
- incompleteness, changes, and delays in the formulation of goals,
- regulations of public authorities (e.g. regarding environmental matters).

Considering that a specific project management structure has to be established for each MOE, we enhance the basic scheme by the determinant *capacity of project management*:

- type of management structure (e.g. representation of project owners, experts, and users),
- expertise of the project managers,
- expertise of the project owners,
- turnover of project managers and project owners' representatives,
- project planning and decision methods (e.g. procedures to evaluate the basic project design of MOEs).

The cost management should concentrate on the production program (project task) and the capacity of project management. They are the *primary determinants* as the project owners' control over both determinants is strong and effective within a short period of time. The importance of the production program (project task) for achieving financial goals is obvious. The determinant "management capacity" is crucial because it directly affects the effectiveness of cost management. As project owners are responsible for the recruitment of the management team, they significantly influence this cost determinant.

2. Empirical Relevance for the Cost-Accounting Approach

The Games in Munich offered us the opportunity to explain the achievement of the financial goals by using the cost accounting approach. For the initial and for the permanent operation a total of 15 new facilities had to be constructed by the project company (OBG). They were treated as separate projects, each serving distinctive sporting functions but were identical regarding the nature of their technical goals (sporting function), the period of planning and completion (from 1967 to 1972), the framework of project management, and the socio-political environment. Therefore, a remarkable number of variables usually restricting the comparison of projects was neutralized. We concentrate on the explanation of the cost of completion (see above table) because explicit and quantified statements on the operation costs (either initial or permanent) have not been available.

Project	Target Costs	Actual Costs	Cost Overrun	
			Absolute	Relative
Canoeing Slalom Track	12	15	3	25
Basketball Hall	15	21	6	40
Cycling Stadium	12	17	5	42
Olympic Stadium	60	85	25	42
Wrestling Hall	15	26	11	73
Olympic Housing (Women)	29	51	22	76
Multifunctional Area	34	62	28	82
Riding Field	22	42	20	91
Press Center	16	32	16	100
Main Sport Hall	35	73	38	109
Swimming Hall	30	69	39	130
Rowing Regatta Center	18	61	43	239
Shooting Field	6	21	15	250
Riding Stadium	5	18	13	260
Tent-Shaped Roof	20	171	151	755
Average	22	51	29	154
Average (Tent-Shaped Roof Excl.)	22	42	20	111

Table 9. Achievement of Financial Goals (Completion) for 15 Facilities of the Olympic Games in Munich (Figures not Adjusted for Inflation)

In order to evaluate the cost accounting approach and to specify the cost determinants we chose 43 variables for a cluster analysis. Eleven factors were identified under the Kaiser-criterion (i.e. the eigenvalues >1). Ten factors could be interpreted separately as well as in relation to the cost determinants *project task* and *capacity of project management*. Two factors ("planning horizon" and "time pressure") could not offer an additional explanation for the achievement of financial goals. Concerning the factor *planning horizon*, the result may be influenced by the fact that the first cost estimates (the date of which was relevant to determine the planning horizon) were made by institutions without project management expertise. Concerning the factor *time pressure*, one has to bear in mind that all construction facilities suffered from similar time pressure because of the invariable date of the initial operation (opening of the Games).

In the following table the remaining eight factors which are significant for the achievement of financial goals are listed according to their eigenvalues.

Factors	Significant Variables (Loadings > 0.8)
F1 Project Task (11.4)	estimated completion costs, number of cost estimates, constructional dependencies of facilities, actual time for construction, actual time for completion (planning and construction)
F2 Intensity of Goal Formulation Process (7.9)	number of activities in the goal formulation process concerning sports-functional or positive/negative or justifying arguments
F3 Structure of Phases (4.7)	accordance with the "ideal" phase scheme
F4 Experience of Project Managers (4.2)	experience with similar undertakings, academic degree in construction science
F5 Influence of Users (3.3)	intensity of user involvement
F7 Achievement of Time Goals (2.2)	estimated and actual date of completion
F8 Speed of Goal Formulation Process (1.6)	speed of goal formulation process adjusted to the actual completion time
F9 Planning Responsibility (1.5)	joint or split responsibility for planning and construction (0.5<loadings<0.8)

Table 10. Factors Influencing the Achievement of Financial Goals of the Games in Munich (Eigenvalues in Parenthesis)

Although our data base failed to meet the requirements of the factor analysis (there have been more variables than research items), the analysis of the data provided some evidence for our list of cost determinants. Additional determinants that might have been relevant for the achievement of the cost goals were either not adequately represented in our sample, e.g. the employment of a general contractor, or were neutralized in this analysis, e.g. the socio-political environment.

In order to specify the influence of the cost determinants on the achievement of the financial goals we carried out a multiple regression analysis using the factors as independent variables. The level of goal achievement (dependent variables) was evaluated on the basis of the actual completion costs, the absolute cost overrun (i.e. actual minus estimated costs), and the relative cost overrun (absolute cost overrun as a percentage of the estimated costs). The results of the multiple regression analysis are shown in the next table.

	Actual costs	Cost Overrun	
		Absolute	Relative
F1: Project Task	+74%	+55%	
F2: Intensity of Goal Formulation Process	+5%	+6%	+27%
F3: Structure of Phases		-6%	
F4: Experience of Project Managers			+17%
F5: Influence of Users			+14%
F7: Achievement of Time Goals		-13%	
F8: Speed of Goal Formulation Process	-6%		
F9: Planning Responsibility	-10%	-4%	-13%
Explained Part of Variance	95%	84%	71%
Level of Significance (p)	≤ 0.001	≤ 0.001	≤ 0.025
Constant	-82.94	-50.69	391.20

Table 11. Results of the Regression Analysis of Cost Determinants

The cost determinants which explain more than one variable of the achievement of the financial goals are in italics to underline their importance.

The explained variance differs significantly for the three variables of goal achievement. By far the best results were achieved for the actual costs, where four of the eight determinants explained 95 % of the variance (note the high level of significance). The explained variance for the absolute cost overrun was still high (84%) and significant. So was the correlation between the actual costs and the absolute cost overrun ($r=0.86$***). Remember: "Big projects, big problems"!

The relative cost overrun shows no significant correlation either to the actual costs or to the absolute cost overrun, and the explained variance for this variable is comparatively low. Nevertheless, we suppose the relative cost overrun to be a useful indicator for the achievement of financial goals as it facilitates a comparison of projects differing in size.

Complexity of the project task (F1) appears to be the dominant cost determinant because it shows the highest explained variance for two variables of goal achievement. The fact that the variable "estimated costs" is loading on this factor indicates the project management's intention for realistic estimates. Nevertheless, excessive overoptimism remains. None of the projects could be completed in line with the target costs, especially the tent-shaped roof, which will be discussed later on.

Apart from the complexity of the project task, *the intensity of the goal formulation process* (F2), which we regard as an indicator of singularity, has considerable influence on the achievement of financial goals. The cost-increasing effect of an intensive goal formulation process is due to the dominance of technical goals. Obviously, the level of aspiration for the technical goals is continuously shifted during the project planning and construction process. One of the reasons for this shift might be the management structure of the project company with split responsibility for technical and financial goals. The committee responsible for technical goals was dominated by the initial users (sports associations, Olympic Committee) and architects. Their influence could be limited neither by other committee members, nor by the financial committee, nor by the board, as all of them lacked the necessary know-how.

The determinants *influence of users* (F5) and *speed of goal formulation process* (F8) also address the process of formulating and changing the goals. The influence of users stands for the involvement of sports associations and the Olympic Committee, both primarily interested in enlarging and achieving technical goals. The findings on the speed of goal formulation process imply that purely accelerating this process does not prevent high actual costs, especially in the case of an over-hasty commitment to the basic design.

The fact that *a joint responsibility for planning and construction* (F9) improves the achievement of financial goals is quite remarkable. Usually, architects have the responsibility for planning but not for construction. Joint responsibility means that either the (planning) architect has the additional responsibility of supervising the construction or the construction company is also responsible for planning. The advantages of this mode are obvious: The planning process is governed by standards which can be met by common construction methods, thereby avoiding re-planning as well as cost and schedule overruns (the amount of replanning is less in the case of joint than in the case of split responsibilities). Therefore, the joint responsibility may reduce the intensity of the goal formulation process (in particular, the tendency to continuously enlarge the technical goals).

The determinants *structure of phases* (F3) and *experience of the project managers* (F4) also deal with aspects of project management. Contrary to the prevailing opinion in the relevant literature (but according to empirical findings on complex business decisions (see Witte 1968), the adherence to the "ideal" phase scheme does not correlate with high levels of goal achievement. Loops in the phase scheme need not necessarily impair the performance. They often reflect the adaptation of the MOE process to new requirements resulting from a change of (especially technical) goals.

At first sight, the findings on the influence of the experience of project managers (F4) are surprising. Our results indicate that the relative cost overrun is higher if project managers are experienced with similar projects. This matches earlier findings on complex business decisions (see Grün 1973, pp.133, 153): Experience with similar tasks can cause a negative learning transfer if the deviations in the task are not considered seriously. In the case of the Olympic Games, such deviations are time pressure, the sports-functional design of the facilities, and the involvement of powerful institutions like sports associations and the Olympic Committee.

The negative sign for the determinant *achievement of the time goals* (F7) indicates that early completion dates correlate with high absolute cost overruns. There is some evidence that the time between completion and initial operation was utilized for an upgrading of technical standards.

The potential of our model to explain the achievement of financial goals is demonstrated in the following table. It shows the actual costs, the costs predicted by the model, and the residuals for 14 sports facilities (tent-shaped roof excluded).

Facility	Actual Costs m	Predicted Costs m	Residuals m
Cycling Stadium	17	31	-14
Olympic Stadium	85	80	5
Main Sport Hall	73	79	-6
Swimming Hall	69	67	-2
Multifunctional Area	62	61	1
Rowing Regatta Center	61	62	-1
Shooting Field	21	22	-1
Riding Field	42	44	-2
Riding Stadium	18	17	1
Basketball Hall	21	20	1
Wrestling Hall	26	27	-1
Canoeing Slalom Track	15	15	0
Press Center	32	22	10
Olympic Housing (Women)	51	46	5
Total	593		
Average	42.4		
SD	24.1		

Table 12. Actual Costs, Predicted Costs, and Residuals of the Absolute Cost Overruns of the Games in Munich (Tent-Shaped Roof Excluded)

The residuals for the cycling stadium and for the press center are remarkably high. In the case of the cycling stadium the high forecast value can be explained by the change of the basic design. The first cost estimate (relevant for our model) was based on the intention to adapt an existing facility for the Olympic Games. This estimate was reduced after calculations had shown that a new facility would be less expensive than the adaptation of the existing facility. In the case of the press center, the values indicate an initial overoptimism. The press center was not included in the list of facilities until December 1970 after a number of provisional facilities had not been accepted by the Olympic Committee.

The tent-shaped roof was considered to be the most ambitious and most questionable facility of the Games in Munich, not only regarding the initial decision, planning, construction, and operation, but also regarding the project costs. As expected, the model could not sufficiently explain the cost overrun of the tent-shaped roof, already identified as a runaway earlier on (actual costs: €171 m, predicted costs: €76 m, residuals: €95 m).

Reasons given by the project management to explain the extraordinary cost overruns of this project have been:
- change of the initial basic design,
- unreasonable cost estimates,
- time pressure preventing the project management from replacing the architect,
- delays in the planning process,
- technical innovations, and
- continuous and substantial socio-political influences.

The empirical findings on the construction facilities of the Olympic Games in Munich prove the relevance of the cost determinants *complexity of the project task* (production program) and *management capability*. Managerial aspects such as clearly defined responsibilities and procedures for the goal formulation process are much more crucial for the achievement of MOE goals than traditional project management tools.

3. Summary and Conclusion

As we expected at the beginning of our research, the achievement of the financial goals has proven to be the crucial issue of MOEs. The fact that in a remarkable number of cases neither the financial goals for completion nor for operation & maintenance were met is striking and calls for greater efforts in both research and management practice. The ensuing discussions have to concentrate on two aspects:
- How to ensure that the financial goals act as a motivator for project management and project owners to the same extent as technical and time goals?
- How to improve the methods of project management to avoid financial disasters in the future?

In principle, project management aims at achieving the technical, time, *and* financial goals. Therefore, failures in achieving the financial goals violate the basic principles of project management, even if this failure can be partially compensated by an overachievement of the technical goals. When the project owners of the Vienna Hospital, e.g., were blamed for the cost overrun, they countered with the argument that the actual project performance would be much better than the planned performance referring to the enlargement of the technical goals. In such cases it would be advisable to abandon the financial goals instead of trying to justify their underachievement.

Lake Placid is a good example of an ex post reassessment of the goals. As mentioned above, the hosts initially insisted on limiting the financial resources. When it became obvious that the financial goals could not be achieved, Spurney, the general manager, changed his mind: "Projects like these don't have economics as their foundation. To me, the production of the event, the translation of the idea within limited resources, is the ultimate challenge" (Fortune, 1980-01-14). Also, the hosts gave up their exclusive local attitude and played the national card in order to receive additional funds from the State and the Federal Governments: "It is a matter of national pride, national spirit." (Newsweek 1980-06-30)

The Games in Munich are another example of goal shifting. In the beginning, euphoria and optimism prevailed and even substantial increases in the estimated costs did not trouble the hosts. After the first shock that followed an exorbitant increase in the estimates for the tent-shaped roof (from €9 to €25 m) a savings committee was set up. Now even €5,000 were subject to detailed discussion and justification. In only a few months the hosts had forgotten the shock and continued to concentrate on the technical and the time performance until an "ultimate" limit of €675m for the Games was set which put an end to the inconsistent cost-consciousness.

The scientific methods useful for explaining the cost overruns of MOEs are still insufficient. So are the methods of cost management. They either lack the ability to avoid cost overruns, or they lack acceptance by the project management. We do have evidence that the methods employed by cost management do not satisfactorily reflect the uncertainty of MOEs (see Wildemann 1982, pp.150). The project management of the Games in Munich only realized the inadequacy of the initial cost estimates after the first cost overrun had become obvious. A contingency fund ("unforeseeables") was created which allowed the project management to offset cost overruns against cost savings without getting the project company board involved. At times, the fund exceeded €50 m!

All projects except for the Munich Hospital ignored the possibility of the design-to-cost concept (DTC) and not a single MOE in our sample was based on the life-cycle concept. The influence of the inflation rate on the completion and permanent costs was not considered in the cost estimates and only mentioned (but usually not quantified) to justify the cost overruns. Efforts were made to draw up reasonable cost estimates (for completion) without establishing a powerful cost management. Most of these efforts turned out to be ineffective, like the creation of a savings committee or the (belated) replacement of the project management. Therefore, the establishment of effective cost management methods must have priority for the current project management.

The only way to deal with the underlying risk as well as the overoptimism in an MOE is to *determine budget ranges*. Budget ranges reflect pessimistic assumptions, e.g. the tendency to enlarge the technical goals and the difficulties of achieving them, as well as optimistic assumptions (including effective cost management skills of the project management). The Apollo Program is an excellent example of budget ranges. When the experts were asked to assess the project costs, they estimated them to be "... anywhere from $20 thousand million to as much as $40 thousand million". In the end the project did cost $21.3 thousand m! (Seamans/Ordway 1977, p.276). Furthermore, the cost information has to be in line with the project management's attitude. A certain amount of "laissez faire" may be tolerated in the formulation of the technical goals as long as the consequences of alternative technical concepts are not known. Once the cost information has been confirmed and the funding limit for the project has been set, the management has to insist on remaining within the budget and avoiding any change in the technical goals which would be likely to jeopardize cost containment. In other words:

The criticality of achieving the financial goals has to be defined by the project owner as a guide-line for the project management.

One dilemma of the financial management of MOEs seems to be unavoidable. The project owners are greatly interested in knowing the actual costs of completion and operation before actually starting the MOE. The question arises: Would they have started the MOE if the total extent of potential cost overruns had been known in advance? A former mayor of Vienna used this argument to defend the decision to build the hospital even after heavy cost overruns had become known to the public: "Without the almost self-destructive willingness of politicians to accept the risk of cost overruns, not even half of the recovery activities after World War II would have been possible" (Die Presse, Vienna, 1976-05-25).

Quoting Flyvberg et al. (2003, p.48), delusion should not be necessary to get projects started " ... because many projects exist with sufficient high benefits and low enough costs to justify building them. ... The problem is that the dubious and widespread practices for underestimating costs and overestimating benefits ... create a distorted hall-of-mirrors in which it is exceedingly difficult to decide which projects deserve undertaking and which not."

E. Overall Performance

Project management is a tool to achieve the technical, time, and financial goals of MOEs. Therefore, the evaluation of any single goal as presented in Chapters B to D is a first step in assessing the overall performance. We will start by discussing some basic methodological problems and continue with illustrating the overall performance by examples.

The overall performance of the Munich and Vienna Hospitals can be summarized in two statements:

- Munich: The time goals were met, the financial goals were met and slightly missed, resp., the technical goals were considerably underachieved.
- Vienna: The time and the financial goals were severely underachieved, the technical goals were partially underachieved (bed capacity) and partially overachieved (net floor space and cubature).

These two statements raise the following questions: Can partial overachievement of one goal compensate for the partial failure of the same goal type, and can overachievement of one goal compensate for the failure of another goal?

Different levels of achievement of the same goal type are very likely because MOEs have to fulfill different functions. With an increasing number of project functions (e.g. initial *and* permanent operation of construction facilities or "multi-functional" use for weapon systems like the Tornado aeroplane) the likelihood of different levels of achievement increases as well. Therefore, it would be desirable to know the priorities of the different sub-goals in order to consider them in the evaluation process, i.e. by using indices of equivalence. This solution is bound to fail when the sub-goals are presented by different groups of interest, all of them convinced that "their" sub-goal is the most important one. A much simpler solution already mentioned is to *state ranges for goal achievement*. Ranges cover different levels of achievement. In view of potential failures in assessing the actual achievement because of limited access to data bases, contradictory figures, etc., ranges express the level of goal achievement more realistically than a single figure.

The second question refers to *different achievement levels compensating for different types of goals*. Is there a clear order of priority and – provided that there is – is there a method of "transferring" different levels of achievement in terms of e.g. currency units? The results of our cases indicate that MOEs usually do not have explicit statements of any priority of goals. For example, the Munich and Vienna Hospitals were intended to provide first-class medical nursing, combined with up-to-date research standards, with early availability of the new facility, and with a cost-efficient operation & maintenance. But, even when the goal formulation had stated priorities, they would be prone to change during the planning and completion process. Olympic Games are an exception in the field of MOEs because the achievement of the time goals has absolute priority from the very beginning and, obviously, cannot be compensated for by overachieving technical or financial goals.

So far we cannot offer a definite solution for the problem in question. In principle, we prefer to analyze the achievement of the technical, the time, and the financial goals separately, according to their separation in the initial goal formulation process. That does not exclude the formulation of qualitative judgements on the overall performance, especially if they are based on empirical findings within the same category of MOEs. Comparing MOEs of the same category is entirely sufficient for project owners. They may decide on the "go" and "continue" or "not go" and "stop" of a university hospital depending on the risk of successful completion; but they cannot, for example, decide to organize Olympic Games instead.

We chose the Olympic Games in Munich and the Munich and Vienna Hospitals to illustrate the overall performance of MOEs. The subject of our evaluation of the *Munich Games* are the newly constructed sports facilities for this event. The time goals were met by all facilities. Minor differences in the dates of completion had no influence on the initial and the permanent operation and are therefore excluded from assessing overall performance. The achievement of the technical goals had to be evaluated separately for the initial operation and the permanent operation and maintenance. The achievement of the financial goals was measured by the actual costs, the absolute and the relative cost overruns.

We have combined ten variables representing the technical goals of the initial and permanent operation with three variables representing the financial goals (actual costs, cost overrun absolute and relative) in thirty crosstables. Only one of these crosstables indicated that the failure to achieve the financial goals was compensated for by a higher level of achievement of the technical goals (initial operation). Obviously, there is no "automatic" compensation between the achievement of the financial and the technical goals, and cost overruns are often not justified by increased achievement levels of the technical goals. In other words: The "technical" performance of MOEs is not only a function of the costs, or, even with limited financial resources a high technical performance is achievable.

Concerning the *university hospitals* we had the chance to compare the Munich and Vienna Hospitals with regard to their technical, time, and financial goals of completion. Contrary to the Olympic Games, though, we evaluated and compared the planned with the actual goal achievement. The achievement level of the three goals is expressed separately, showing the "gap" between the actual and the planned level. The zero-line indicates that the actual and planned levels are identical. Negative deviations express underachievement (cost overruns, delayed completion, decreased technical performance), positive deviations express over-achievement (cost savings, early completion, increased technical performance. The following diagram shows the achievement levels for all three goals. The ranges in the diagrams reflect different levels of achievement of sub-goals as well as different sources and calculation methods (see above).

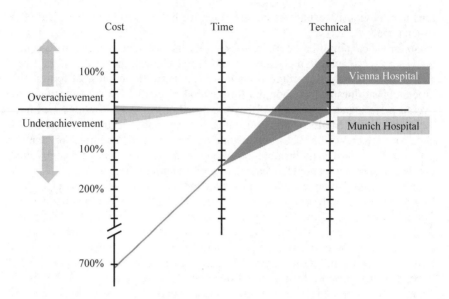

Fig. 13. Overall Performance of the Munich and Vienna Hospitals (Completion)

The deadlines for the first and second start-up phases of the Munich Hospital were met. Therefore, the *time goals* were fully achieved. The analysis of the Vienna Hospital is based on an estimate of the completion date made in 1972 with 1985 as date of completion. Given the actual completion date of the hospital in 1994, the schedule overrun is 144%. We consider this figure to be rather low as we have already disregarded optimistic estimates made in earlier years which would result in a much greater schedule overrun.

The ranges of the *technical goals* refer to different levels of achievement of sub-goals. For the Munich Hospital we calculated an underachievement of the technical goals of 37% (based on the number of beds). The evaluation of the Vienna Hospital also varies, depending on the base of reference: the number of beds decreased by 12%, the net square increased by 157%.

The evaluation of the *financial goals* achievement differs significantly for the two hospitals. Munich showed an achievement ranging from a cost overrun of 34% to cost savings of 5% referring to different dates and cost estimates. The cost overrun of the Vienna Hospital amounted to 710% (figures adjusted for inflation).

Fig. 13 illustrates the overall performance based on quantitative data. Even if the evaluation refers to the same sub-goal dimensions, like beds or other items in a university hospital, the comparison between different levels of achievement is still subject to qualitative judgements. First of all, failure and overachievement may differ in relevance. An additional cost overrun of 10 % is much more critical, if the financial funds of the project owners are already exhausted. Overachievement raises similar problems. A capacity of 1,500 beds has proven to be a crucial limit for hospitals. When exceeding this limit, the supposedly "positive" overachievement may cause serious operation problems for the oversized hospital. Therefore, the qualitative judgement should not only consider under- and overachievement but also constraints. Moreover, the evaluation has to consider whether the level of aspiration for the initial goals was low or high, as high levels are more likely to be missed than low ones.

Part Three: Success Factors

F. Strategies for Selecting Success Factors

Our discussion of the goal achievement of MOEs in Part Two has shown that not one of the projects studied in detail was successful as far as the overall perform-ance is concerned (achievement of technical *and* time *and* financial goals). The following chapters (G to J) focus on the success factors of goal achievement.

The identification of success factors is a common subject of project manage-ment discussions. The efforts for improvement increased with the growing number and significance of failures. Concentrating on empirical approaches, the findings of Murphy et al. (1974) may serve as a framework, though only a few of their pro-jects match our definition of MOEs.[13] The findings are based on 646 responses to a questionnaire. The sample includes projects from different fields: construction (43%), hardware or equipment (22%), new processes or software (14%), and stud-ies, services, and tests (11%). The study was carried out to identify the determi-nants of cost and schedule overruns in public and private sector projects. The de-terminants and their relationships are shown in the following figure:

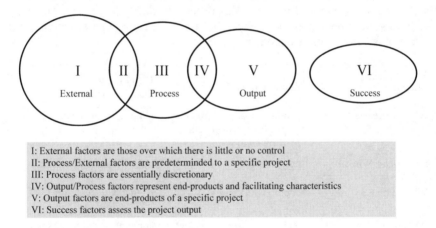

I: External factors are those over which there is little or no control
II: Process/External factors are predetermined to a specific project
III: Process factors are essentially discretionary
IV: Output/Process factors represent end-products and facilitating characteristics
V: Output factors are end-products of a specific project
VI: Success factors assess the project output

Fig. 14. Determinants of Project Success (Murphy et al. 1974, p.10-11)

---

[13] Lechler 1997 presents an overview of 44 empirical studies and the results of his own empirical study of 448 projects, which concentrates on the success factors top management, project manager, project team, participation, information/communication, and plan-ning/controlling; see also Gemünden 1990; Fenneberg 1979 presents studies on R&D pro-jects. Schultz et al. (1987) develop a ten-factor model with three factors representing the strategy phase and seven factors representing the tactical phase. For another ten-factor model see Pinto/Slevin 1998, pp.386.

The analysis of Murphy et al. (1974, p.70) proves that cost overruns highly correlate with the size of the project. Schedule adversities and resulting schedule overruns are supposed to be the primary determinants of cost overruns.

The essence of their research findings based on a series of multiple regression analyses is illustrated in a path analytical diagram. This diagram shows the interaction of a large number of variables. The strength of the relationships is measured by path coefficients (see Fig. 14). "The most significant conclusion to be derived (from the path diagram, note of the author) is that a project manager faced with one or more adversities need not and should not adopt a defeatist approach to the management of the project. Even when combinations of adversities exist, moderate success levels can be achieved if heavy emphasis is placed upon appropriate strategies for the situation and the environment as well as upon diligent pursuit of the project goals."

Despite the differences in the nature of projects ("normal" vs. MOE) the findings of Baker et al. serve as a valuable guideline for the research on success factors of MOEs: The number of success factors is remarkable, the success strategy has to be linked to the specific context and – most important – the success factors are manageable. Our primary concern is to focus on the factors that are most crucial for MOE success. Unfortunately, the important success factors are not earmarked but are mentioned in lists which differ remarkably in volume. Therefore, we have to develop a strategy to select the crucial variables. Our selection procedure is based on the following criteria:

Criteria	Important Success Factors	Less Important Success Factors
What is Success?	avoiding disasters/affecting all projects goals (overall performance)	gaining excellence/affecting selected project goals
Success for Whom?	project owners	other project participants
Which Focus?	coping with causes	coping with symptoms
How Many Success Factors?	number adjusted to project management capacity	comprehensive set of success factors

Table 13. Criteria for Selecting Success Factors

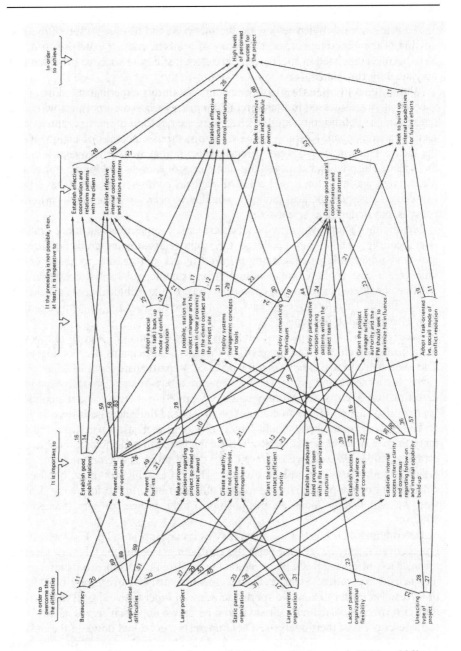

Fig. 15. Contingent Strategies for Successful Projects (Baker et al. 1988. p.930)

What is success? When reviewing the literature and headings used in the discussion of the effectiveness and efficiency of projects, enough expertise seems to have been accumulated in specifying the factors that ensure success, provided that they are duly considered.[14]

With respect to MOEs we have our doubt about this expertise, as most of the success factors discussed in literature are empirically based on projects which do not match our definition of MOEs. Therefore, the question of the relevant success factors remains open. Keeping in mind the disastrous outcomes of many MOEs, the factors that can avert severe or total project failure are worth investigating. If the Vienna Hospital had achieved the same level of success as Munich, for example, a huge waste of funds and a lot of political controversies could have been avoided and the new medical facilities would have been available much earlier for patients, physicians, and scientists.

Identifying factors which avoid disasters is less ambitious but more realistic than identifying factors for excellence. Our approach is still ambitious because we aim at avoiding failures concerning *all MOE goals,* not just the technical or the time or the cost goals. Correspondingly, for example, substantial cost overruns must be considered as disasters, even if the time or the technical goals are met or overachieved. Therefore, the success factors have to be analyzed with regard to their effects on all three goals.

Success for whom? Typical of MOEs is the involvement of a great number of participants. Obviously, the interests of the MOE participants are not identical. The main reason for a *contractor*, for instance, to participate in an MOE is to increase his turnover and profit. He may employ a buy-in strategy (intentional underestimation of costs, see Murphy et al. 1974, p.89) in order to obtain a contract. He may also support efforts to enlarge the project and thus increase his profit.

The *project owner* has (should have!) different interests: Apart from the primary interest in the undertaking itself, he is interested in realistic and reliable cost estimates, although we have observed a tendency towards overoptimism or even infantile enthusiasm of project owners. The project owners may oppose an enlargement of the project, owing to their limited funds. In the following discussion we will mainly focus on the position of the project owners (see Kelley 1982b).

Determining their position is not as easy as it may appear to be. The interests of project owners may be (at least partially) conflicting. Hosting the Olympic Games, for instance, offers the host city or region the opportunity to improve its infrastructure and its reputation. State or federal governments, however, may only grant limited subsidies for distinctive sports facilities. In order to avoid goal conflicts of project owners, a basic arrangement has to be drawn up which serves as an "official" description of their interests. These interests can be laid down in the bylaws of the project company which may be amended only with the consent of all project owners.

---

[14] Rubenstein et al. (1976) recommend differentiating between facilitators and barriers to project success and failure, respectively.

Our focus on the project owners' position reduces the number of success factors. Many management techniques, like the network analysis, may be crucial to contractors (e.g. to construction companies) but are less important from the project owners' point of view. Therefore, such techniques are not relevant to our study.

Which focus? Having clarified the interests of the project owners (i.e. to complete or carry on the MOE) and the intention of our analysis (to avoid disasters) we have to narrow down our further investigations by keeping in mind that we are looking for crucial success factors. We target the *causes of project disasters rather than the symptoms*. Dealing with the symptoms may be easier but is less effective. Imagine, for instance, that the project owners have paid too little attention to crucial decisions like the enlargement of the technical goals. Changing the legal form of the project company in order to enlarge the power of the owners' representatives in the decision-making process, as in the case of the Vienna Hospital, is merely curing the symptoms. The cause was not a lack of formal authority but the lack of courage to stop the continuous goal-changing process. Literature on project management presents a lot of examples where the symptoms were tackled instead of the causes. Excessive discussions of network techniques rather than the creation of "healthy" time pressure is one of the most striking examples.

Similar to the question of symptoms or causes is the question of *initial impediment or failure correction*. An initial impediment of MOEs like power plants and airports may be the strong involvement of the socio-political environment. In these cases, the involvement of external parties seems to be unavoidable. Delaying the establishment of a project company, however, – as we have experienced in some cases – is by no means unavoidable (for details see Chapter J). Providing an adequate management structure from the very beginning of the project is much more effective than replacing incompetent managers during planning or completion.

How many success factors? Our last question refers to the number of success factors. The number of success factors in a model is always a trade-off between scientific proof and practical application. This holds true especially if research results are intended to be used in the practice of project management. We believe that *management's capacity* of handling the success factors is just as important as a comprehensive list of factors. In this context, the well-known *Kiss-rule* ("Keep it *s*imple, *s*tupid") may not only be appropriate for determining the basic design (see Chapter H) but also when making recommendations to the management of MOEs.

To assume that MOE management can pay attention to any number of success factors shows lack of realism. By concentrating on crucial success factors we seek to reduce their number to help avoiding an overload of recommendation on the part of the project owners and the project management.

It should be kept in mind that management capacity is not only limited in quantity. Qualitative limitations may refer to the ability of project owners or project management to control success factors. Some examples may illustrate the problems involved: The contractors' equipment (in terms of quantity and quality) is an important determinant of the project costs. Poor equipment often is the reason for cost overruns. Unfortunately, project management has only restricted possibilities to influence the contractors' equipment (see Chapter D.III). On the other hand, the socio-political environment – often taken for granted by the project management –

can doubtlessly be managed. The demanding position of the general manager has tempted a number of authors to ask for a "champion" who is able to cope with this special kind of management challenge (see Horwitch 1979b and Chapter I). We will discuss only those success factors which can be controlled either by the project management or the project owner.

Summing up, our selection focuses on success factors which:
- avoid project disasters,
- emphasize the interests of the project owners,
- influence the causes of failures, and
- do not overtax the capacity of the project owners and the project management.

We believe that the following success factors meet all the criteria listed above:
- goal formulation and change of goals (Chapter G),
- basic design (Chapter H),
- socio-political environment (Chapter I),
- management structure and capacity (Chapter J).

All these success factors have been subject to extensive discussion in the literature on MOEs and have proven their relevance in our case studies. We strongly believe that they have the potential to avoid project disasters as all of them are able to describe and explain MOE disasters very convincingly.

The four success factors are discussed by using the same three-step scheme. In the first step we clarify the substance of each success factor. The second step deals with the influence of the success factor on goal achievement. The third step deals with managing the success factors.

We assume that the intention to start a specific MOE is given. Strictly speaking, this intention should depend on the evaluation of the chances of successful goal achievement. The basic decision may be revised if the crucial variables indicate the probable failure of the project. Our discussion of success factors will, therefore, include situations which necessitate a revision or even the cancellation of this basic decision.

G. Formulation and Change of Goals

Goal formulation and change has been repeatedly addressed throughout this book. The discussion of the goal structure of MOEs shows that goal formulations may be incomplete at the beginning of the planning process. Initial incompleteness requires the goal formulation process to be continued after the project planning has started (Hauschildt 1977, pp.98).

Kharbanda/Stallworthy (1983, pp.252), who have studied a widespread field of projects – most of which match our definition of MOEs –, see goal change as "always expensive" and suppose "the later change occurs, the more expensive it becomes." They refer to a dilemma which typically occurs when dealing with MOEs. On the one hand, the necessary extensive planning process generally delays completion. On the other hand, projects often have to be completed under time pressure.

We, too, have demonstrated with our cases that unlimited changes of goals, especially the enlargement of the technical goals, are responsible for failures in goal achievement (see Chapter B). Goal change should not be mixed up with goal specification. Due to the long-term character of MOEs it is unrealistic to expect all goal specifications to be made at the beginning. The initial goals may serve as a framework for further specification but the process of goal specification may also lead to a change of the initial framework.

We will analyze the processes of goal formulation and goal change and how the two processes are related. We will then concentrate on the reasons for goal change. A concluding note will deal with the management of both the formulation and change of goals.

I. Overlapping of Formulation and Change of Goals

Under ideal circumstances, the goal formulation process is finished (i.e., all goal dimensions are determined) by the time the problem solving process has been started. This assumption is realistic for routine decisions. Obviously, in undertakings like MOEs the goal formulation overlaps with problem solving.

The theory of project management deals with this problem by determining distinctive phases (life cycle). Assuming a scheme of five phases with a conception, definition, design, development/production, and a utilization/turnover/start-up phase, the first two phases are primarily dominated by the goal formulation process (see Archibald 1992, pp.25, Kerzner 2001, pp.558, Morris 1982, pp.155). The *conception phase* involves the following activities:
- recognizing the need for a project,
- defining the expected results,
- explaining and defining the resources, and
- establishing a project management.

Goal formulation is even more intensive in the *definition phase* which includes:
- specification of the project results (physical characteristics, performance criteria, evaluation standards, cost and time limits, specification of the resource requirements),
- determination of constraints (like environmental regulations).

The goal formulation process may be continued even in later phases of the project. When it becomes evident that the initial goals cannot be achieved they have to be changed.

The process of formulating the goal framework can show different levels of complexity. In the case of the Olympic Games, the protocol of the International Olympic Committee dictates the dimensions of various facilities and detailed equipment requirements (e.g. length of runs). Due to this quasi-standardization a lot of expertise can be utilized to ensure a reliable goal framework. Other MOEs, like university hospitals, show high levels of complexity as the variety of options, the influence of local interests, and numerous constraints prevent a standardized approach. The inherent likelihood of goal changes for these undertakings is much higher than for Olympic Games.

Our further discussion is based on the assumption that the initial goal framework is established by the time project owners hand over planning activities to external experts and consultants. The employment of external planning and engineering capacity marks a significant milestone in the life cycle of the MOE because:
- the intention of the owners to start a specific MOE is manifest and public;
- the structure of ownership is determined and the owners have the chance to declare their interests in the MOE;
- the size of the MOE, usually determined by user units (beds, spectators) or other output specifications (production capacity, etc.), is declared;
- the location (like downtown or outskirts for a university hospital) is clarified.

These specifications may be based on formal, internal commitments of the project owners (sometimes laid down in voting trust agreements or in the bylaws of the project company).

II.   Types of Goal Change and their Impact on Goal Achievement

As mentioned above we have to distinguish the formulation and specification of goals from the change of goals. The key element in explaining the reasons for and the processes of change is a balance of goal formulation and the driving forces.

A *balance in the goal formulation* requires the technical goals to be consistent with the time and the financial goals. If the initial goal framework is unbalanced, corrective actions have to be taken until a balance is reached. The *driving forces* may either enlarge or reduce the goals. A typical example of driving forces are users calling for an enlargement of the technical goals, either concerning completion or operation or both. The architects who planned the tent-shaped roof in Munich were also a driving force, insisting on their design even when the technical diffi-culties of construction became obvious. Project owners may also act as driving forces if they try to enlarge their advantage at the expense of other project owners (remember the representatives of Lake Placid who were eager to improve their in-frastructure and facilities to boost the tourism industry). A special driving force is technical progress which significantly influenced the goal changing process of the university hospitals because their planning and completion periods were very long and the technical standards changed rapidly. An example of impeding forces are environmental influences.

By combining the key elements of change (balance and driving forces) we can distinguish four different types of goal change.

Driving Forces / Initial Goal Framework	Controlled	Uncontrolled
	Type A	**Type C**
Balanced	preserving the initial framework (some Olympic sports facilities)	reformulating the initial goal framework (tent-shaped roof Munich; Lake Placid)
	Type B	**Type D**
Unbalanced	balancing the initial framework (Munich Hospital)	derailment of the initial goal framework (Vienna Hospital; Tornado)

Fig. 16. Types of Goal Change

The *A-type*, characterized by a balanced goal framework from the beginning and by controlled driving forces ("stabilized framework"), is the most favorable. As the following figure shows, the final goal framework is almost identical with the initial goal framework.

------ Initial Goal Framework

—— Final Goal Framework

Fig. 17. A-Type: Preserving the Initial Goal Framework

The A-type, obviously, does not apply to large and highly innovative MOEs. We observed this favorable kind of (no or minor) changes only in connection with some Olympic sports facilities.

The *B-type* of goal change is characterized by an unbalanced initial goal framework but controlled driving forces.

------ Initial Goal Framework

—— Final Goal Framework

Fig. 18. B-Type: Balancing the Initial Goal Framework

A typical example of the B-type is the Munich Hospital, where the initial technical goals could not be achieved under the given time and financial constraints. Therefore, the technical goals had to be changed (reduction of the bed capacity and the number of clinical departments). If you recall the tendency towards overoptimism, reducing technical goals means replacing "wishful thinking" with realism. Another quite common case is the ex-post correction of overoptimistic time estimates. The B-type of change is still acceptable, as we have learned from the studies of MOEs: First of all, failures in the initial goal framework appear to be the rule when dealing with innovative undertakings and second, the change affects only one of the three goal dimensions. The B-type, therefore, means balancing the initial goal framework by reformulating only one goal.

The C- and D-types differ from the A- and B-types since the driving forces are out of control. The *C-type* may start with a balanced initial goal framework, but the driving forces make it necessary to change the goal framework.

------ Initial Goal Framework

——— Final Goal Framework

Fig. 19. C-Type: Reformulating the Initial Goal Framework

The Olympic Games as a package of projects (like sports facilities, competitions etc.) are vivid examples of the C-type. In Munich and in Lake Placid were strong driving forces to enlarge the technical goals, especially regarding the infrastructure, the capacity of the facilities, the standard of the equipment, the buildings (new ones instead of reconstructing existing facilities), and various art programs. Quoting Peter L. Spurney, the general manager of the Games in Lake Placid (ENR, 1979-02-22): "There was an original assumption that the 1932 facilities (left over from the Olympics held in Lake Placid that year) would suffice... . Then people thought, let's do it right; let's do refrigeration; let's make a good facility, a great one. You just walk on up the ladder." The constraints imposed by the limited funds were not strong enough to stop the goal enlargement process. Finally, the invariable time limit for the Games brought the process of goal changing to an end.

The *D-type* of goal change has the most destructive impact on goal achievement. The driving forces are so strong that the project management is unable to reformulate the goal framework. An additional impediment is the unbalanced initial goal framework (a symptom of insufficient goal formulation awareness). The process develops a momentum of its own and ends up in uncontrolled change, that we may call a "derailment" process.

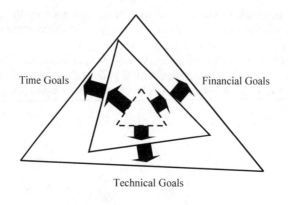

Time Goals

Financial Goals

Technical Goals

------ Initial Goal Framework

—— Final Goal Framework

Fig. 20. D-Type: Derailment of the Initial Goal Framework

The Vienna Hospital is a striking example of the D-type change. In Vienna the ambition to build the most modern university hospital in Europe with the most up-to-date technical equipment – together with the obligation to fully comply with user requirements – was responsible for the project management's loss of control over the goal change process. The Tornado project (Multi-Role Combat Aircraft, MRCA) went out of control because of the conflicting interests of the project owners.[15]

If goal changes happen too often and within short periods of time, the reformulation of the framework (especially adjusting the financial and the time goals to reflect the changes of the technical goals) overtaxes the management capacity. Even more harmful is the fact that the goals lose their mandatory force.

III.   *Managing Formulation and Change of Goals*

If you recall the reasons for goal change there are two crucial elements: Establishing a balanced initial goal framework through feasibility studies and controlling the driving forces.

The *establishment of a balanced initial goal framework* is the basic responsibility of the project owners and should not be delegated to consultants or other external experts. The demand for a balanced framework corresponds to literature calling for realistic goal estimates. But who would want to carry out an unbalanced or non-realistic framework? Therefore, more useful recommendations than just the demand for realism or balance are necessary.

---

[15] See Köppl 1979

(1) The first recommendation is to *spend enough time on the initial goal formulation*. This advice may be modified if there is time-pressure, especially in the case of invariable time goals. But even then project owners can never spend enough time on this process since failures in the initial goal framework will create continuous difficulties throughout the planning and completion process. In order to ensure enough time, the determination of optimistic (maximum) and pessimistic (minimum) levels of goal achievement may be required (see above). Our recommendations as well as those by Kharbanda/Stallworthy (1983, p.251) are: "Take the time to make a sound assessment of project cost and duration before you start" and "Always ask yourself to what extent this project is a 'development' project, and if it is of that nature allow for it in terms of both cost and time". This recommendation implies a *need for feasibility studies* in order to adequately consider technical, time, and financial goals. The authors concede that, on average, three to five percent of the total project costs need to be expended for realistic estimates of the project outcome. They expect fewer overruns in cost and time if the initial estimates are more realistic. Therefore, they call for a step-by-step approach to reduce the change rate (Kharbanda/Stallworthy 1983, pp.252; see also Harrison 1992, pp.201):

1. "Complete the basic project definition;
2. Do not proceed with detailed engineering and procurement until the process flowsheets and line diagrams have all been finalized;
3. Delay start on site until detailed design and procurement for the whole project is within six to nine months of completion."

(2) The second recommendation is to *state ranges in the initial goal framework*. Ranges reflect the uncertainty of MOEs in a realistic manner. We have gathered enough empirical evidence on MOE disasters to justify pessimistic levels of goal achievement, especially regarding the time and financial goals, and the contractors' attitude to underestimate. "The one thing that is never said, though so often true, is: 'We underestimated because we wanted to do the job'" (Kharbanda/Stallworthy 1983, p.258).

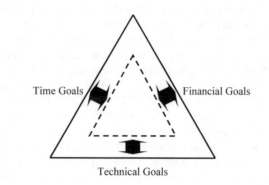

Technical Goals

------ Optimistic Level of Achievement

——— Pessimistic Level of Achievement

Fig. 21. Stating Ranges in the Initial Goal Framework

(3) The third recommendation, which aims at achieving a balanced goal framework from the beginning, is to *establish an internal obligation among the project owners and an external obligation to the public*. As mentioned above, the internal obligation can be achieved by a formal commitment of the project owners and by bylaws of the project company. In addition, the procedure for reformulating the initial goals should be impeded by specific regulations such as the principle of unanimity. Concerning the external obligation, officially informing the public and requiring the owners to justify any intended changes can establish the basis for public awareness of goal change. The idea of personalizing MOEs, meaning that the development (and success) of the MOE is linked to the careers of well-known public persons – e.g. leading politicians – is tempting but cannot necessarily prevent goal expansions or disastrous results. Remember Montreal and the mayor's (Jean Drapeau) identification with the Olympic Games in 1976, calling them "his" Games. He was neither able to manage them nor to finance them successfully (Auf der Maur 1976).

(4) Even if project owners fail to establish a balanced initial goal framework it may be stabilized later on by successfully *managing the driving forces* (managing the change). Some driving forces must be eliminated from the very beginning, especially forces that aim at achieving the highest currently available technical standards or the obligation to fully comply with the requirements of the users or other project participants. Such intentions are likely to fail. The long completion time of MOEs may cause a never-ending spiral of new demands and, therefore, affects the whole MOE negatively. In order to deal with driving forces, a separate "change management" structure and procedure has to be established (Seamans/Ordway 1977, pp.290). A lesson may be learned from the Apollo program and the Munich Hospital, where controlled project change ensured the acceptance of unavoidable changes without jeopardizing the goal framework. Instead of offering incentives for goal changes (such as contracts which allow architects to increase their fees as

the costs of the MOE increase) mechanisms that penalize changes should be inserted. As a minimum requirement, individuals and institutions asking for changes should be recorded and made known to the public if the change would affect the time or financial goals. Furthermore, the management structure should provide for obligatory channels and procedures to be followed before the change is approved.

Another way to blunt the influence of the driving forces is the establishment and strengthening of opposing forces. The financial goals which are supposed to be a limiting force have failed repeatedly. One reason is the often delayed or incomplete calculation of the financial consequences of changes. Therefore, the only real limiting force – apart from the socio-political environment, which may even bring an end to the MOE – is time, and the first question is not how to finish within a limited time but how to establish a time limit. Deadlines for the process of goal change (such as "frozen zones" in the production of heavy equipment) are easier to establish under a given time pressure as in the case of Olympic Games. Even then strong tendencies to extend the decision period could be observed. "Waiting for Mexico" was a common slogan used by the Munich hosts (Games 1972) to justify decision delays because of the chance to gain experience from the Mexican Games in 1968. Therefore, effective time management is the most promising method of managing goal change and, subsequently, of ensuring proper goal achievement.

H. Basic Design

The basic design determines how (technical) goals are to be achieved. The same technical goals may be achieved with different basic designs (e.g. a one- or two-block design for university hospitals, a bridge or tunnel as a link). In this case, the financial or the time goals may be decisive for the choice of a specific basic design. The basic design of MOEs is crucial for project success:

- It immediately determines the performance of the technical goals which have a dominant influence on the overall performance.
- If the basic design does not comply with the interests of the project owners and the users, the whole undertaking will encounter substantial changes during all phases, including the initial operation and permanent operation & maintenance of the project.

I. *Meaning and Variety of Basic Design*

Viewed logically, the technical goals (the results) have to be formulated before the basic design (the means) can be fixed.[16] Typical of MOEs is that their technical goals are innovative and that they may be changed if the analysis of their achievement as well as the basic design indicates potential difficulties. Consequently, the relationship of basic design and technical goals is neither one-sided, nor final, but rather dynamic and likely to change in a process as shown in Fig. 22.

The initial basic design (1) which is derived from the initial technical goals (1) leads to a change of the technical goals (2). There may be a revised basic design (2) which corresponds to the requirements of the revised technical goals. Further analysis may generate the basic design (3), inducing further revisions of the technical goals (3). The process comes to an end when the final technical goals (n) and the final basic design (n) match.

Due to its interdependence with the technical goals, the basic design should always reflect the fact that the technical goals are likely to be incomplete, too, a problem we already discussed in Chapter B. Defining the basic design may help to overcome incomplete goal formulations.

---

[16] That means a goal-driven instead of a solution-driven approach, see Flyvberg et al. 2003, pp.115.

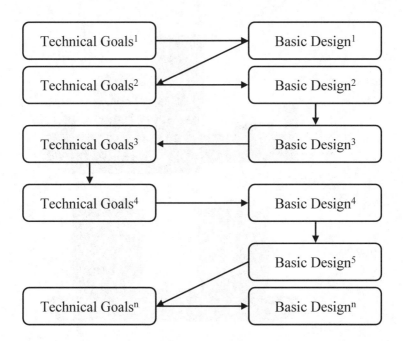

Fig. 22. Relationship between Technical Goals and Basic Design

The Olympic Games as well as the university hospitals are good examples of the process of deriving and fixing the basic design. Let us turn to the *university hospitals* first. When the hospitals in Aachen, Munich, and Vienna were started in the 1950s and early 1960s, the prevailing opinion was that only the so called "block-type building" (in contrast to the traditional pavilion design; see Fig. 24) would be able to meet the requirements of sophisticated medical and technical standards because:

- block-type buildings facilitate the cooperation between the clinical and non-clinical departments, a cooperation which generally suffers from continuous specialization on both sides;
- block-type buildings are best suited to ensure the high utilization of the expensive infrastructure and equipment;
- block-type buildings are suitable for adapting the bed capacity to the changing requirements of the various departments (instead of equipping all departments with a fixed number of beds);
- block-type buildings were believed to be more convenient for patients, physicians, and scientists because the distances between the departments and facilities were kept to a minimum. As a side effect, labor costs were expected to be reduced.

Although the advantages of the block-type buildings were not undisputed from the beginning, the Munich and the Vienna hospitals were designed this way.

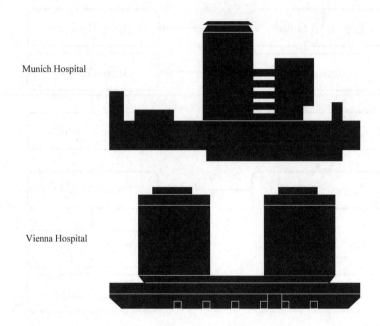

Munich Hospital

Vienna Hospital

Fig. 23. Block-Type Design of the Munich and Vienna Hospitals

The Munich and Vienna Hospitals (see Fig. 23) are very similar in design apart from their significant difference in size (the usable floor space of the Vienna Hospital is twice of that of the Munich Hospital and the building volume three times). It should also be mentioned that the Vienna Hospital has a two-block design which has proven to be more useful than the one-block design in Munich.

The *Olympic Games* demonstrate different options for the basic design, not only regarding the overall design but also the design of the individual facilities. The Games in Munich (1972) and Montreal (1976) were both influenced by the concept of short distances between the various facilities. The significant differences in the basic design were due to a different technical goal in Munich, requiring "open-space Games". This goal ruled out a concentration of solid construction facilities on a single site.

Major differences in the basic design of facilities serving the same technical goals can be illustrated by comparing, for example, different ski-jump facilities. The ski-jump competitions at the Games in Lake Placid were held on man-made ski-jumps in contrast to so called natural jump facilities using the gradient of the  hill as a run-out. Minor – but no less effective – differences in the basic design were various standards in the technical equipment, such as snow and ice making equipment.

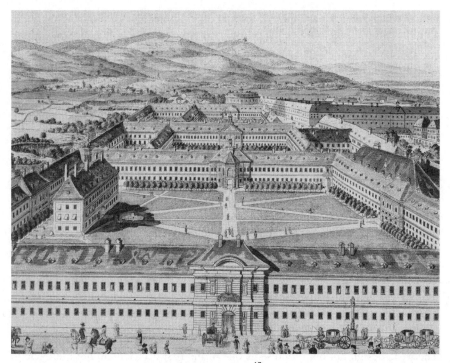

Fig. 24. Pavilion Design of the Old Vienna Hospital[17]

So far we have demonstrated that the basic design is not a mere "translation" of technical dictates but *subject to an explicit decision*. This decision has long-term consequences. A city hosting Olympic Summer Games is faced with the basic decision of whether the stadium should be covered by a roof or not. On the one hand, the roof may be less important for the initial operation during the summer period; on the other hand, it may become a crucial factor for the permanent operation, especially when long winter periods call for special accommodations. Even after this basic decision has been made, there is still a wide variety of options regarding the design, fixation, and material of the roof.

Several options also have to be considered when deciding on the location of MOEs. In Vienna, for instance, the university hospital is located in the center of the town, whereas the Munich University Hospital is located on the outskirts. Deciding in favor of the latter may generate additional demands on the infrastructure, especially the transportation system.

The decision on the basic design deals not only with options but also with important *constraints*. For any type of construction work the availability of suitable sites represents an important constraint. In Calgary, the hosts of the 1988 Games chose sites for the sports facilities which experts qualified as inadequate because of the local weather conditions. Therefore, the choice of locations for events or fa-

---

[17] Wyklicky/Skopec 1984, p.8

cilities which require very specific sites is often limited. Not a physical but rather a political constraint could be the refusal of a region or city to host a special event or facility (such as airports, power plants, or recycling plants). Conversely, a city may insist on participating in events or facilities in order to improve its infrastructure or to receive additional taxes.

It has become evident that the decision on the basic design is a very complex and time-consuming process. The basic design of the Olympic Village in Munich, for example, was fixed after screening fifty-seven alternatives (!) which were subsequently reduced in a step-by-step procedure without changing the technical goals. Screening has to be continued until the achievement of the technical goal is ensured and a specification of the time and financial goals is possible. The dilemma between never-ending (delayed) and over-hasty decisions is obvious and requires further attention (see Chapter Q. II. 1.).

We assume that the *high complexity* of basic designs has *negative effects on their consistency*. Obviously, complex systems require a long time to be completed, giving the project participants the chance to press for changes. The reasons for changing basic designs are not only technical but also financial ones. At the Munich Hospital the basic design was changed in order to reduce the complexity of the building and thus to meet the time and financial goals.

II.   Impact of Basic Design on Goal Achievement

The basic design not only represents one of the first decisions in the life cycle of an MOE, but also has a dominant influence on goal achievement. The effect which the different types of basic designs have on goal achievement can be amply demonstrated by the *university hospitals* in Munich and Vienna.

Both hospitals were started at approximately the same time and had comparable technical goals. The number of similarities decreased as the planning and completion phases proceeded, resulting in a rather satisfactory achievement of the completion and operation goals in Munich and extraordinary cost and schedule overruns in Vienna. The main reason for the unequal goal achievement was the development of two different basic designs. In Munich the design was more or less fixed with remarkable efforts to reduce complexity. The Vienna Hospital experienced a prolonged uncertainty about the basic design plus the tendency to expand the basic design and its complexity. The development of the basic designs is illustrated in the following figure.

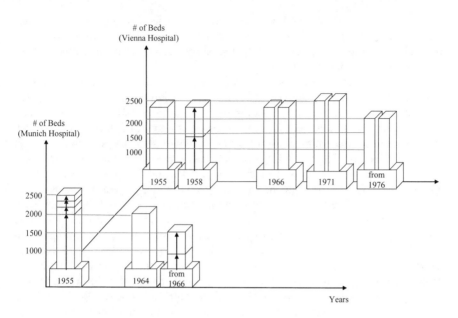

Fig. 25. Change of Basic Designs of the Vienna (top) and Munich (bottom) Hospitals

Comments on the Munich Hospital:
- In 1964 the project owner decided to reduce the basic design by cancelling major parts of the project, which meant giving up about one quarter of the whole facility and about 500 beds.
- In 1966 the project owner reduced the capacity to about 1500 beds thus compensating for the cost overruns. The whole complex was divided into nine sections, enabling an almost independent work on the separate sections, and into two completion phases: Conservative departments (completion and start-up in 1974) and surgical departments (completion and start-up in 1980).
- In 1966/67 and 1974 minor corrections were made to the requirement specifications.

Comments on the Vienna Hospital:
- In 1955 a new building for only one clinical department was planned.
- In 1965 the two-step-completion approach of 1958 was replaced by a one-step approach.
- In 1974 the first of the four sections was completed.
- In 1976/77 the decision in favor of one of the six alternatives for the central building and the annexed buildings, which together represented about 80 % of the whole hospital (the so called fourth section) was taken.

In general, the basic design of *Olympic Games* caused fewer problems. The nature of the event as well as the interests of the permanent users favored decentralized solutions and allowed for a reduction in complexity. Partial failures occurred none the less, as the Olympic Games in Munich demonstrated. The design of the architect, which was approved by the project owner, included one roof for three different facilities (Olympic stadium, main sport hall, and swimming hall). The serious difficulties caused by the design of the tent-shaped roof significantly hindered the planning and completion of these facilities.

There is another lesson to be learnt from the Games in Munich. A well known characteristic of complex decisions is that the decision-making activity is spread over the total problem-solving process resulting in a series of preliminary decisions. These preliminary decisions may be seen as a tool to reduce complexity by dividing the problem into portions which facilitate stepwise solutions. Yet an over-hasty fixation on preliminary decisions has to be avoided and a compromise between the pressure to make decisions and the demand for free options has to be found. At the Games in Munich, the project owner, the project management, as well as the public were very pleased with the ambitious design of the planning architects. The architects successfully insisted on the completion of their design by the project management. The conflict between the architects and the project management was inevitable when technical problems and cost and schedule overruns arose, especially in the case of the tent-shaped roof. As the project went on, the interests of the project owners began to conflict with the interests of the architects, as aptly described by a member of the project company's board: "We are told all the time that the interests of the project owners are met in a unique manner, including the functions of the facilities. Yet the project owner is more or less forced to comply with the ideas of the architect" (Grün 1975a, p.43). Finally, the "cooperation" between the project company and the architect ended in a lawsuit over the architect's fee.

The case of *GROWIAN* is another striking example of the negative impact of an early fixation of the basic design (concerning the size of the rotor) on goal achievement (see also Flyvberg et al. 2003, pp.89).

III.   *Managing Basic Design*

The following chapter deals with the methods of influencing the basic design. There are four essentials to be considered for the management of the basic design:

- Limiting the risk,
- Breaking down the technical goals,
- maintaining consistency, and
- ensuring the project owners' responsibilities.

1. Limiting Risks

If risks cannot be limited by the basic design, crisis management is often the only way out. Limiting risks does not mean risk avoidance because risk is a characteristic of MOEs in general. It reduces, however, the likelihood of MOE disasters, and primarily refers to technical aspects, especially the size, complexity, and singularity of the MOE. Risk limiting should include the following aspects:

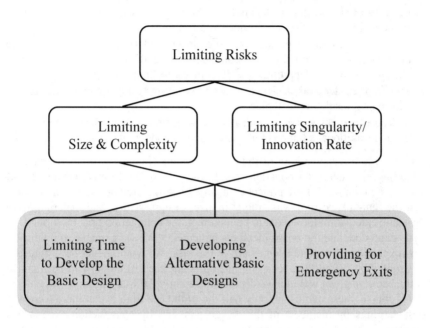

Fig. 26. Strategies for Limiting Risks in the Development of the Basic Design

Limiting size must not be mistaken for a plea for small undertakings. We have to be aware, however, that there are boundaries or limits which cannot be exceeded without facing substantial difficulties. It has been shown, for instance, that 1,500 beds are the crucial limit for university hospitals of a block-type design. *Limiting complexity* is even more challenging than limiting size as complexity cannot be measured in quantitative terms such as user-units (beds, spectators), area, or cubature. We can only distinguish different levels of complexity when comparing alternative basic designs, such as the block-type compared to the pavilion design for university hospitals. Unfortunately, the proponents of sophisticated solutions – deliberately or not – tend to underestimate complexity. Complexity in conjunction with (over)size can be disastrous, as the Vienna Hospital has shown. The block-type design is a typical result of the trend that dominated the 1960s, favoring gigantic undertakings and unlimited confidence in technology. Later on, experts stated: "Nowadays such a monster (the new Vienna Hospital, note of the author) would not be built any more" (Kurier, Vienna, 1980-02-24). The block-type design even failed to meet its basic idea, which was to centralize all facilities. The actual design with an increasing number of annexed buildings located in the vicinity of the main building can be interpreted as a renewal of the traditional pavilion design.

Calling for *limiting the innovation rate* may not be very popular. On the other hand, unlimited innovation rates can wind up creating a disaster. Despite the availability of state-of-the-art technology, the project owners of the Munich Hospital decided in favor of simple, almost "old fashioned" solutions:

- They excluded the expensive self-supporting walls and were satisfied with brick walls to save money. This construction was flexible enough to allow for changes of clinical departments without major technical difficulties.
- The front facade was designed to save energy by using small-sized windows and special insulating materials.
- Instead of expensive and technically sophisticated systems they preferred simple and traditional solutions for waste disposal and on-site transportation.

The minimum responsibility of the project owners should be complete frankness regarding the intended innovation rate. In the case of the Munich Games, for instance, the members of the project company's board were not told (or not aware?) that the tent-shaped roof was unique in size, design, statics, and material. When the static calculation turned out to be incorrect, the completion time multiplied, the costs exploded, and the board members lamented: "We were unable to predict the cost explosion. If we had been aware of this risk, we would never have agreed to this roof". Or: "If all facts regarding the costs and the difficulties had been known at the beginning, we would have decided differently." (Grün 1975a, S. 46)

Of course, these quotes tell only half the truth. The truth is that there were serious warnings by members of the design jury and by construction experts who pointed out the risk of cost explosions. The members of the project company's board, however, ignored the weak warning signals in view of the challenging and impressive design of the tent-shaped roof. Complaints by skeptics were of no avail because constant time pressure prevented a change of the basic design. In this context, we should note that time pressure has not only objective but also subjective effects. The objective effect of the time pressure on the Olympic Games, for example, was further increased by the subjective impression that there was not enough time for the serious planning and discussion of alternative basic designs.

Once again, *time management* proves to be crucial for MOE success. The basic design is affected by time as extensive periods for the development of the basic design may be misunderstood as an invitation for change. Remember the differences in time to determine the final basic design and the management of change for the Munich and the Vienna Hospital, respectively. While Munich required about ten years to determine the final basic design (1954-1964), the same process took about nineteen years in Vienna (1957-1976). The reduction of size in Munich resulted in a cut in capacity of about 1,000 beds. Vienna also cut its bed capacity by about 500 beds but at the same time increased the building volume from about 1m cubic meters (1957) to about 2m cubic meters (1976) and finally about 2.8m cubic meters (1980)! The complexity of the hospital was further increased when users enforced the replacement of the two-step completion plan by a one-step completion approach in 1965. This decision may have been the most significant management mistake in the life of this undertaking. The mistake was committed by those faculty members whose departments were scheduled to be finished in the second completion phase. They feared that the cost overruns of the first completion step might prevent the execution of the second step. With regard to these negative effects of change, especially of "late" changes, it is advisable to set a time limit for the development of the basic design. This time limit is even more effective in the case of time pressure. If the basic design cannot be developed sufficiently for serious cost estimates within a limited period, there is strong evidence that the risk is too high as far as the overall performance of the MOE is concerned.

Aside from time management, *parallel planning* is an essential tool for the project management and the project owners to ensure the proper development of the basic design. Some cases indicate a strict "all-or-nothing" strategy (the Vienna Hospital, the Munich Games, and GROWIAN, for example, were committed to the block-type building, the tent-shaped roof, and a special rotor type, respectively). The only way to limit the risk and to ensure choice is to *develop alternative basic designs*. It would have been desirable for the university hospitals to develop a pavilion-type design simultaneously to the block-type design. There were also several alternatives for the tent-shaped roof in Munich. The common argument that there was not enough time or capacity (or both) for parallel planning was rather weak. The time and capacity actually spent on making the basic design work was much more than the time necessary for planning alternatives, not to mention the cost overruns resulting from sticking to one plan. Therefore, the project owners have to ensure sufficient management and planning capacity from the beginning to allow for the serious development and screening of alternative basic designs by means of feasibility studies.

Providing for "emergency exits" is a third method to limit the risks. Emergency exits are needed to ensure that even if MOEs fail to achieve their original goals, the project can function as a viable torso by achieving less ambitious or other goals. An impressive example of the emergency exit approach is the Pentagon in Arlington, Va (U.S. Defense Department). It was originally designed to accommodate veterans from World War II. According to this approach, the design of university hospitals should allow for alternative uses like nursing homes or office buildings.

2. Breaking Down of Basic Design

The breakdown approach is closely linked to the risk-limiting approach. Breaking down the MOE into manageable subparts reduces and limits the total project risk. In such a way MOEs which are gigantic in size and show high levels of singularity and complexity can be tackled. Breakdown means separating the elements of the basic design in terms of substance and sequence. The aim is to decrease the rate of interdependence among the MOE parts, thus reducing the overall complexity. The work-breakdown structure (WBS) is a classic in the arsenal of project management tools. When WBS is applied to MOEs, however, the operation as well as the completion phase and the interdependence among the parts in terms of time and sequence have to be considered.

Breaking down the completion phase, a proper balance between the various MOE parts in terms of size, singularity, and complexity has to be ensured. This criterion was significantly violated in the case of the Vienna Hospital: Whereas three sections accounted for only 20% each showing low levels of size, complexity, and singularity, the remaining fourth section accounted for almost 80% of the total project. The initial basic design of the Munich Hospital was also unbalanced, with one section representing about 75% and three sections only about 25% of the total project. This mistake was revised in the final basic design by having two relatively well balanced sections.

As mentioned above, the breakdown also affects the *operation* of MOEs. In the (initial) operation phase of Olympic Games, different users (like sports associations) operate different facilities for different purposes at the same time. The breakdown must consider such a "horizontal" aspect of operation and should enable simultaneous uses without mutual interference. Interferences can be avoided best, if all facilities are adequately fitted with infrastructural and technical equipment as well as administration units.

The approach for the operation of university hospitals is quite different. Hospitals need a basic design which allows turning over individual sections to operation as they are completed. In Munich the architects complained that half of the patients' block was left unused for several years. This could have been avoided by breaking down the basic design into more than two sections. Due to their experience with the Munich Hospital, the architects and a senior project manager were of the opinion that more than two sections should have been planned, completed, and operated separately.

Our discussion of the basic design for completion and operation strongly indicates the importance of *sequence aspects* in the breakdown approach. Here, the *milestone concept* is worth mentioning. It is a means of reducing the complexity of processes and of facilitating the feedback on the level of goal achievement. The milestone concept is designed for successive action in linear processes. The general question is: Which course of action will minimize the dependency of the later actions on the preceding ones? Or asking more precisely: Does the initial "go" decision exclude "no go" decisions in the future, meaning that once a project is started, it must be completed under all circumstances?

Common but partially contradictory rules of thumb are:
- complex components first (as it is easier to make up time lost on complex parts by working on the simple ones);
- simple components first (to create and benefit from learning effects which may facilitate the following work on the complex components);
- urgent components first (replacing old facilities, like clinical departments which suffer from the worst conditions);
- parallel completion of (all) project components.

It should be noted that in practice these strategies are rarely found in their pure form, but rather as combinations.

An *"all-or-nothing"* strategy (Fig. 27) results in a long completion time and a late start of operation. The risk of this strategy is that failures in the completion phase delay the operation of all project components. The strategy of the Vienna Hospital came close to this strategy, with the exception of minor project parts which were completed earlier and turned over to operation.

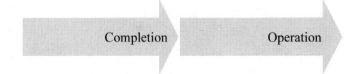

Fig. 27. "All-or-Nothing" Strategy

The *Indian-file strategy* (Fig. 28) tries to avoid risks by delaying further completion until experience with the operation of finished components has been gained. The completion time remains the same, but finished components can go into operation without delay. The "Mercury" project is an example of such a strategy where all steps were based on the experience gathered in the preceding steps (Swenson et al. 1966, pp.638).

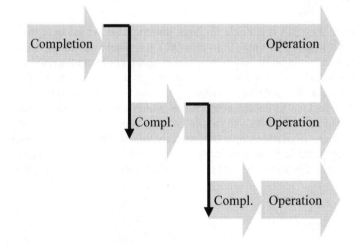

Fig. 28. Indian-File Strategy

The *overlapping strategy* (Fig. 29) reduces the completion time by starting the completion of later following components without waiting for the feed-back on the operation of earlier components. Therefore, the final operation can start sooner compared to the "all-or-nothing" and the "Indian-file" strategy. The capacity requirements and the risks are comparatively higher. The Munich Hospital came close to this strategy although it suffered delays in operation resulting from the block-type design which complicated the project breakdown.

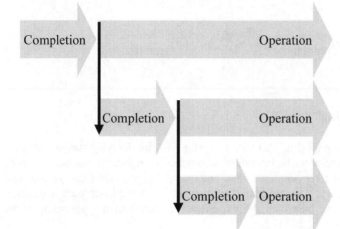

Fig. 29. Overlapping Strategy

The *parallel strategy* (Fig. 30) is suitable for large undertakings which have to be finished within a short period of time (time pressure) and where operation has to be started simultaneously. Capacity requirements during the completion period are high. The risk is considered to be average as the likelihood of all components failing is rather low. A good example of this strategy are the Olympic Games. Time pressure makes it necessary to design components which can be planned, completed, and operated simultaneously. The parallel strategy requires the components to be balanced in terms of size, complexity, and singularity to ensure (almost) equal completion times. Since these criteria were disregarded Montreal the Games in 1976 had to be opened without the ambitious umbrella roof having been completed.

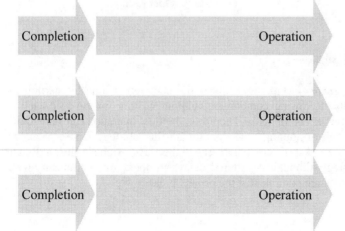

Fig. 30. Parallel Strategy

The ratings of the four strategies are summed up in the following table.

Breakdown Strategy	Criteria			
	Completion Time	Date of Operation	Capacity Requirements (per Period)	Risk
All-or-Nothing	long	very late	low	high
Indian-File	long	early/ medium/late	low	low
Overlapping	medium	early/medium	low/medium	low/medium
Parallel	short	early	high	medium

Table 14. Evaluation of Breakdown Strategies

3. Maintaining Consistency

Like the breakdown approach, the consistency approach complements the effort to limit risks. It aims at preventing endless changes of the basic design. We can distinguish change required by project owners and change necessitated by technical problems. Accordingly, we have to deal with two directions of consistency, the forward consistency affecting the contractors and the backward consistency affecting the project owners. Both aspects are closely related.

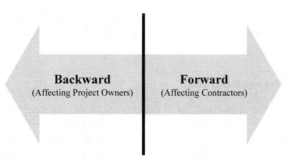

Backward
(Affecting Project Owners)

Forward
(Affecting Contractors)

Fig. 31. Directions and Subjects of Consistency

The consistency of the basic design is endangered if it fails to meet the technical standards or cannot be performed within reasonable financial or time limits. The *requirements of forward consistency* are met when all serious doubts regarding the technical feasibility as well as the achievement of the time and financial goals have been eliminated. Traditional planning methods require for a determination of the basic design before potential contractors are involved, e.g. construction companies are invited for tenders. These methods increase the likelihood of changes of the basic design or missing the goals. The only way out is to ensure overlapping planning and completion know-how and responsibility.

At the Olympic Games in Munich several members of the project management strongly advised to create a joint responsibility pact for the tent-shaped roof that would include the (planning) architects and the engineering and construction companies. They argued that the planning capacity and the construction know-how of the architects were not sufficient for large innovative buildings. This proposal was rejected because a majority insisted on finishing the planning process first and then making a formal invitation for tenders in order to strictly comply with the regulations on public procurement. With hindsight from the tent-shaped roof problems, the project management then changed its mind. By that time, however, it was too late to gain realistic cost estimates and serious plans for implementing alternative basic designs.

The *backward consistency* primarily addresses the project owners. Project owners tend to determine the basic design early (as the tent-shaped roof in Munich or GROWIAN have shown), and to continuously change basic designs in order to meet new (usually increasing) user requirements. If the MOE is subject to severe time pressure, the tendency to determine the basic design early is remarkable; conversely, there is a tendency towards unlimited change if explicit time limits are missing. Assuming that the project owners are responsible for the final decision on the basic design they need to be fully included in the discussion process. Once the decision makers, especially the opinion leaders, are convinced that they are fully informed about all relevant alternatives, their identification with that decision will be higher and the tendency to press for changes will decrease. To quote a member of the project company's board of the Games in Munich: "The stepwise selection procedure (starting with 57 alternatives for the basic design of the Olympic Village, note of the author) reassumes me that our decisions are on the right way. Furthermore, this procedure saves more time than any other method" (Grün, 1975a, p.40).

4. Project Owners' Responsibilities

As mentioned earlier, it is the responsibility of the project owners to determine the basic design. Project owners' responsibility cannot (or should not) be delegated. The problem is that a lot of persons and institutions – apart from the project owners – are very much interested in the basic design. They may call for an enlargement (as users and contractors) or for challenging designs (as architects). When making a final decision, project owners will need the help of experts, especially if the innovation rate of the project is high.

If the worst comes to the worst, the basic design reflects the different interests of the project owners without offering a solution for the conflicting views. This dilemma not only provokes further discussions among the project owners but also encourages the other participants to pursue their own interests. The stepwise performance of projects, broken down into separate components, and the incremental upgrading of the actual standard, is more favorable than the one-shot performance of huge and highly innovative MOEs (see Hall 1980, p.272).

The project owners' responsibilities include the awareness of their key role, which is – in our framework of the four success factors – the determination of the basic design. All project participants (i.e. the members of the project management, planning and engineering experts, consultants, contractors, and users) are not faced with and committed to the original goals but the basic design. Even the "external participants" from the socio-political environment often do not question the goals but rather fight the location and the size of an MOE. The basic design acts as an "interpreter" and "multiplier" of the goals. Interpreter means that the basic design should be understood as the authentic representation of the project goals. Multiplier means that mistakes or misunderstandings in the basic design will cause additional failures in the following planning and completion phase.

I.   Socio-Political Environment

Until the 1980s the socio-political environment was not discussed in project management. In the past years, however, it has proven indispensable to analyze the socio-political environment when dealing with MOEs. Our analysis includes the various spheres of the socio-political environment (I), its impact on goal achievement (II), and the question of how to manage this success factor (III).

I.   *Various Spheres of Socio-Political Environment*

The term socio-political environment was introduced in response to the awareness of forces outside the immediate influence of project owners and project management. Since we believe that these forces are not necessarily given but rather subject to management awareness and action, we will analyze the various spheres of the socio-political environment, especially regarding the sources and actors which cause, represent, and form them.

Ritterbush (1982, pp.113) distinguishes two different but interrelated "spheres" of the socio-political environment: the project environment and the country environment. Due to the special characteristics of MOEs we split up the project environment into the sphere of (1) the MOE, (2) the parent organizations (of the project owners), and (3) the contractors. We will solely concentrate on the socio-political aspects and neglect physical and technical aspects, such as the availability and the quality of local materials or equipment.

1. Nature and Development of MOEs

Discussions of the socio-political environment often neglect that it is strongly dependent on the MOE activity. The socio-political environment reacts to MOE activities, e.g. changes of the MOE basic designs.

Project management in the 1950s and 1960s was initially applied to weapon systems. These undertakings as well as their end products were virtually of a *non-profit* nature, and a "protective national defense cloak" shielded them from outside criticism (Horwitch/Prahalad 1982, pp.17). The Apollo program basically was a civil and non-profit project. Recent MOE activities focused on more controversial areas like transportation, communication and energy systems, economic development, and civil aviation. The end products of these MOEs served a *more commercial* purpose than those of the 1950s and 1960s. Return on investment calculations and profitability analysis became an important part of the decision process. Additionally, governments altered their R&D funding. They reduced their commitment in the field of hardware development, leaving it to the private sector and tried to sell "their" projects to private users, e.g. using the space shuttle in the telecommunications industry. As a result, the relationship between the public and private sector has become more complex.

Munich offers a striking example of extremely different reactions of the socio-political environment, depending on the nature of the MOE. To the distaste of the planning architects the university hospital was eclipsed by the Olympic Games in 1972. The Games were "a capricious child, cared for with extravagant and forbearing love" (Eichberger/Schlempp 1977, p.61). With hindsight, the university hospital can consider itself lucky not to have been the focus of public attention.

A comparison of the Munich and Vienna Hospitals leads to the conclusion that the influence of the socio-political environment depends not only on the technical goals (which were identical in their nature) but also on the success and failure of MOE activities. Whereas Munich was not subject to significant socio-political influence, the Vienna Hospital experienced it very intensively: Investigations by public accounting offices, by special parliamentary committees, and by the courts, daily news headlines, parliamentary debates, and resignations of politicians. The lesson to be learnt from this is that the kind and intensity of the socio-political influence depend on how the MOE develops. Successful MOE management can obviate or at least reduce this influence thus avoiding the pretext for political intervention.

Summing up, we have to keep in mind that the subdued and tolerant environment of MOEs in the 1950s and 1960s was a reflection of the projects that were carried out at that time. This restraint had almost disappeared by the late 1960s due to social and cultural changes (remember the student revolts in 1968). The socio-political environment caused impediments and setbacks that, for example, "... the Defense Department never dreamed off" (Baker et al. 1988, p.923). But the loss of the "protective cloak" may also be explained by changes of MOE activities and by failures in the management of MOEs.

2. Parent Organizations

For MOEs a special organization has to be set up which is responsible for planning and completion. Usually the project company, founded by the project owners but run separately from the parent organizations, is the adequate organizational framework for MOEs. Regardless of the legal form of the project company, the project owners are responsible for nominating the top project managers and their representatives on the various committees (board, etc.).

This nomination is an important source of socio-political influence. The nomination itself is often more of a political matter than a question of project management expertise, which will be discussed later on (see Chapter J). If the representatives of the project owners on the boards are politicians (as in almost all our cases), the MOE decisions are very likely to be influenced by political considerations. These considerations sometimes refer to the trade-off between the short-term maximization of votes versus the long-term viability and welfare of the project. Decisions likely to be objected to, e.g. by environmental protection organizations, are frequently delayed. This *influence by nomination* can be even more dysfunctional if the representatives of the project owners are members of different (political) parties or even different wings of the same party. According to media reports, the opposition to the Tornado aircraft was supported by the left wing of the German Social Democratic Party, while the Minister of Defense, a member of the same party, approved the project. Statements and actions are likely to be changed, if a political party loses or gains governmental power during the life of MOEs.

Apart from the influence by nomination, there may also be socio-political influence from the sphere of the project owners by *ad-hoc interventions*. Political ad-hoc intervention is very common when public sector MOEs have experienced (or are expected to experience) a crisis. The Concorde was supported by the British and French government although there was no doubt that the project would not achieve its economic goals. In Austria two referenda, both resulting in a rejection of the MOEs, prompted opposite governmental reactions: A nuclear power plant near Vienna (about $500m completion costs in 1978) was suspended when practically completed and finally terminated, whereas the Vienna International Center was completed as planned. Another example of political intervention was the Vienna Hospital. After the scandal had reached its peak – extensively exploited by the opposition parties, of course – a former chancellor insisted on establishing special internal control procedures which contributed to control overkill and caused further schedule overruns (see Chapter J.I.3).

Additionally, the *media* may play an important role in the process of initiating, blowing up, but also in calming down political discussions on MOEs. They surely cannot be blamed for that. The topics for their headlines are not necessarily essential problems (like cost explosions or schedule overruns), but rather side aspects (like corruption) which can be "sold" more effectively. The choice is often left to chance.

3. Contractors

As mentioned above, we will not deal with the role of contractors in terms of technical and economic performance, such as the availability and quality of materials, equipment, skills, and financial resources. These aspects are very important, especially for international project but are not typical of MOEs. We focus on socio-political problems caused by contractors (see Flyvberg et al. 2003, p.45).

Contractors intend to create *pressure to start MOEs* in the first place. A lot of MOEs deal with industries which are dominated by only a few suppliers that make a remarkable – sometimes the dominant – part of their turnover and profit by contracting with public clients. This dependency on public clients (potential project owners) may be found in the weapons, the aerospace, the aircraft, and in the construction industry. Contracts with (public) project owners are attractive for contractors as they ensure not only a basic capacity utilization over a long period of time but also the chance to make profits by gaining from almost inevitable changes of MOEs. The pressure to start MOEs is very strong if public interests can be asserted. Typical arguments include the creation and safeguarding of jobs (often supported by contractors as well as by labor unions), keeping up with the international technological standard (this argument was especially favored by the British and French aircraft industry to promote the Concorde project), and strengthening international competitiveness. The pressure increases if the potential contractors are fully or partially owned by public sector organizations.

The same arguments that are employed to start MOEs may be used to *enlarge or to finish* them. The arguments and actions used by contractors to enlarge MOEs are rather sophisticated. They may support the initial overoptimism or offer more advanced technical systems and solutions during the planning and completion phase, or they may recommend systems which require sophisticated engineering and maintenance assistance during the operation phase.

A third type of influence is linked to the *choice of contractors*. As our cases as well as other studies have shown, project owners are encouraged if not urged to employ local, regional, or domestic contractors even if other contractors have submitted better bids. This preferential treatment may include planning experts (like architects) and engineering, construction, and equipment companies. Once again, arguments like the creation and safeguarding of jobs or even "national security" are used to justify local, regional, or national preferences. Contractors can also try to influence the recruitment of the project managers or nominate their own representatives for the project management. It should be mentioned that local preferences are not typical of MOEs. The engagement of a local but not sufficiently qualified contractor, however, can cause many more difficulties for a one-shot undertaking than for repetitive processes.

4. Local, Regional, and National Institutions

Local, regional, and national institutions can exercise political, legal, social, and cultural influences on MOEs. Sometimes genuine *political considerations* are the reason for starting MOEs and even participating in them as project owners, not to mention "defense-policy" considerations in connection with weapons, transportations, and communications systems. The decision of the German Federal as well as the Bavarian State government, for instance, to support the City of Munich in getting the Olympic Games of 1972 awarded was heavily influenced by their ambition to present the image of a new democratic and wealthy society to the world and to erase all memories of the fascist regime which dominated the Games 1936 in Berlin. The attempts of developing countries to host Olympic Games or other international events like world fairs may be based on similar intentions. Undertakings may also be carried out to maintain a leading position in international competition or to respond to challenging MOEs in other countries. The Apollo program, pushed by J.F. Kennedy in the 1960s, is a striking example of such political-economic influence on MOEs, where the very best US scientists and engineers were engaged to achieve the president's vision and to demonstrate America's world-wide leadership in science and engineering. Due to the increasing influence of the economy on politics, economic aspects are an important driving force for MOEs.

The *legal influence* (federal and state) is most advanced and formalized in the field of environmental protection.[18] The following comments on US legislation are

---

[18] For environmental impacts and risks see Flyvberg et al. 2003, pp.49.

to illustrate the kind and strength of this influence on MOEs (see Hoyte 1982, pp.39). The National Environmental Policy Act (NEPA) is a "national policy requiring that all federal agencies give comprehensive consideration to environmental impacts in planning and carrying out agency programs". An Environmental Impact Statement (EIS) is required for every major federal act that might significantly affect the quality of the environment. This calls for a discussion of alternatives and for the adequate circulation of the results in order to enable comments from the people and institutions involved. The Environmental Protection Agency (EPA, established in 1970) has to review and comment on all EISs. The EPA is also engaged in the Clean Air Act, which regulates the emissions from stationary and mobile sources of air pollution. The State Implementation Plan (SIP) aims at achieving and maintaining the national standards. There are other federal regulations like the Federal Clean Water Act (FCWA). The EPA has laid down a number of limitations (required by the FWCA) for each industry, based on the various levels of technology. The Resource Conservation and Recovery Act of 1976 is supposed to prevent environmental damage by regulating the disposal of both hazardous and non-hazardous waste.

Numerous state regulations also deal with the review and approval of projects that might have a significant impact on the environment. The Massachusetts Environmental Protection Act (MEPA), for instance, calls for the filing of an Environmental Notification Form (ENF) and for an Environmental Impact Review (EIR). The following figure illustrates the process of how the ENF and the EIR are handled:

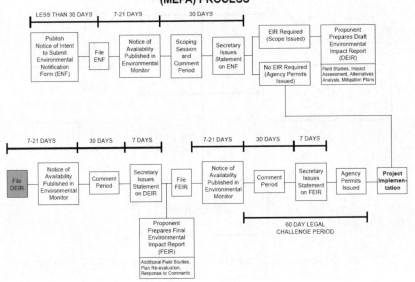

Fig. 32. MEPA Process Flowchart (City of Boston/Town of Brookline 2003)

Some of the regulations mentioned above affect all MOEs with (at least partially) public ownership. Other MOEs, like power plants, are subject to special regulations. The Nuclear Regulatory Commission (NRC) and the Department of Energy (DOE) have significant influence on the initial MOE decision and on the site selection through the Federal Energy Regulatory Commission (FERC, since 1972).

Although most of the regulations represent the demands of environmentally minded groups, and residents' participation in the project development process has been institutionalized, there is another impact on MOEs which may be even more effective than the impact of legal regulations. Residents who are directly affected by project locations as well as environmentalists like the World Wide Fund for Nature (WWF) or Greenpeace, and professional activists (some of them traveling around the world to oppose every major new undertaking) have made headlines with their opposition. Individuals and groups who claim to represent the general public are at work, using the regulations as an instrument for campaigns against MOEs. These "new participants" are equipped with their own data sources and (sometimes self-appointed) experts. They cause an increasing number of interventions and they have even founded their own parties (the "green" parties) with the express mission of protecting the environment.

The relationship between the spheres of the MOE, the parent organizations, the contractors, and the local/regional/national institutions are shown in the following figure:

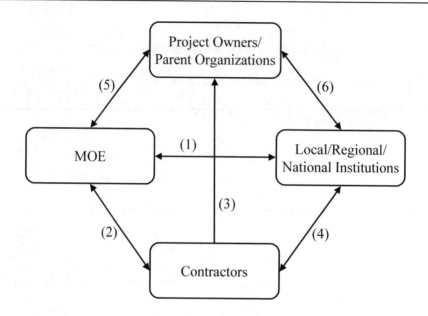

Fig. 33. Relationship between Various Spheres of the Socio-Political Environment

MOEs and the local/regional/national institutions are closely interrelated (1). On the one hand, MOEs are subject to existing regulations (like approval procedures) and to ad-hoc interventions. On the other hand, the MOE may be the reason for establishing additional regulations (such as the introduction of special auditing features after the scandal in Vienna). If local, regional, or national interests can be proved, the project owners/management can expect special support like additional funds or the provision of sites (6).

MOEs may stimulate extraordinary efforts by contractors (2) to establish new subsidiaries, cooperatives, or even new businesses. They may also try to influence the parent organizations and the local/regional/national institutions. Their influence on the parent organizations aims at starting and enlarging the MOE and at controlling the key decisions (3). The range of means includes the nomination of local politicians for the committees of the project company and perhaps even bribes to decision-makers. A common method used by the contractors to influence the local/regional/national authorities (4) is lobbying by individuals, groups, or associations (sometimes by forming a coalition of employers and unions).

The socio-political influence of the *parent organizations* on an MOE (5), apart from its official influence through the project company) depends mainly on the amount of attention which the parent organizations pay to the MOE relative to other undertakings they are involved in.

II.   Impact of the Socio-Political Environment on Goal Achievement

Since the 1980s, the relevant literature has been showing a significant impact of the socio-political environment on goal achievement. Apart from the almost classic environmental restrictions which Kharbanda/Stallworthy (1983, p.255) call an "ever increasing and ever more significant factor in both the initial capital cost of the plant and also in running costs", there are other constraints on the achievement of the MOE goals.

The impact of the socio-political environment on goal achievement differs in kind and strength and varies with the goals to be achieved. A nuclear power plant or an airport, for instance, are likely to be subjected to more environmental influence than a project in developing countries or the Olympic Games. Concerning the strength of the impact, there is some evidence that the importance of the socio-political environment for goal achievement correlates with the size of the MOE (Kelley 1982a, p.13).

The influence of the socio-political environment is described in the relevant literature as an *increasing lack of predictability* of both the process and the outcome of an MOE. Concerning the *process*, some effects may be predicted fairly well. The proliferation of governmental regulations primarily influences the duration and costs of the MOE. Hoyte (1982, p.54) points out that a detailed environmental evaluation of alternative sites and the regulatory agency's review of a coal-fired power plant, for example, may take years even without regulatory complications. Infighting in established environmental agencies as well as in local or state authorities may also increase the length of the process. Therefore, further governmental regulations are assumed to be dangerous and undesirable for projects (see Sykes 1982, p.150). In Lake Placid the ski-jumps were accused of causing "sight pollution" and some replanning was necessary to meet the environmental regulations (which increased the time pressure and the project costs).

Another regulation which protracts the process are *auditing systems*. They are established to safeguard public interests, especially the proper compliance with regulations regarding bid procedures. Auditing systems often act in an oversophisticated and bureaucratic way causing substantial delays in planning and completion.

Other types of socio-political influences on the process prove even more dysfunctional because the date, strength, subject, and objective of the influence are not predictable. *Political events like elections* may delay or accelerate the MOE process. The Rhine-Main-Danube Canal project, for instance, was suspended by the German Social Democratic Government. It was only continued after the Christian Democratic Party had come to power. The reconstruction and operation of the wind power prototype GROWIAN was only possible after the state government had changed.

Limited predictability of the outcome of MOEs refers to their size, their location, and even to the whole undertaking. Frequently, the impact of the socio-political environment can be cushioned by changing the initial goal framework, especially by reducing the technical goals or the basic design. Sometimes socio-political influence is exerted to obtain a change in the location of an MOE. The "nimby" (not in my backyard) -argument is often used by residents to prevent an MOE from being located close to their properties. Unpopular MOEs such as refuse disposal sites or power plants are then shoved around from one city or state to the next (like challenge trophies) until the ultimate decision to stop the MOE altogether becomes inevitable. One of the most striking cases of environmental influence – already mentioned – was the first and only Austrian nuclear power plant. It could not go into operation because a narrow majority of voters had declared itself against the plant, which at that time had already been completed.

III.   Managing the Socio-Political Environment

The idea that the socio-political influence on an MOE is not only subject to reaction but also to action is widely shared in the literature on project management: "I suggest that the project manager's ability to manage these so-called uncontrollable factors will be the key to project success in the 1980s. I am saying *manage*, I choose my words carefully, because I believe that to seek to control rather than manage these factors is not only futile but dangerous. To attempt to control or manipulate today's environmentally aware and sensitive citizenry, for example, is likely to turn a poorly informed project skeptic into an embittered project opponent" (Hoyte 1982, pp.37).

Although the importance of this determinant is undisputed, we are facing a significant lack of management tools to handle it (in contrast to the very sophisticated techniques like the network analysis employed for the management of less important issues). The following recommendations refer to (1) establishing a framework and (2) formulating procedures for action, as well as (3) eliminating pretexts for possible interventions.

(1) Establishing *a framework for action* concerning the socio-political environment includes awareness of the management's responsibility, the adaptation of the management structure, and special expertise of project managers and staff. *Awareness of the project management's responsibility* for the socio-political environment can be ensured by means of special mention in the formulation of the project goals and in the bylaws of the project company. The environmentally orientated goals need to be transferred into an appropriate managerial perspective and set of attitudes; "appropriate" meaning with a sense and understanding not only for technical or economic questions but also for environmental and political issues (which includes dealing with bureaucracy, with competitive MOEs, and with growing and changing political attractiveness). This awareness pays off: "The Trans Alaska Pipeline survived as a project because its senior project management was incredibly sensitive to the political realities of Congress and the importance of being environmentally responsible; the American program failed because its management was politically unsophisticated and failed to get support if needed in Congress. The Apollo program succeeded because of the political protection given by NASA, the White House, Administrator James Webb, and, perhaps more im-

portant, a tidal wave of public support" (Morris 1982, p.160, see also Horwitch 1979a).

The *management structure* has to be set up according to the kind and strength of the socio-political influence. In general, the management system has to ensure a good balance for the consideration of the technical, economic, and socio-political perspectives of MOEs. Special committees or external consultants can contribute advice. In the case of the Games in Lake Placid, for example, the dominance of local representatives and the manner of (public) discussion and decision-making in the committees was rather unfavorable as far as the socio-political environment was concerned. It blurred the borderline between private and project responsibility and enhanced the tendency to overestimate local interests.

The framework for socio-political action cannot be effective without *environmentally sensitive project managers*. It is recommended, therefore, to engage individuals who represent a variety of backgrounds and views. Kharbanda/Stallworthy (1983, pp.255, 257) agree that the project management's experience with similar project situations avoids pitfalls. But their general outlook is not very optimistic: "expect the worst, even if you dare to hope for the best." Special attention should be paid to the top manager, the "project champion". His capabilities should include (Horwitch/Prahalad 1982, pp.32):

- effective communication with several culturally distant and distinct groups and even with representatives of the potential opposition;
- integration of people who speak "another language";
- motivation of people for voluntary involvement (remember the hundreds of volunteers supporting the project management of the Games in Lake Placid);
- recognition of the legitimacy of dissent and change in the socio-political environment while completing the project.

(2) The *formulation of procedures* for managing the socio-political environment should provide for *feasibility studies* to identify from the beginning the relevant socio-political surroundings and its forces. Different assumptions on the socio-political situation can be simulated by means of scenario techniques. In-depth feasibility studies on the environmental implications of different locations have proven to be essential. In heavily populated areas, for example, the completion of an MOE is frequently almost impossible without disturbing everyday life and, consequently, provokes the opposition of the individuals affected. Their opposition has to be weighed against the advantages of an existing infrastructure in providing project resources and services. Avoiding major centers of population creates substantial infrastructural problems for an MOE, e.g. the housing of employees and their relatives. On the other hand, the likelihood of an adverse public reaction in suburban locations is lower; the residents in those areas may even welcome the MOE because of its stimulating effects on the local economy.

Obviously, the procedures require external monitoring throughout the project completion and turnover phase. *Early warning systems* to identify and assess the signals from the socio-political environment have to be established. All projects which failed because of socio-political influences showed a remarkable ignorance concerning early warning signals such as diverging opinions of the project owners on cost-sharing, doubts about the management capacity, lack of enthusiasm for the MOE, etc.

Procedures also affect the communication process. The necessity of informing and communicating with the socio-political environment is evident: "Owners increasingly are having to answer for their projects in the political area" (Morris 1982, p.160). Information and communication have to consider the number and variety of participants which increase with the size and complexity of MOEs: Politicians, judges, users, local citizens' action groups, representatives of similar MOEs, labor unions, public accounting offices, etc.

(3) In general, *project failures*, such as heavy schedule overruns or significant changes of the goal framework, tend to attract public attention. It is not surprising that socio-political influences increase with growing project difficulties. The inverse correlation between MOE success and socio-political influence has been sufficiently proven in our cases (see the Vienna versus the Munich Hospital; or see the American SST-program, where the missing of technical and economic standards as well as turnover in top management caused the external influence, see Horwitch 1979a). These observations are further evidence that the socio-political environment can be managed in two ways: Direct management of the external influences once they occur, and their indirect management by preventing them from arising.

The socio-political environment offers another opportunity for project management. The restricting forces of the socio-political environment may be regarded as a potential countervailing power to balance the driving forces. The tendency towards overoptimism and goal enlargement has proven to be extremely risky for goal achievement. It depends, therefore, on the project management whether the influence of the socio-political environment will be a productive, destructive, or at least a neutral force.

J. Management Structure and Management Capacity

The importance of management structure and management capacity as success factors is undisputed and has been adequately shown by a literature survey (Wildemann 1982, pp.101, Kerzner 2001, pp.161, Cleland/King 1988, pp.269) as well as by our own empirical studies.

Apart from the establishment of a project-specific company which is almost indispensable for MOEs, issues like the integration of project owners and/or experts into the management system have to be considered. Different structures represent different potentials for action. Management capacity depends not only on the structure, however, but also on the project managers and other participants acting within this structure. A lack of managerial capacity can endanger the MOE's success, just as unbalanced and changing goal frameworks, overcomplex basic designs, and strong or neglected environmental influences can.

Yet, management structure and management capacity differ significantly from other success factors because project management has to cope with goal formulation and change, with the basic design, and with the socio-political environment. If, for instance, the basic design lacks consistency, it is the responsibility of the project management to take the necessary steps to achieve it. Therefore, project management is (should be) the most important actor in the development of MOEs. Without sufficient management capacity even the most sophisticated management tools will not be effective. In other words, the concentration on a suitable management structure and an adequate management capacity avoids discussing details like the choice of contractors or leadership style, because skilled project management has experience with the standard requirements and tools. We, therefore, understand project management as a potential source of action with a multiplying effect on other success factors.

Since the management structure does not exist at the beginning of an MOE, its establishment has to be initiated and led by the project owners. This shows that project management is not only a subject but also an object in the development of MOEs. Establishing the management structure must be seen as a separate task which is crucial for MOEs and very time-consuming.

I. Elements and Variety of Management Structure and Management Capacity

Generally, the management structure (representing different management capacities) should deal with the:
- type, time of establishment, and size of the project company;
- organizational structure (including levels of hierarchy, number and type of organizational units, and task responsibility);
- integration of contractors, experts, consultants, and auditors;
- recruitment of the project managers and project staff;
- problem of staff turnover in the project company.

Various management structures that may prove to be appropriate will be illustrated by our cases and by selective extracts from the literature on project management.

1. Type, Time of Establishment, and Size of the Project Company

The project-specific company (see Fig. 2) is the most appropriate *type of project organization* for MOEs. Such companies are founded for the sole purpose of planning, completing, and financing MOEs. In the case of Olympic Games, the project company's responsibility involves primarily the completion of the facilities and the initial operation (i.e., organizing the Games). The responsibility can also cover the permanent operation & maintenance of the facilities. The operation & maintenance responsibility is an additional reason for the establishment of the project company even if the planning and completion activity alone would not justify this type of project organization.

The project company is the appropriate type of organization for MOEs, because several institutions share the project ownership and are, therefore, demanding influence according to their equity share. Separating the project company from the parent organizations facilitates the cooperation of the project owners who may belong to different sectors (e.g. public and private) or industries with different levels of know-how, different management structures and procedures, as well as different wage and social benefit systems.

International projects in the weapon and aircraft industry demonstrate that even with project companies the difficulties due to conflicting project owners' goals, different backgrounds of the project managers, and different national socio-political environments (including rivalries on the location of the project company, and the choice of suppliers) are hard to overcome. Therefore, it may be advisable to delegate the planning and completion responsibility to one project owner called the lead owner.[19] In this case, the management structure of the project-owner company can be smaller and less complex, and the management procedures can be much simpler, allowing for a speed-up of decision-making processes. At the Munich Hospital, for instance, the federal government did not insist on being involved in the project management structure. It was sufficient, therefore, to merely provide for a separate organizational unit (called "construction office") within the state administration.

Existing and/or preceding organizations facilitate the establishment of the project company as the Olympic Games in Lake Placid illustrate (see dotted lines in Fig. 34).

---

[19] "The first rule, therefore, is to keep the direct participants to an absolute minimum". (Sykes 1982, p.143)

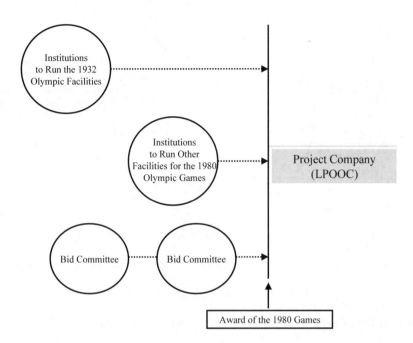

Fig. 34. History and Development of the Project Company for the Olympic Games Lake Placid 1980

Among the preceding organizations were the ones that had operated the facilities remaining from the Olympic Games in 1932. Other preexisting institutions were responsible for facilities which were built after 1932 and designated for later Games. The bid committee can also be regarded as a predecessor of the project company (Lake Placid Olympic Organizing Committee, LPOOC). The bid committee had its own predecessors as Lake Placid had applied for the Olympic Games ever since 1954.

Fig. 34 shows that the project company was established immediately after the start of the MOE. In most cases, however, its establishment is not a one-step event. In the early phases of the project, when the goal framework and the basic design are determined and feasibility studies are carried out, other types like the "pure project management" may be sufficient. Changes of the project task, however, ought to entail changes in the type of organization (remember the fit of the type of organization and the type of project task in Fig. 2).

The management structure of the Vienna Hospital was changed repeatedly. Most of the organizational changes, however, responded insufficiently to the changes of the project task. The following figure shows the most important steps in the development of the project company, which add up to an impressive list of changes, a fact not considered beneficial to the project.

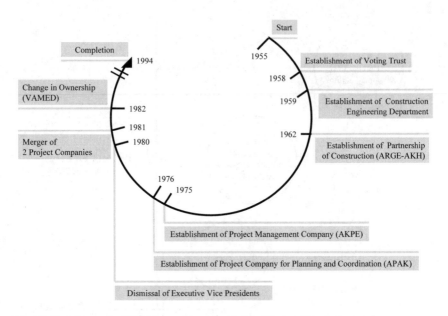

Fig. 35. Development of the Project Company for the Vienna Hospital

The project management company (AKPE) was not established until 1975. Prior to its establishment, the project was not separated from the parent organizations (state/federal); all project owners had equal rights and nominated federal and state ministers for the board. Even after the establishment of the project company in 1975 only a few employees but many consultants were engaged. The MOE responsibility was shared by two project companies, and no general manager was appointed for the MOE. Later on top executives had to be replaced (in 1982), a "token general manager" was nominated, and bureaucratic regulations concerning responsibility encumbered management action.

This case demonstrates that not only the type but also the *time of establishment* of the project company is crucial for MOE success. The relevant literature strongly recommends (Horwitch/Prahalad 1982, p.33, Malouf et al. 1980, pp.320) the establishment of the project organization as early as possible in the life of the project. The following table shows that this recommendation was often ignored in our cases.

MOE	Final Decision to Start the MOE	Establishment of the Project Company	Delay in Months
Olympic Games Munich 1972	1966-04	1967-07	15
Olympic Games Lake Placid 1980	1974-10	1974-12	2
Vienna Hospital	1962-04[2]	1975-09	161
Munich Hospital	1961-03[1]	1967	72

[1] Acceptance of the feasibility study by the state parliament
[2] Decision by one project owner (City of Vienna) to build a new Vienna Hospital (first section)

Table 15. Time of Establishment of Project Companies

The delays in the establishment of project companies for Olympic Games are considerably shorter than for university hospitals. Four reasons are worth to be mentioned:

- the existence of preceding organizations required for the approval procedure;
- models from previous Games provided and required by the International Olympic Committee (IOC);
- a comparatively clear conception of the goal framework as well as of the planning and administrative capacity necessary to achieve the goals;
- the inherent time pressure for Olympic Games.

Although these conditions may facilitate the early establishment of project companies, other potential failures need to be considered. Due to lengthy negotiations among the project owners, the delay in Munich was much longer than in Lake Placid. The project owners in Munich insisted on detailed and finalized contracts prior to their signing of the establishment agreement. Delays in decisions crucial for the time schedule (e.g. the space and functional program of the main facilities) could have been avoided, if the project owners had started project activities according to their basic commitment to the undertaking.

None of the four reasons mentioned above are applicable to the university hospitals (especially regarding the inherent time pressure). This may explain the enormous delays compared to the Olympic Games. Yet the striking delays in establishing the two project companies require further analysis. In the case of the Vienna University Hospital the greatly delayed establishment of the project company may be explained by the initial technical goal to reconstruct only one clinical department. The project company's development always lagged behind the enlargement of the project task, and changes of the company structure were not implemented until project crises made them indispensable. It took about 13 years until politicians realized that it was impossible to manage this huge undertaking as a sideline, spending just a couple of hours on the board. For the same reason the civil servants who had managed the hospital on a part-time basis were replaced by full-time managers. As for the Games in Munich, the negotiations between the project owners concerning the establishment agreement lasted several months. Another six years (!) were necessary to finalize the agency contract between the project owners and the project company. This is rather surprising in view of the fairly good experiences with MOEs in Austria (like the Tauern Highway) run by project companies.

In addition to the type and time of establishment, the *size of the project company* is an important determinant of management capacity. It can be measured by the number of employees. A comparison of the employee numbers may prove difficult, because the companies differ in their legal form, internal structure, lifespan, and in the extent of project management functions delegated to external companies, experts, and consultants. Despite these qualifications, a comparison of the project companies of the Olympic Games in Munich and of the Vienna Hospital may demonstrate that the management capacity of the Vienna Hospital was definitely not sufficient.

Project	Size		
	Total Costs[1]	Max. # of Company Employees[2]	Employees per €100m of Costs
1972 Munich Olympic Games	€675 m	126 (1971)	19
Vienna Hospital	€3,090 m	215 (1981)	7

[1] Adjusted for inflation
[2] Maximum refers to the highest number during the planning and completion period

Table 16. Project Company Size of the Olympic Games in Munich and the Vienna Hospital

The comparatively low management capacity in Vienna may be justified by the argument that the project company of the Vienna Hospital had a much longer lifespan than the project company of the Olympic Games. Conversely, it may be argued that the planning and completion time of the hospital could have been reduced if the management capacity of the project company had been larger.

The Munich Hospital, e.g., showed greater awareness of possible shortcomings regarding the size of the project company. The capacity of the internal and external project management was enlarged in order to cope with the workload of the detailed planning to avoid schedule overruns.

2. Organizational Structure

The organizational structure refers to the internal division of authority in the project company and its interface with the external project participants. The structure, as shown in the following organizational charts, is characterized by the:
- type of job specialization,
- number of hierarchical levels/span of control,
- outsourcing of project management functions to external participants,
- interface with the project owners.

We will start with an analysis of the Olympic Games (1) and then compare them to the university hospitals (2) in order to determine common characteristics.

(1) The charts of the Games in Munich and Lake Placid are shown in Chapter L and M (see Fig. 48 and Fig. 50). The interface of the project companies to the project owners is illustrated separately in the following two figures.

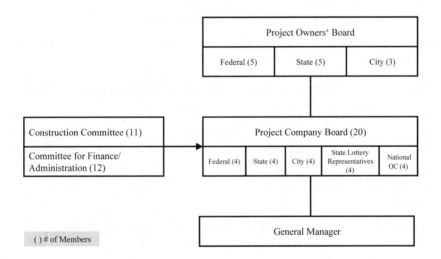

Fig. 36. Interface of Project Company with Project Owners of the Olympic Games in Munich

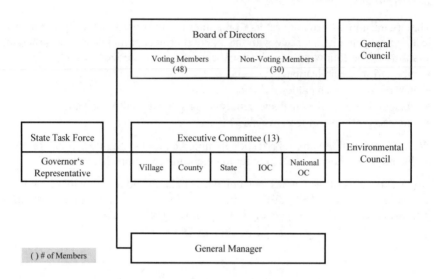

Fig. 37. Interface of Project Company with Project Owners of the Olympic Games in Lake Placid

The characteristics of the two structures are summarized in the following table.

Project Company	OBG (Munich Olympics 1972)	LPOOC (Lake Placid Olympics 1980)
Responsibilities	facilities	facilities and initial operation
Job Specialization	facilities + functions	functions
# of Hierarchical Levels/ Span of Control	5/medium	4/large
Outsourcing	planning/construction to experts/construction companies	planning/construction to general contractor
Interface with Project Owners	board	executive committee

Table 17. Organizational Characteristics of Two Olympic Project Companies

Type of job specialization/outsourcing: In the case of the Olympic project company in Munich the principles of object-orientation (facilities, installation, equipment, contracts) and functional specialization were combined. The project company in Lake Placid, on the other hand, was predominantly divided into (management and operational) functions. One reason for this remarkable difference can be derived from the divergent *outsourcing strategies*. Whereas in the case of Lake Placid the planning and construction of the facilities was delegated to a construction company acting as general contractor, in Munich this function was delegated to various external experts and companies. Each facility was managed by an internal project manager, with total or partial responsibility for various components (like roofing). The responsibilities for the necessary installations, equipment, and contracts were concentrated in separate organizational units.

In Munich an Organizing Committee (OC) was responsible for the initial operation, whereas the Lake Placid Olympic Organizing Committee (LPOOC) carried out the initial operation with specialists for various functions (like sports or protocol). The set-up of a separate marketing department reflected the substantial efforts of the project company to obtain external funds.

Number of hierarchical levels/general manager's span of control: The Munich company had a five-level structure whereas the hierarchy in Lake Placid was flatter with only four levels. Both companies experienced a change in the top management structure. The Munich company started with four levels and the responsibility was shared between a technical and a commercial vice president. A fifth level was added when the company board hired a general manager to put an end to the rivalries among the technical and commercial vice presidents and to improve the internal coordination. The Lake Placid Olympic Committee hired a general manager after the existing top management structure had collapsed and little time was left until the opening of the Games. The flatter hierarchy at Lake Placid meant a huge span of control for the general manager. Twelve managers directly reported to him, whereas only four managers reported to the Munich general manager (yet ten reported to the technical vice president).

Interface with the project owners (see Fig. 36 and Fig. 37): Legally, the Munich company was a private limited company. Its board, however, resembled that of a public limited company, representing the three project owners (city, state, federal), representatives of a state lottery, and the National Olympic Committee. The board was supported by two sub-committees (one for construction and another for finance and administration). The sub-committee system proved effective although some responsibilities overlapped and most of the board's decisions were predetermined by the subcommittees. The style of cooperation between the board and top management (interface with the project owners) changed during the course of the Games. In the early phases, project management insisted on the full commitment of the board even when minor problems were discussed. Due to the limited availability of the prominent board members, arranging board meetings was rather difficult. The workload for the project management – responsible for ensuring proper minutes – was said to be remarkable and the full involvement of the board in the project management process proved inefficient. Subsequently, the project management demanded more and more responsibilities while the board members accused management of neglecting its information duties.

The development in Lake Placid was similar to that in Munich. Prior to establishing the position of a general manager, the decision-making process in the executive committee was cooperative. Since nobody within the project company was authorized to make day-to-day decisions, the committee was constantly engaged in the "nitty-gritty" of routine issues. Furthermore, the decision-making process was impeded by its public discussion mode. "When we decide something, any one of our neighbors can come up to us on the street and say we're crazy. They wouldn't do that to a stranger" (Fortune, 1980-01-14). The influence of the executive committee, dominated by the project owners, was restricted by the appointment of a general manager.

(2) The organizational structure of the two *university hospitals* is less suitable for comparison as the only constant element of the structure in Vienna was its change. The Vienna Hospital is a perfect example of the difficulties resulting from an unclear structural design and from continuous changes in the organizational structure. The following explanation may help to better understand the case:

Vienna Hospital's project owners refused to engage a general contractor either for planning or for completion. Instead, two companies were established, the project company (AKPE) and the planning company (APAK) located in the same office building. The cooperation suffered from vague and frequently overlapping responsibilities as well as poor communication and information systems. The "benefits" of this cooperation deficit accrued to the contractors and the users. The contractors successfully claimed that the mistakes were due to unclear and inconsistent directions by the project and the planning company; the users took the existence of the two institutions as an excuse for promoting their own increasing demands.

This cooperation was at its lowest when responsibility for failures in the MOE process had to be allocated. Continuous structural changes led to an extraordinary turnover of senior project managers, board and committee members, many of them politicians. Their pat excuse for declining responsibility was: "When I took this position (on a committee, e.g., note of the author) things had already gone too far" (Die Presse, Vienna, 1976-05-21). After the disaster became obvious and known to the public by detailed auditing reports, the question of responsibility could not be evaded any longer. Quoting a politician who made the following remark in 1976 (!) when the peak of the scandal was still to come: "I don't believe that we are able to identify anybody who is responsible – as the lack of responsibility is the reason for the disaster of this project" (Die Presse, Vienna, 1976-05-12). Since public opinion could not be fobbed off with such statements, a new category of responsibility was invented: political responsibility. Political responsibility, however, is judged only on the occasion of political elections, when MOE-events (especially its failures) are mixed up with completely different issues like job or infrastructure programs. From the project management's point of view, this kind of responsibility leaves much to be desired and strengthens the demand for clear regulations.

In contrast to the Vienna Hospital, the Munich Hospital experienced no comparable problems with the organizational structure although it involved a remarkable number of institutions. Especially the *interface with the project owners* worked well in Munich. Some characteristics of this cooperation are worth mentioning:

• The State of Bavaria was the lead project owner, because the federal administration had delegated its authority to the state government. The federal interests were secured by formulating specific standards for size, costs, and evaluation procedures. By insisting on these standards it was possible to limit the federal funds.

- The state set up a separate inter-departmental committee to relieve the over-taxed top politicians and to avoid lengthy parliamentary debates, both causing delays in the decision-making process. Indeed, it empowered the committee to concentrate on decisions regarding the requirement specifications and their changes.
- The intervention of project owners focused on only a few but crucial issues of the MOE:
  - approval of the initial project,
  - approval of the requirement specifications,
  - cost reduction programs (managed by a separate commission),
  - administrative construction conditions (acting as building authority), and
  - concurrent auditing and controlling.

The restricted intervention by the project owners must not be mistaken for a "laissez faire" attitude. When basic interests of the owners were infringed, powerful reactions followed immediately. The reduction of the technical goals in order to avoid cost overruns is a convincing example of this attitude.

The strategy pursued by the project owners in Munich combined with experiences from other university hospitals and the Olympic Games enable us to draw a *first conclusion concerning the organizational structure*. Obviously, there is an initial tendency towards a strong involvement of project owners in the project management structure and process. This tendency results in a complicated organizational structure and procedures which cause decision delays as well as confusion about authority and responsibility. Once the disadvantage of this tendency becomes evident, the structure needs to be changed, leading to additional difficulties.

It is strongly recommended, therefore, to establish a structure which avoids excessive involvement of project owners and compel them from the very beginning to concentrate only on their basic interests.

---

3. Integration of Contractors, Experts, Consultants, Users, and Auditors

The size of MOEs requires a substantial and lasting involvement of all project participants. Therefore, their integration into the project management structure is a major issue. The basic question, already raised in an earlier context, is: How much and what kind of project work can or should the company delegate to external participants (source out)? The project company may decide to delegate all but the essential project management functions to external participants. The other extreme is a fully staffed project company with only small external support.

(1) Usually, the *contractors'* contribution to the MOE (like construction work) cannot be performed by the project company. What needs to be done by the project company, though, is the coordination of the contractors. The following figures indicate that this coordination may be organized in different ways (Wildemann1982, p.230; Barrie/Paulson 1992, pp.25).

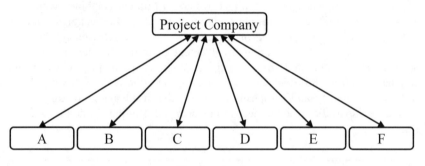

Contractors

Fig. 38. Coordination of Contractors by the Project Company

If the project company aims at retaining full authority over the coordination of contractors, it has to provide for sufficient management capacity. The project company of the Olympic Games in Munich, e.g., coordinated most of the contractors itself. If, for any reason, the capacity of the project company is restricted, external institutions should be entrusted with the coordination. There are different options to delegate: to special companies (as in the case of the Vienna Hospital, "APAK"), to planning experts (like architects), or to contractors, as shown in the following two figures.

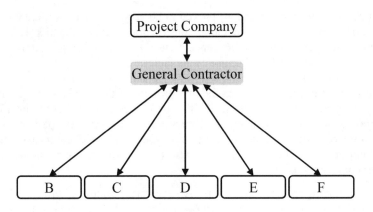

Sub-Contractors

Fig. 39. Coordination of Contractors by a General Contractor

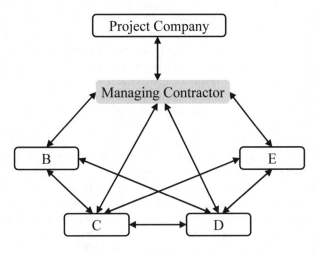

Contractors' Corporation

Fig. 40. Coordination of Contractors by a Managing Contractor

The project company in Lake Placid coordinated the sub-contractors through a general contractor. This contractor was engaged after screening seventeen offers. Unlike for the Games in Munich, the general contractor in Lake Placid was also responsible for planning. He established a separate project management structure with a "super manager" in charge of nineteen project managers. Delegating the responsibility for planning and completing the facilities to the general contractor (including technical assistance during the initial operation and adaptation of the facilities for permanent operation) proved to be very effective. While the contractor was able to draw on his planning, construction, and coordination experience, the project owners were able to concentrate on other major project issues like marketing and the post-Olympic use of the facilities.

Coordinating operations by a managing contractor is similar to the general contractor-type arrangement as far as the involvement of the project company is concerned. Project owners have to deal with only one contractor, but the internal cooperation among the contractors is different. This cooperative-type is commonly used in the construction industry, especially when only a few contractors (usually equal in size) share the contract. It can also be used for planning, engineering, or construction supervision.

(2) Employing external know-how is necessary because of the singularity of MOEs. The integration of *experts and consultants* raises the following two problems. First, the quantity of external expertise has to be determined. Second, the balance between the experts' influence and their responsibility needs to be considered. The tent-shaped roof of the Olympic Games in Munich is an example of the intensive involvement of experts because of the board members' lack of technical expertise. The dominant role of the planning architect who designed the tent-shaped roof has already been mentioned. Other experts were necessary to evaluate the technical feasibility and to calculate the statics and the costs of the construction. All crucial project decisions were based on the recommendations of external experts, as internal experts were either not available or their arguments were too weak. In the beginning, the architect was present at most of the board meetings and had the opportunity to directly influence board members when he disagreed with the project management. The public support for his tent-shaped roof design was so tremendous that project management could not make any changes to the design without risking a public uproar. At the Munich and Vienna Hospitals, external experts were engaged even to make the requirement specifications. In Vienna external experts held a powerful position not only because of the high technical standard of the hospital but also due to the small and often changing project management capacity. In the case of GROWIAN scientists enthusiastically supported the idea of constructing a large wind energy converter and to build the rotor blades in a composite manner. The ideas of the academic experts proved to be too ambitious at that time and caused the failure of the MOE.

The almost unlimited influence of experts and consultants[20] based on their technical know-how is frequently not balanced by a matching responsibility. The case of the Games in Munich may serve as a lesson because the members of the board – not the experts! – were formally criticized by a commission of the Bavarian State Parliament. The experts are not financially liable even if the facilities cannot be completed at all (as with the umbrella roof for the stadium in Montreal) or if significant cost overruns (in the completion or operation phase) turn out to be

---

[20] The consulting architect of the Montreal Games 1976 had a privileged position with the Major of Montreal. "He was thus able to interfere in many areas normally not the concern of a consulting architect: for example, the selection of contractors and professionals ... " (Malouf et al. 1980, Vol. II, p.328).

the result of their advice. This absence of serious penalties has been responsible for many of the high-risk designs at the expense of the project owners. Furthermore, we have to realize that engaging experts in controversial decisions is time-consuming and very expensive. Therefore, our primary concern is to find a suitable management structure or other means to control the influence of external experts and consultants.

(3) The influence of the *users* has been analyzed for Olympic Games as well as for university hospitals. A successful integration of the users is crucial for goal achievement, and the management structure should ensure the following:
- User requirements must be articulated in time. Obviously, this is rather challenging if the project is under time pressure and if the often conflicting requirements of the initial and permanent users need to be coordinated.
- Changes in user requirements during the project planning process should be limited.
- Initial and permanent users should be equally represented.
- Influence, authority, and responsibility of the users should be well-balanced.

Project management generally tends to be less aware of long-term goals (permanent operation) compared to short-term goals (completion and initial operation). Therefore, special attention must be paid to representing the permanent users in the management structure. By looking at the Games in Munich and Lake Placid we identify different forms of representation with formal and informal interventions in favor of users' requirements.

The representatives of the initial operation were the National and International Olympic Committees (NOK and IOC) and the National and International Sports Associations. Formal interventions went through the project company board where the National Olympic Committee held four out of twenty seats (the other seats were held by federal, state, and city representatives). This procedure was to prevent self-willed actions by single sports associations and the opportunity of directly contacting the project management.

For several reasons this formal procedure did not work. Sports associations or board members submitted their specific requirements to the project management without involving the NOK board members. Problems also arose due to the delayed specification of requirements. The number of athletes, e.g., was determined only a few weeks before the opening of the Games.

In contrast to the initial operation – their goals were submitted by a special organization, the Organizing Committee (OK), with representatives on the board – the representatives of the permanent operation of the Olympic facilities in Munich had no consolidated position in the management structure of the project company. Although Munich applied for the Olympic Games partly to improve the city's infrastructure and sports facilities, the institutions in charge of the permanent operation were nominated only after the project company had been established. Several attempts to promote the permanent users' opinion (such as an expert opinion of a public accounting office) could not compensate for the permanent users' disadvantage of lacking a formal position in the management structure. In addition, the project owners tried to avoid getting involved in post-Olympic affairs for fear of being blamed for high operation costs. The only exception to the general underrepresentation of the post-Olympic goals was when the project owners' intentions coincided with those of the permanent users.

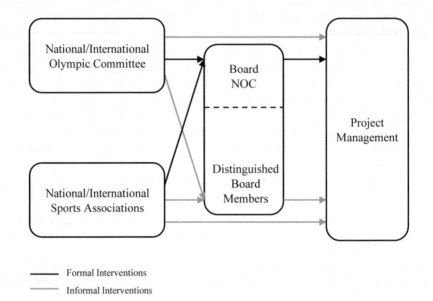

Fig. 41. Formal and Informal Interventions by Users at the Munich Games 1972

In contrast to the initial operation – their goals were submitted by a special organization, the Organizing Committee (OK), with representatives on the board – the representatives of the permanent operation of the Olympic facilities in Munich had no consolidated position in the management structure of the project company. Although Munich applied for the Olympic Games partly to improve the city's infrastructure and sports facilities, the institutions in charge of the permanent operation were nominated only after the project company had been established. Several attempts to promote the permanent users' opinion (such as an expert opinion of a public accounting office) could not compensate for the permanent users' disadvantage of lacking a formal position in the management structure. In addition, the project owners tried to avoid getting involved in post-Olympic affairs for fear of being blamed for high operation costs. The only exception to the general underrepresentation of the post-Olympic goals was when the project owners' intentions coincided with those of the permanent users.

Unlike in Munich, the project company in Lake Placid managed both the completion phase and the initial operation of the Olympic facilities (see Fig. 47, Fig. 48). All Olympic users were represented on the executive committee. Because of the permanent users' participation during the planning and completion process, the delayed establishment of the institution to manage the permanent operation was not a serious issue. This is due to the fact that the residents of Lake Placid – who had the majority on the executive committee and the board – insisted on a facility design which would primarily be suitable for post-Olympic use.

We have already mentioned the almost unlimited influence of users on the Vienna Hospital although they were not officially represented in the project management structure. The strength of influence does not always correspond to a formal position in the organizational structure. The users' influence in Vienna was based on the project management's obligation (enforced by the project owners and numerous interventions by various politicians) to ensure a permanent and full commitment to the users.

The management structure of the Munich Hospital was intended to limit the influence of the users and to provide special measures for channeling their influence. The school of medicine was required to approve the initial basic design and set up a separate building commission ("user conference") to be engaged in the equipment and operation planning. This commission acted as a consultant to the faculty, the project management, and the administrative head office of the hospital (see Fig. 60). The most important task of the committee during the completion process was to coordinate user requirements and to ensure a continuous flow of information and communication between the parties involved. The administrative head office, which was set up very early in the process, was designed to serve as an additional interface with the users. It included a medical administration unit to coordinate the interests of the users, the project management, and the planning architects. The start-up of the hospital was prepared by a special commission under the direction of the administrative head office. It worked in close cooperation with the building commission of the medical faculty. All these measures, together with an advanced recruitment policy, guaranteed the early, explicit, and official statement of user requirements.

(4) Our final integration issue deals with *project auditing*. Both the Olympic Games in Munich and the Vienna Hospital were subject to thorough investigations and examinations throughout the completion and start-up period. Montreal and Lake Placid also faced substantial post-Olympic investigations.[21] The public auditing of the Munich Hospital reported no serious inconsistencies.

The audits of the Munich Games and the Vienna Hospital resulted from serious MOE failures. Substantial cost overruns in Munich, caused by the tent-shaped roof, initiated the investigations which were later extended to cover all facilities. In the case of the Vienna Hospital doubts regarding the proper ordering process for the masterplan of operation led to a public auditing which was then also broadened to other areas.

The results of the various project audits were more or less the same. So were the immediate reactions: Public attention grew significantly and the pressure by the socio-political environment increased. The project management, especially the senior management, was compelled to spend much of its time commenting upon the detailed reports and justifying its actions. (The Vienna City auditing report, for instance, had a volume of almost 1000 pages.) The auditing, once started, devel-

---

[21] See for Montreal: Malouf et al. (1980)

oped a momentum of its own and ended in a formidable "audit overkill," including excesses like a quasi competition in Vienna between the federal and city public accounting office.

Some of the comments and conclusions in the auditing reports are certainly noteworthy and would meet the standards of scholary treatises. They included criticism, however, that would be applicable to day-to-day business and bureaucratic performance standards but not to innovative undertakings like MOEs. The reports assigned equal weight to the treatment of essentials and of details.

The vital point, however, was that the auditing started only after the crucial decisions had been made, most of them being irreversible with regard to the status of planning and completion. It took a long time before the MOEs, which were subject to investigation, were able to return to business as usual, the real failures still uncorrected. We believe that the harm caused by these audits nearly offset their potential benefits. This raises two questions. Firstly, to what extent can traditional control procedures currently in use – compared to other measures, such as sophisticated recruitment policies (see next chapter) – contribute to project success? And secondly, what kind of control procedure will not harm the MOE (see Chapter Q.V.).

4. Recruitment of Project Managers and Project Staff

Recruitment is closely related to the management structure and to staff turnover (see next section). Well-designed structures cannot work unless the persons involved are skilled and motivated. Incorrect recruitment policies have often proven to be the reason for fast turnover of staff.

In the literature on project management you will find listings of skills for project managers, especially for top managers (Gaddis 1959, Sayles/Chandler 1982, Slevin/Pinto 1988, Wilemon/Baker 1988, pp.848, Kerzner 2001, pp.173). Our studies have shown that even basic standards of recruitment were often neglected. The most serious recruitment problems in MOEs were caused by a preference for:
- local personnel,
- personnel from public authorities,
- political representatives on the board, and
- technically oriented managers.

We will first illustrate the genesis of such recruitment mistakes by some cases and then turn to the Munich Hospital which can serve as a recommendable model for recruiting MOE personnel.

We have already mentioned the *preference for local personnel* in our discussion of the management structure (especially the interface with the project owners). The Games in Lake Placid suffered the most from this preference. It was the basic understanding of the Lake Placid residents that the Games were "theirs". Therefore, an important criterion for nomination was to be a Lake Placid resident. When the president of the executive committee had to be nominated, the former local postmaster, Roland M. MacKenzie (he was already retired and in his 70s), was elected. His expertise (a promoter of the Olympic Games since 1962, an enthusiastic winter sportsman, and experienced in organizing local sport events) was believed to be sufficient. Other important positions in the senior project management were also held by local residents, especially by owners and managers of the tourist industry who were greatly interested in the post-Olympic use of the facilities. They were described as "nearby good ol'boys, who are not likely to make waves" (Skiing 1979, p.60). Local preferences also dominated the recruitment of personnel on the middle and junior management level. The preference for local personnel resulted in a lack of professionalism. "A small group of Lake Placid's proud citizenry is staging the event, in much the same way local civic clubs put on car washes or bake sales" (Fortune, 1980-01-14). The management capacity was simply too weak and this was, in our opinion, the crucial weakness of the Lake Placid Games.

When the Lake Placid Games experienced a crisis, a "stranger" (Spurney) was hired for the position of general manager. He was nominated for the job because he had successfully managed large events before. His know-how for the Lake Placid project stemmed from his consulting services to the hosts. He was said to have serious problems with the residents in the project company and, therefore, tried to back his position by nominating a marketing manager who had worked with him on previous assignments. Regardless of his merits for overcoming the crises, however, he remained a "stranger" all along.

A *preference for hiring personnel from public authorities* was obvious at the Games in Munich and the Vienna Hospital. The project management of the Munich Games frequently argued that their commitment to the salary standards of public authorities prevented the recruitment of highly skilled personnel from private firms. Consequently, they pursued a rather thrifty recruitment policy. The question of whether a less thrifty policy would have had a significant impact on the expertise of the management staff must be left open. We should note, however, that the newly appointed general manager was allowed to disregard public salary standards. At that time, however, most of the staff had already been hired and the competitiveness of the project company on the labor market had decreased with the economic recovery in the late 1960s. Owing to the initial salary regulations the project company also lost some of its most skilled managers who moved to more attractive jobs in the life of the MOE. Considering the total project costs, though, such a rigorous salary policy is not very convincing.

Preferring personnel from public authorities caused additional side effects. Sometimes the staff experienced conflicts between their current employer (the project company) and their former and possibly future employers (e.g. the same or other public authorities). Another side effect was the tendency of former public employees to prefer challenging technical solutions. An explanation for this may be the fear of those employees of appearing narrow-minded if they were in favor of conservative concepts. Thus, the recruitment policy even increased their risk propensity concerning technical goals (risky shift).

For the Vienna Hospital the project owners favored top management applicants experienced in public administration. They tried to justify this preference by their objective of ensuring a certain degree of continuity in the management of the project. The expertise of such applicants for positions in this enormous undertaking was questionable. After a series of investigations had revealed numerous cases of corruption, the demand for civil servants (in public MOEs) became even stronger along with considerations regarding an appropriate legal form of MOEs which would guarantee a sufficient influence by the public on them.

The preference for personnel from public authorities and the limited attention given to their skills in some of our cases is very probably an indicator of the insufficient separation of the project company from the (public) owners' parent organizations.

The *preference for political representatives on the board* was most striking at the Olympic Games in Munich and the hospital in Vienna. The problem of such a recruitment policy is best illustrated by the Munich Games case. Most of the board members were high-ranking politicians, including mayors and ministers from the state and federal governments. Although some of the board discussions were held on a highly sophisticated level, the *lack of technical and project management skills and experience* regarding MOEs can be shown by quoting one of the board members: "And in the reports (to the board, note of the author) there are a lot of comments which I am not able to understand". Another board member wanted to know whether orders beyond €10m were realistic! The board tried to compensate for this lack of expertise by engaging numerous experts. Unfortunately, the most important issues resulted in diverging expert opinions. Now, the high technical qualifications, which the board members lacked and which had made the engagement of the experts necessary in the first place, were required to deal with the diverging opinions. It was not surprising, therefore, that the board members felt rather uncomfortable in the end and blamed the experts for failing to provide the "right" expertise.

An additional problem caused by politicians on committees and boards is their constant orientation towards changing public opinion. They often respond to it even if this response only distracts from the real problems of MOEs. Another disadvantage of having political representatives on the board is their commitment to local contractors.

The *preference for technically orientated managers* was particularly striking in our European cases. This preference may be justified by the challenging technical goals which are characteristic of most MOEs. The technical argument was naturally supported by the experts who mostly came from technical areas. Lake Placid and Los Angeles, however, have proven that not the technological but the managerial skills are crucial for the success of MOEs. Whereas project management can delegate most of the technical activities to external participants, management functions cannot be outsourced.

The Munich Hospital was the only case in our sample that performed exceptionally well with regard to the recruitment policy. There was no particular preference, neither for residents nor for personnel from public authorities, political representatives, nor technically orientated managers. The project owners insisted on senior management experienced in planning and completing university hospitals. The administrative head office was staffed with managers who had both managerial as well as medical skills. The user requirements were represented by those faculty members who would be the first to move into the new hospital and would actually have to live with their previous decisions and requirements.

Other examples of effective recruiting policies are the Olympic Games in Squaw Valley (1960) and the Games in Los Angeles (1984). Squaw Valley aimed at recruiting the best qualified personnel, ignoring local preferences (Skiing 1979, p.60). In Los Angeles, professional head-hunters searched for a general manager. After screening hundreds of potential candidates for the job, including renowned top managers like Lee A. Iacocca, they came up with Peter Ueberroth (Reich 1986).

The Los Angeles Games as well as other MOEs underline the importance of highly skilled general managers ("champions") and the advantage of a general manager compared to joint responsibilities in committees.

---

5. Staff Turnover in the Project Company

An almost unbelievable staff turnover continued to trouble the Vienna Hospital. By 1984 the hospital had worn out eleven members of the executive committee and twenty-two members of the board! The list of ministers in office and responsible during the planning and completion period of the hospital seems to be endless: nine ministers of finance, four ministers of construction, five ministers of science and research, five ministers of social and health affairs, five mayors, three city counselors of finance, two city counselors of health affairs, and two city counselors of building affairs (press release by the opposition party of 1984-09-20).

At the Munich Games most of the staff turnover affected the board of the company. While all state representatives kept their mandates until the project company was wound up, changes in the city and federal governments led to a replacement of their board representatives. This turnover made close cooperation on the board and in its subcommittees rather difficult as new members had to be first integrated. It also affected the cooperation of the board with the top management of the project company and eventually encouraged top management to limit the board's involvement in the decision-making process.

In the case of GROWIAN different phases of the MOE were dominated by different project management teams and contractors. There was no continuity in personnel, and follow-up groups could always justify their failures by decisions made during preceding phases by preceding teams.

Although turnover of staff cannot be eliminated, every attempt should be made to minimize it. Turnover affects one-shot events far more than routine business, especially, when top managers are concerned. Reasons for staff turnover are:

- changes in the management structure, sometimes leading to month-long vacancies in top management positions;
- appointment of politicians or top managers with close ties to political parties as board members (politicians are liable to be replaced due to election results);
- poor expertise of top managers.

6. Summary

The five variables of the success factor "management structure and management capacity" are closely interrelated:

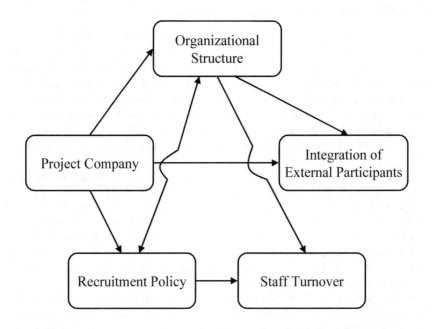

Fig. 42. Interdependence of the Variables of Management Structure and Management Capacity

The *project company* (type, time of establishment, size) influences the organizational structure, the integration of external project participants and the recruitment policy.

- The *organizational structure* tends to be more complicated if several project companies are involved in the MOE.

- The influence of the project company on the *integration of external partici-pants* varies. If its establishment is delayed, the influence of external partici-pants on the MOE may become uncontrollable and their subsequent integration harder to manage. Especially small-sized project companies face the need to in-tegrate numerous external project participants.
- The project company also influences the *recruitment policy*. If the project com-pany type, e.g., fails to allow for a sufficient separation from the (public) parent organizations, civil servants and individuals with close ties to political institu-tions will be favored.

The *organizational structure* may affect the recruitment policy, the rate of turn-over of staff, and the integration of external participants.

- Its relationship with the *recruitment policy* is mutual. Changes in the organiza-tional structure may be caused by an inadequate recruitment policy. These changes in turn can influence the rate of *turnover* of project company members. Staff turnover, however, may also be caused by overlapping and conflicting re-sponsibilities.
- Concerning the relationship between organizational structure and *integration of external participants* we have learned that the number of project functions delegated to external participants (outsourcing) varies. This influences the number of hierarchical levels and possibly even the internal specialization, as our comparative analysis of the Munich and Lake Placid Games has shown.

Finally, the *recruitment policy* significantly influences the *turnover of staff*. Inade-quate skills, apart from thrifty recruitment policies, are one of the most important reasons for turnover. Recruitment policies that emphasize expertise as their only criterion of selection are, therefore, likely to avoid turnover.

II.   Impact of Management Structure and Management Capacity on Goal Achievement

There are direct and indirect effects of management structure and management ca-pacity on goal achievement.[22] The following examples may illustrate these effects.

The delayed establishment of the project company for the Munich Games is said to have been one of the reasons for the cost overruns, because the delay cre-ated additional time pressure. But time pressure need not always be a cost driver. We assume that time pressure was the reason for adhering to the initial basic de-sign, as there was not enough time for an extensive redesign.

The close involvement of local residents in the project company of Lake Placid had lasting effects on the goal formulation process. Their heavy emphasis on the post-Olympic operation may explain the rather successful permanent operation of the Olympic facilities.

The turnover of board members of the Olympic construction company in Mu-nich gives an idea of how turnover affects the overall goal achievement:

---

[22] Larson/Goebel 1989 analyze the significance of project management structure (like functional/project matrix and project team) for the success of R&D projects.

- Staff turnover impeded potential learning curve effects (no accumulation of expertise);
- the group of board members with the highest turnover had the least chance of promoting their interests.

An early involvement of the contractors is likely to prevent unrealistic technical goals, can help to gain more reliable cost estimates in the early phases of the project, and obviates continuous goal change. Obviously, management structure/capacity determine the goal formulation and the change process and – in an indirect way – goal achievement.

III.   Guidelines for the Design of Management Structure and Management Capacity

Our cases demonstrate a wide range of options for designing the management structure. Some principles may serve as rough guidelines:

1. *Early establishment of project management capacity:* MOEs generally lack management capacity. This lack is especially detrimental in the early phases of projects when the most important decisions, e.g. the formulation of the basic design, have to be made. The project company, including a definite management structure and management capacity, is not likely to be established prior to the final commitment by the project owners to start an MOE. The establishment of the project company may be delayed for several reasons and it takes some time before the management structure and its capacity work effectively. We recommend overstaffing at the beginning rather than risking any kind of insufficient management capacity later on. As the project tasks develop, management capacity needs to be adapted to ensure an optimal fit. After project completion, the management structure of the project company has to be altered to meet the requirements of permanent operation or the project company has to be wound up.

2. *Safeguarding project owners' responsibility:* It is the sole responsibility of the project owners to establish the project management structure. This responsibility should be more than just an annoying obligation since it is one of the most effective opportunities for the project owners to implement their interests.

3. *Outsourcing:* All activities which can be outsourced by the project company should be delegated to contractors and external experts. Outsourcing relieves project management capacity and enables it to concentrate on its core tasks. Successful outsourcing requires, among other things, sufficiently skilled contractors (Lake Placid decided on the general manager after screening seventeen applications) as well as a clearly defined goal system. The project owners of the Munich Hospital recommended a general contractor for buildings that took up to two years to complete. The buildings should not be too complex and not strongly interrelated with other project components. Using modern techniques, complex projects can be broken down to meet these requirements. We doubt that there are benefits in delegating the planning process to separate planning

companies, as it was done in the case of the Vienna Hospital. Delegating the planning of MOEs to architects or to other external institutions increases the likelihood that project owners and project management lose control over the project. The supervision of the construction of the Olympic facilities in Munich was successfully delegated to external engineering companies. In the case of the Munich Hospital, however, the costs and the potential negative effects on the cooperation between the planning architects and the project owners prevented the project management from taking this measure.

4. *Balanced internal and external capacity:* Despite the positive effects that outsourcing has on the utilization and costs of project management capacity, it is unrealistic to pursue this strategy beyond a certain point. Our discussion of the experts' integration has shown that an unlimited substitution of external experts for internal capacity is a constant source of trouble. A balance of internal and external project management capacity, therefore, is absolutely crucial. As we have learned from the tent-shaped roof in Munich the project owners and the project company will lose control over the project if the internal capacity is too small. In the case of the tent-shaped roof, internal experts failed to counter the influence of external experts. Even details are important for an effective balance. If planning architects or other experts are allowed to take part in board meetings, the internal experts should also have access to these board meetings.

5. *Early involvement of contractors:* The EIP concept (Early Involvement of the Production) has proven very effective in avoiding development activities which generate problems in the process of production turnover (Wheelwright 1995). An early involvement of contractors (EIC) aims at avoiding basic designs which could be completed only with substantial schedule and cost overruns. It is not surprising that the contractors made more realistic cost estimates for the tent-shaped roof than the planning architects and other experts. Another advantage of this principle is access to the engineering capacity of contractors.

6. *Balanced authority and responsibility:* The effects of unbalanced authority and responsibility have been illustrated with some cases of our sample. The prime beneficiaries of this imbalance are the users and the external experts. Therefore, the formal responsibility of these groups has to be established and their integration into project groups as well as into the board is an important issue.

7. *Establishing links:* Much attention has been paid to the ("vertical") cooperation of project owners with project management, contractors, experts, and other external institutions. Yet the ("horizontal") cooperation between contractors and experts for planning or other project activities has been neglected. Links should be established to intensify interaction between these groups. This applies especially to the coordination of planning and completion activities. "Traditional" procedures are based on formal regulations and planning activities separate from completion activities by time and institutions. In the case of the Games in Munich, however, the opposite has proven advantageous: joint authority and responsibility for planning and completion (at least for the supervision of construction). The planning architects favored to split up the planning and comple-

tion responsibility owing to the size and duration of the project but size and duration of MOEs can be reduced by breaking down the whole project into components which allow for a joint planning and completion responsibility.

8. *Avoid recruiting politicians:* Recruiting politicians as representatives of the project owners has proven disadvantageous (remember their susceptibility to public opinion or their turnover due to political changes). Having politicians on the board increases the likelihood of nominating executives with close ties to political parties. The interests of the project owners are much better served by representatives who have no direct obligation to the public. For the Munich Games high-ranking civil servants (like permanent secretaries) proved much more effective than ministers as they did not have to be replaced in the event of political changes. A special investigation by the German public auditing office came to the same conclusions (Bundesrechnungshof 1972, pp.14)[23].

9. *Championship for top positions:* As far as the general manager of the project company is concerned, it is advisable to nominate a single person instead of a committee. This "champion" needs to be a promoter with excellent managerial skills (even charisma) and the highest possible commitment to the project task. He should have faith in the MOE and should be able to transfer his conviction to the project management staff and to other project participants. Drapeau, the former mayor of Montreal and "father" of the 1976 Games, was a phantast but not a champion of the MOE. After serious schedule and cost overruns in 1975 the project ownership was shifted from the City of Montreal to federal authorities in Quebec (Die Presse, Vienna, 1975-11-24).

---

[23] "The Mayor of Montreal ... had neither the aptitude nor the knowledge necessary to take over the direction of an undertaking of such magnitude" (the Summer Olympics, note of the author). ... "The first magistrate of a city, and for that matter anyone holding public office, should not act as director of a project sponsored by public authority" (Malouf et al. 1980, Vol. II, pp.321, 323).

K. Success Factors and Goal Achievement

This chapter is to show the mutual interrelation of the success factors of MOEs and their interdependence with goal achievement. We start by summarizing our findings on success factors.

I.   *Summarized Empirical Findings on Success Factors*

Our summary is structured according to success factors (first order) and MOEs (second order).

(1) Formulation and Change of Goals
- *Balance and consistency of goal formulation:* The Olympic Games experienced significant enlargements of their technical goals causing a reformulation of the initial framework. Contrary to the Munich Hospital, where only the technical goals had to be reformulated, the hospital in Vienna faced a continuing "derailment" of the initial framework. The technical goals of GROWIAN aimed at maximizing size and were not redefined in time.

(2) Basic Design
- *Complexity:* The basic designs of the Olympic Games were less complex than those of the university hospitals due to inherent tendencies towards local decentralization of the facilities. The designs of the Munich and Vienna Hospitals were rather complex considering the block-type buildings. The design of the hospital in Vienna was even more complex because of its size. In the case of GROWIAN an early fixation on size and a specific technical solution increased the complexity.
- *Consistency:* The consistency of the basic designs of the Olympic Games was quite satisfactory. The Munich Hospital faced a change in its basic design but this was directed at reducing complexity, thus facilitating efforts to stabilize the goal framework. The Vienna Hospital underwent continuous changes, all of them jeopardizing the stability of the framework. In the case of GROWIAN and the tent-shaped roof (Olympic Games in Munich) the inflexible basic design proved the decisive failure.

(3) Socio-Political Environment
- *Nature and Development of MOEs:* Events like Olympic Games or environmental initiatives like GROWIAN usually mobilize supporting forces. These forces were offset in the case of the Munich Games by troubles caused by several facilities, especially the tent-shaped roof. The Munich Hospital experienced no marked influence from the socio-political environment. The analysis of the hospital in Vienna has shown that the political turmoil did not affect the MOE until severe failures occurred.

- *Parent organizations:* The Olympic Games in Munich and Lake Placid and the Munich Hospital experienced no significant socio-political influence from the parent organizations. The Games in Lake Placid were marked by quasi-public meetings of the project management which interfered with the necessary separation of the project company from the parent organizations. The Vienna Hospital was burdened by questionable nominations of executives, frequent ad-hoc interventions, and intensive public auditing activities. Politicians and scientists were strongly involved in the case of GROWIAN.
- *Contractors:* The Vienna Hospital is the case where contractors (especially publicly owned contractors) had a dominant influence on the MOE. In the case of the Summer Olympics in Munich, planning architects exercised an intensive and lasting influence on the basic design of key facilities, esp. the tent-shaped roof. Concerning GROWIAN contractors rejected project ownership which was offered to them by the public project owner.
- *Local/regional/national institutions:* None of our cases suffered from opposition or obstruction as encountered by, for example, power plants. The Olympic Games even benefited from a strong local, regional, and national lobby. The lobby of the Vienna Hospital aimed at retaining or re-establishing the great reputation of the Viennese medical school. In the case of GROWIAN federal politicians pressed for the maximization of technical goals.

(4) Management Structure and Management Capacity
- *Project company (type/time of establishment/size):* At the Games in Lake Placid, the project company was established early. At the Games in Munich, the establishment of the project company was delayed, but the type and size were adequate. The project company in Vienna was established late and was understaffed. In the case of GROWIAN the project company was set up after the decision on the goals and the basic design had been made.
- *Organizational structure:* The Munich Games provided for a good balance between authority and responsibility but had some problems concerning the interface with the project owners and the structure of top management. The Lake Placid Games suffered substantially from the "democratic" mode of decision-making in the executive committee until a general manager position was created. The management structure of the Munich Hospital provided for clear responsibilities from the beginning and for the adaptation of the management capacity according to the workload. The Vienna Hospital and GROWIAN suffered from continuing changes of the organizational structure and a severe imbalance between authority and responsibility.
- *Integration of contractors, experts, consultants, users, and auditors:* The Olympic Games and the university hospitals show completely different results. The Munich Games dealt only poorly with some aspects of the integration issue while the Lake Placid hosts did an excellent job with respect to the integration of contractors. The Vienna Hospital and GROWIAN had

problems with the integration of contractors, experts, and users, while the Munich Hospital integrated them successfully, especially the users.

- *Recruitment of the project manager and project staff:* The Munich Hospital is a model of a proper recruitment policy since the project owners relied solely on proficient project managers. The Vienna Hospital – once again – was the exact opposite with strong preferences for politicians and employees from public authorities. The Munich Games also showed a tendency towards employing politicians and civil servants, but not to the same extent as Vienna. In the case of GROWIAN, the hundreds of private and public institutions involved hindered a consistent recruitment policy. The Lake Placid Games were impeded by the extreme preference shown for employing local residents.

- *Turnover of staff in the project company:* The senior project management of the Vienna Hospital and the board of the Games in Munich experienced a significant turnover of staff. In the case of GROWIAN, the turnover was caused by changing responsibilities in different phases of the MOE. The Lake Placid Games and the Munich Hospital were not affected by remarkable turnover problems.

II.   *Interdependence of Success Factors*

In complex systems like MOEs mutual relations between the success factors are not surprising. Yet, the interdependence of the success factors is challenging for managing MOEs. MOE management has to deal not only with the unilateral impact of success factors on goal achievement but also with their mutual effects.

The following comments refer to the interdependence of success factors as illustrated in Fig. 43.

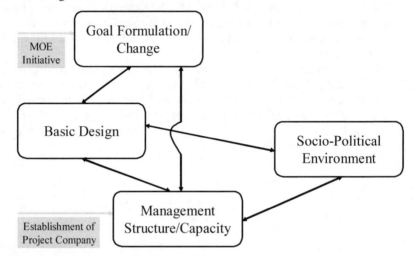

Fig. 43. Interdependence of Success Factors

MOE initiative: The basic idea of an MOE, including vague formulations of the goal framework, is born prior to its official start. These first formulations may stem from planning architects, contractors, or users. However, they still lack the commitment of the potential project owners to engage in the MOE. In the course of the planning process, the initial idea is likely to change.

Management structure/capacity and *goal formulation/change:* The impact of the management structure on goal formulation should be governed by the following principles:

- Complete goal formulation: Management structure serves as a tool for project owners to ensure that their interests are sufficiently considered in the goal formulation. It depends on the management structure whether all aspects of the goals are taken into account and whether different scenarios (based on optimistic and pessimistic assumptions) are transferred into ranges of goal achievement.
- Balanced goal framework: A balanced goal framework requires continuous cross checks to ensure a fit of technical, time, and financial goals. To achieve a balanced goal framework is a time-consuming process. To avoid cutting short this process it is advisable to involve a sufficient number of project par-

ticipants with different interests and to follow formal procedures (e.g. special tender procedures).

- Framework consistency: The management structure should ensure the goal formulation process, including the search for alternatives, until the project owners commit themselves to the goal framework. After this general commitment, the management structure should restrict and channel the driving forces that intend to alter (in most cases to enlarge) the goals. Further, it should facilitate the identification of project management with the initial goal framework and the control of driving forces, e.g. by establishing a special change procedure.

Management structure/capacity and *basic design:* Owing to the interdependence of goal formulation and basic design, management structure influences the basic design indirectly. Management structure should encourage the development of alternatives at the beginning and oppose changes after decisions on the basic design have been made. The basic design determines the management structure and capacity, especially the size of the project company and the know-how requirements of the staff.

Management structure/capacity and *the socio-political environment:* The management structure should allow the project management to anticipate and respond to possible interference by the socio-political environment (e.g. by integrating representatives of environmental groups). The influence of the socio-political environment on management structure is manifold. It can require a change of the management structure (to ensure more public or environmental influence), or a replacement of untrustworthy project managers. The fact that the socio-political environment affects the management capacity of MOEs has not been sufficiently considered in our discussion so far. Environmental regulations may take up management capacity as they require additional reports and evaluations. Other activities adding to the workload are press conferences, hearings, and even law suits. In some cases, the project management – usually its senior members – is even unable to concentrate on the "real" MOE problems because it is tied up with socio-political issues.

Goal formulation/change and *basic design:* We described the basic design as a specification of technical goals and a rough outline of how to achieve them. We also demonstrated that there is a continuous process of mutual adjustment between technical goals and basic design (see Fig. 22). The interdependence is assumed to be strong at the beginning and to become less important in the course of planning and completion.

Goal formulation/change and *the socio-political environment:* On the one hand, goal formulation determines the basic level of awareness of the socio-political environment regarding MOEs. On the other hand, the socio-political environment can also be seen as a possible constraining force on goal change.

Basic design and *the socio-political environment:* Generally, the socio-political environment does not interfere with MOEs until their basic design has been determined. Relevant for the socio-political environment are the kind of undertaking (including its environmental side-effects, such as pollution, ruining the landscape, etc.), its size (big projects attract more public attention than smaller ones), the structure of its ownership (causing possible conflicts of interests), and its location, which is likely to mobilize local residents. Even public awareness in the case of failure (danger of scandalization) is influenced by the basic design since the likelihood of failure increases with the complexity and singularity of MOEs. Socio-political influence on the basic design can cause a change of size and/or location, or even the abort of MOEs. It should be kept in mind, though, that the socio-political influence is not only an opposing force but may also have a promoting influence on the basic design (i.e. regarding the location).

III.   Interdependence of Success Factors and Goal Achievement

So far we have assumed that the relationship between the success factors and the variables of goal achievement is unilateral and that goal achievement has no influence on the success factors. This assumption would be legitimate if goal achievement could not be determined until final project completion. We know, however, that measuring goal achievement is a step-by-step procedure. Estimates and objectives are provided from the very beginning of projects and can be compared to actual figures long before final project completion. This holds true for technical goals (e.g. output specifications for building sections in terms of volume, installation, and equipment), for time goals (e.g. deadlines for the completion of sub-projects), and for financial goals (e.g. budgets for sub-projects or phases). Such comparisons may be impeded by delays in information processing and/or accounting procedures. Precise evaluations of the achievement of the technical goals, generally, cannot be made until the MOE has gone into operation. But even biased information about goal achievement during completion has (or should have) substantial feed-back effects on the success factors.

We have to extend our framework of interrelated success factors by including the variable *goal achievement*. This extension of our basic framework creates additional interdependencies as shown in Fig. 44.

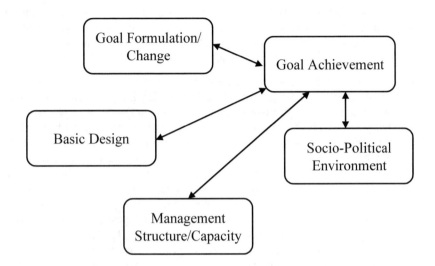

Fig. 44. Interdependence of Success Factors and Goal Achievement

Management structure/capacity and *goal achievement:* Different management structures offer different possibilities for tracking and responding to goal achievement. The attitude of project management to goal achievement depends on four conditions:

- First, the actual goal achievement has to be determined. This requires an adequate information and accounting system (standard tools of project management).
- Second, the information on actual goal achievement has to be passed on to project management and project owners. Whether this transmission is successful depends mainly on the management structure. By delegating project management functions (like planning) to contractors, the transmission process and subsequently the project management's ability to react to goal achievement may be impeded. The link between project owners and project management is another crucial issue to ensure that project owners are informed about actual goal achievement.
- Third, the information has to be evaluated by comparing it with the planned goal achievement. Even with a basic commitment to a planned goal achievement, the evaluation is subject to different interests and different (i.e. optimistic or pessimistic) attitudes. Different management structures may lead to different evaluations, as the structure determines the number and variety of participants involved as well as their positions within the management structure.
- Fourth, the reaction to (potential) goal achievement depends on the commitment of the project management and project owners to a planned goal achievement. Their commitment to the goals of MOEs is not self-evident. The well known design-to-cost concept, for instance, is much more than a technique. It

represents a distinctive attitude of project management. Whether the management structure enforces or hinders action in favor of the planned goal achievement depends, for example, on the number and influence of project managers with either a technical or financial background.

Our cases have shown that these conditions for effective feedback from goal achievement are often missing. Instead, poor reporting systems, selective perception of information, overoptimistic evaluations, changing patterns of reaction, and the tendency towards feeble reactions when facing failures have been observed.

The influence of goal achievement on the management structure depends on the probability of good performance. In the case of (potential) success, existing structures are likely to be reinforced and stabilized. Too much stability, however, can make structures inflexible and cause delays in adapting to the development of the project task. (Potential) failures, on the other hand, may destabilize the management structure. Our findings show a great variety of changes: concerning the type of project organization, the interfaces with project owners, the outsourcing of project management functions, and procedures of project control. Such changes may even require the replacement of managers, especially top managers.

Goal formulation/change and *goal achievement:* Logically, goal achievement cannot be assessed without first defining the goals. Goal change may be necessary to correct mistakes in the initial framework, especially if the goals lack realism or balance. Even if the initial goal framework has been thoroughly checked for its potential success, later developments (e.g. the influence of the socio-political environment) may necessitate its adjustment. Empirical findings, however, demonstrate that changes tend to have a negative impact on goal achievement. Frequently changed goals lose their function of controlling the planning and completion process.

Anticipating (potential) goal achievement influences the formulation of goals according to the theory of goal adaptation (Cyert/March 1992, pp.171). There is evidence that goals will not be reformulated, unless a change of the basic design has proven inevitable.

Basic design and *goal achievement:* The basic design not only specifies technical goals, but also influences the time and cost estimates. Remember that the estimated costs of the Olympic facilities in Munich, which we expected to be a suitable approximation of the basic design, explain approximately 75% of the variance of actual costs (see Table 11).

Information indicating MOE success will increase the consistency of the basic design. In the case of strong indications that goals cannot be achieved, changes in the basic design should be considered. The basic design is difficult to change if completion has reached an advanced stage or no technical alternatives are available. We expect, at least, substantial feed-back delays, when MOEs experience failures. Especially contractors or users will not be interested in pushing project owners or project managers to reformulate the basic design because it might result in the reduction of the technical goals or the establishment of cost limits.

Socio-political environment and *goal achievement*: The literature on project management has paid much attention to the impact of the socio-political environment on goal achievement. Remember the delays and cost overruns caused by environmental laws. This holds true particularly for public opposition to distinctive technical goals or locations of MOEs (see Chapter I). As mentioned above, involvement of the socio-political environment usually starts with decisions on the basic design. Additional information on (potential) goal achievement is also likely to stir up socio-political reactions. These reactions will either support the project opponents by confirming their doubts or strengthen the proponents of the MOE. The latter may be the case if aborting the project cannot be accepted for political reasons or if terminating information on the goal achievement points to successful results.

Concerning the influence of (planned) goal achievement on the socio-political environment, our empirical findings as well as other studies have proven that the likelihood of socio-political involvement correlates with the actual level of goal achievement. Failures are likely to stimulate opposing forces, while success is an effective shield against socio-political interventions. The relationship between the socio-political environment and goal achievement is not only mutual but also very volatile. Therefore, the strength and direction of the influence of this success factor is hard to predict and requires close attention from project management.

Table 18 gives evidence of significant and different interrelations between success factors and goal achievement in our case studies. For details see Part Four.

Success Factors	L. Olympic Games Munich	M. Olympic Games Lake Placid	N. Vienna Hospital	O. Munich Hospital	P. Large Wind Energy Converter GROWIAN
Goal Formulation/Change	goal formulation process dominated by architects of key facilities	reformulation of technical goals (upgrade of facilities' standards, increased # of spectators, reduced access to transportation system); enlargement of financial goals	almost unlimited change, mostly towards enlargement, enforced by users and politicians	decrease in technical goals; goals determine basic design	technical goals dominated by scientists' and politicians' will to maximize dimensions; lacking goal flexibility; after-failure justification of goals
Goal Achievement	early warning signals by cost overruns ignored; later on cost explosions mobilised socio-political environment	budget overruns caused changes in senior project management and change of goals	ignored or delayed feedback: 1974 call for stop by an adviser to project owner; no learning transfer from early completed components	early detection of budget overruns for completion goals (1963)	construction problems (composite and hybrid materials) not taken as a chance for adaptation of technical goals and basic design
Basic Design (Complexity/Consistency)	a daring design (esp. for the tent-shaped roof) caused serious technical problems and cost overruns	basic design determined by permanent operation	blocktype design/flexibility dominate technical goals and cause goal changes	close feed-back to goal achievement; two-step completion mode	early fixation on size, specific design, and technical solutions (rotor blades)
Management Structure/Capacity	delayed establishment of project management company; general manager no-minated to overcome rivalries between engineering and commercial divisions	preference for residential managers; lack of professional management until 1978 (collective decision making); successful involvement of general contractors	chaotic until 1975 with part-time project managers; overlapping responsibilities; insufficient management capacity; questionable recruitment policy, dominance of users	proper adaptation to project development; high recruitment standards; single project owner; successful user involvement	continuous and fundamental changes of project management; private industries refuse participation in project ownership
Socio-Political Environment	the Games experienced an unusual "friendly" environment until cost overruns caused interventions (external auditing)	strong influence owing to recruitment policy for project managers; public decision making until 1978	uncovering of corruption (1980) and budget overruns cause strong interventions	no significant influence	strong interventions by scientists and politicians

Table 18. Interdependence of Success Factors and Goal Achievement

Part Four: Case Studies

L. The Olympic Summer Games 1972 in Munich

A huge volume of empirical sources enabled us to analyze almost 100 variables describing this MOE in all its phases from the initial idea to host the Games to the permanent operation of the facilities after the Games. The main sources were files of the project management and the board (including minutes, budgets, drawings, and organizational charts), periodic reports to the project owners, auditing reports and press releases.[24]

I. Characteristics of the Summer Games 1972

When the XXth Olympic Summer Games 1972 were awarded to Munich on April 26, 1966, the city was named the unofficial capital of the Federal Republic of Germany because of its Bavarian flair and its attractiveness for economic activities. The State of Bavaria as well as the City of Munich were known for their long tradition of hosting guests from all over the world. Munich was also chosen to represent the "New Germany" in contrast to the Olympic Games in Berlin during the Nazi Regime in 1936.

The hosts' guiding principles for the Games were:
- "enjoyable Games", calling for fun and fraternity among competitors and spectators;
- "green Games" with a parklike architecture ("open space") instead of monstrous facilities prone to become post-Olympic ruins;
- "bright and simple Games", combating the tendency towards oversophisticated technical solutions and bureaucratic procedures;
- "Games of short distances", avoiding long commuting between the different sites of competitions.

The above list does not include any cost aspects. We, therefore, conclude that the project owners (City of Munich, State of Bavaria, Federal Republic of Germany) ranked financial goals behind technical goals and the invariable time goals.

Our case concentrates on construction activities. About €675m were required to adapt existing facilities and to build new ones. Fifteen sports facilities, almost 60% of the whole construction activity, are the subject of our in-depth analysis. These facilities were selected for the following reasons:
- they could be analyzed as separate projects of the Olympic Games, each facility representing a substantial volume in size and costs;
- they were sports facilities not infrastructural ones;
- they were new constructions, not adaptations of existing facilities;
- they were intended for permanent operation;

---

[24] See Organisationskomitee, OK (1972a, b), (1973-1976) and Olympia-Baugesellschaft, OBG (1974); for details and additional references see Grün (1975a) and (1977).

- they were managed by the Olympic Construction Company (OBG).

The facilities and their actual costs are listed in Table 9.

II.   Achievement of Goals

When we started our research program with the Olympic Games in Munich we believed the level of achievement to be rather poor. Further analysis revealed, however, that not only the achievement of technical and time goals was reasonable, but also the achievement of financial goals was rather satisfactory, apart from the cost explosion of a single facility, the famous tent-shaped roof, which proved to be a runaway cost and will be discussed separately.

1. Technical Goals

The *goals of completion* were fully achieved. All the ambitious standards of capacity, technical equipment, comfort, and design could be met. Some facilities, which initially were intended for renovation or for provisional adaptation, were replaced by new constructions. Only the eastern part of the roof of the Olympic stadium was planned but never finished.

The *initial operation* was evaluated regarding the functionality of the facilities for Olympic competitions. We asked 46 sports journalists and representatives of the hosts to judge the initial operation. Each facility was rated from "excellent" (1) to "poor" (5), regarding the different competitions and events which took place in the specific facility. The overall ratings were very high: the journalists' judgment averaged 1.7, the hosts' judgment averaged 1.6 with some reservations concerning the capacity of the facilities.

No major problems were reported concerning the housing of spectators. The infrastructural capacities of Munich and the surrounding communities were sufficient to temporarily host a total of more than 3m spectators, including 140,000 with overnight accommodations. Transportation worked well because a new subway system was developed as part of the infrastructural improvement program. This program proved to be one of the benefits for the host City of Munich.

The *permanent operation* was evaluated by representatives of seven different users. The results were less favorable. The average rating (same scale as above) was 2.5, including technical standards of the facilities, their fit of capacity, their infrastructural contribution, and their functionality. On average, the number of different functions for post-Olympic operation was five, ranging from one to thirteen functions. Although the permanent operation was rated lower than the initial operation, it was still adequate. These results reflect favorably the intention of local and state representatives to benefit permanently from the Olympic Games, to avoid "post-Olympic ruins", and to enable the post-Olympic users' to market their facilities.

2. Time Goals

Owing to the invariable date of opening, most facilities were finished in time even allowing for extensive pre-Olympic trial runs. The average rating for the achievement of time goals was 1.6. A more detailed analysis shows that some projects suffered from severe time pressure because of an ambitious integrated design (especially the tent-shaped roof, see III.2). Not all facilities were handed over to the post-Olympic users in time. The impact of time pressure on the achievement of financial goals will be discussed in the following chapter.

3. Financial Goals

Financial goals refer to completion (construction) costs and costs of permanent operation & maintenance. We start with *construction costs*, illustrated by cost estimates, actual costs, and cost overruns.

The average cost overrun concerning 15 facilities was 111% (72% without the tent-shaped roof; adjusted for inflation, for details see Table 9). The cost overrun for the whole project (including all facilities and the initial operation) amounted to 138% (€260m estimated costs versus €675m actual costs; adjusted for inflation). The project company tried to justify these overruns by the following reasons:

- innovative (partially integrated) design of facilities, lack of technical experience;
- continuous enlargement of technical goals;
- prestigious nature of the project;
- incomplete and delayed establishment of space and functional requirements;
- inadequate cost estimates;
- construction activities during the winter season, simultaneous planning and construction activities;
- lack of competition among construction companies;
- increased costs due to construction regulations and rise in salaries;
- managerial failures like late establishment of the project company, split responsibility for planning and construction supervision, inadequate cooperation between board committees, insufficient skills and high turnover of board members, and insufficient decision-making procedures.

More striking than the average amount of cost overruns is their range. Especially the overrun for the tent-shaped roof (722%) calls for an explanation. Originally designed for the German pavilion at the World Fair in Montreal (1967) the tent-shaped roof had been multiplied in size for the Olympic Games. Despite the doubts of some experts who questioned the feasibility and the estimated costs of the design, the project management refrained from searching for alternatives. In the end, the roof had to be finished at any price because there was no time left to develop alternative designs (see later).

The evaluation of *permanent costs* proved difficult because there was only one official cost estimate for the permanent use of all facilities. Therefore, we had to rely on the post-Olympic users who were asked to judge the appropriateness of the costs of permanent operation in terms of comparable facilities.

Project	Rating
Basketball Hall	1.5
Shooting Field	2.0
Olympic Stadium	3.0
Multifunctional Area	3.0
Cycling Stadium	3.5
Press Center	3.5
Rowing Regatta Center	4.0
Wrestling Hall	4.0
Canoeing Slalom Track	4.0
Swimming Hall	4.5
Tent-shaped Roof	4.5
Main Sport Hall	5.0
Riding Field	5.0
Riding Stadium	5.0
Olympic Housing (Women)	5.0
Average	3.8
Standard Deviation	1.1

Table 19. Rating of the Operation & Maintenance Costs of Facilities, Munich Games 1972 (Scale Running from 1=excellent to 5=poor)

Only two out of fifteen facilities were rated "good" or higher (≤ 2.0). Six facilities were rated "poor" (>4.0)! This was by far the worst achievement of all goal dimensions of the project.

4. Overall Performance

Project success requires favorable levels of achievement of the technical, time, and financial goals. In the case of the Olympic Summer Games in Munich, the achievement of technical and time goals was excellent and good, respectively, while the achievement of financial goals was rather poor. High construction costs could not be justified by low costs of the permanent operation. In order to test the interrelationship between technical and financial goals of the various facilities we correlated ten variables representing different dimensions of technical goals with three variables representing financial goals. No significant interrelationship could be ascertained.

III.   Success Factors

We focus our analysis of success factors on the reasons for the achievement of technical and time goals and for the underachievement of financial goals. Special attention is paid to the tent-shaped roof.

1. Formulation and Change of Goals

(1) The most important formulation and change problems were reported concerning *technical goals*. The rules of the IOC stipulate the competitions to be held whereas the international sports associations (neither the project owners, nor the project management) define the minimum standards of the sports facilities. Project owners, on the other hand, are responsible for determining the following:

- capacity of facilities for competitions, press activities, and accommodation depending on the number of athletes, coaches, officials, spectators, and journalists;
- location of facilities;
- technical standards of facilities, ranging from minor adaptations of existing facilities to construction of new ones;
- requirements of the post-Olympic users of facilities.

In this case technical goals dominated financial goals, and short-term goals for initial operation dominated long-term goals for permanent operation. The dominance of technical goals over financial ones can be quantified by analyzing the goal-formulation activities. The ratio between activities referring to technical aspects (especially sports functions) and those concerning economic aspects was 3.4 to 1! Another analysis shows a positive correlation of the actual costs of facilities with the level of activity of the project management directed towards those facilities. Obviously, project management became aware of rising costs and discussed them but was unable to control them in their crucial phases because of insufficient technical expertise (see below).

The preferential treatment of short-term over long-term goals can be explained by motivational as well as rational aspects. Organizing glamorous and unique Olympic Games seems to be more attractive and offers quicker feedback than being responsible for an appropriate post-Olympic operation. As to the rational aspect, information on long-term operations are considered to be less precise and less influential than information on events in the near future. In general, project owners tend to overestimate the financial means of post-Olympic users.

Three major *driving forces* were responsible for increasing the technical goals. *Sports associations* (initial users) strongly influenced the decisions on the capacity and technical standards of facilities. They constantly aimed at increasing the technical goals based on the assumption of increased numbers of athletes and other participants, new international standards, or more sophisticated technical equipment. Representatives of sports associations were able to exert their influence on goal formulation without having formal authority in the decision-making process because the board and its committees lacked the necessary expertise of sports functions.

Project owners were another driving force. They favored new constructions even in cases where existing facilities could have been adapted, or they promoted facilities even though their necessity for initial operation was questionable. Especially the local (City of Munich) and the state (State of Bavaria) project owners pushed their post-Olympic interests and finally compromised only at the expense of the third project owner (federal government).

Architects were a third driving force. The design of the architects for the main facilities, including the tent-shaped roof, was favored by the jury because it integrated key facilities into one homogeneous unit. This integration turned out to be a handicap because construction difficulties and design changes of one facility automatically affected other facilities. Besides these "design-inherent" problems the architects – assisted by some planning experts and by the media – successfully prevented changes in the technical goals, even when their redefinition seemed inevitable for constructional and financial reasons (see also "Basic Design").

Limited technical expertise of the project management, especially of board members, made it difficult to control the driving forces. The fixed *time goals* (a 6-year period between the date of award and the date of opening) may have prevented further changes (enlargements) of the technical goals and, consequently, an increase in costs. Apart from this invariable time limit, other time goals had to be formulated, especially deadlines for the space and functional requirements of the facilities. Early calls for a frozen zone to avoid further changes occurred in 1968, only two years after the start of the project. These calls were ignored to allow further analyses and experience transfers from the Summer Games 1968 in Mexico City. Therefore, crucial decisions were delayed – possibly even "forgotten" – or made under severe time pressure (e.g. decisions concerning the space and functional requirements and the nomination of permanent users). Other decisions, made very early, were neither questioned nor abandoned. Finally, there was confusion concerning planning because it was not in line with the actual progress of the project.

(2) The increase in and change of technical goals had continuous and substantial impact on the *formulation of financial goals*, as shown in the following table:

Estimated by	Date of Estimate	Cost Estimate (m€)
Project Owners	1966-12	260
Project Management	1968-02	410-432
Savings Committee	1968-05	380-425
Financial & Administrative Committee of the Board	1968-05	380
Project Management	1969-04	393
Project Management	1969-05	400
Project Management	1969-11	575
Project Management	1970-12	675
Financial & Administrative Committee of the Board	1971-03	675

Table 20. Cost Estimates of the Olympic Games in Munich 1972

The initial commitment of the project owners in 1966 set a cost limit of €260 m. After the project company was established and had made a first estimate of the project costs in 1968, this commitment became obsolete. Despite efforts by a savings commission to reduce costs (1968), these increased substantially and peaked at €500m in 1969/70. Finally, the costs were fixed at €675m (equal to actual costs) at the end of 1970.

The extreme *uncertainty* of early cost estimates can be demonstrated by three estimates for the *tent-shaped roof,* dated from April to July 1969: Planning architects estimated €20.5 m, an engineering office for construction supervision estimated €42 m, and the bids of construction companies ranged from €50.5m to €65 m. We can see from these figures that the estimates made by institutions with construction responsibility were far more realistic (actual costs €85.5 m).

> A lesson from this case is to involve institutions with responsibility for construction (more generally: for completion) in order to gain reliable cost estimates.

Two facilities, the basketball hall and the rowing regatta center, illustrate different types of *consistency* in the goal formulation.

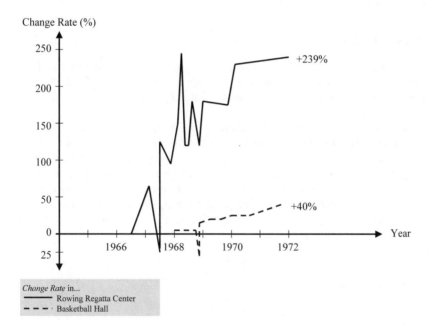

Fig. 45. Cost Estimates for Two Facilities of the Olympic Games in Munich (Initial Estimates as Zero-Line)

While the cost estimates for the basketball hall grew moderately from 1970 onwards, the estimates for the rowing regatta center developed erratically.

The formulation of financial goals was not only inconsistent but also *incomplete*. Important cost items (e.g. the overhead costs of construction supervision, the operation costs at the construction site) and the rate of inflation were not included. Overhead costs amounted to about 15% of construction costs and anticipating the inflation rate would have decreased the cost overrun. The goal formulation was also incomplete because the project owners and project management failed to turn estimates into budgets. No binding cost limit was set for the architects. The president of the board was right to remark: "Common sense doesn't allow us to start an invitation for tenders without any constraints on the architects' playful creations and their financial implications. If you offer them a hunting ground without boundaries you cannot expect them to meet the planned figures by lucky coincidence or merciful fate" (Grün 1975a, p.56).

Another weakness of cost management resulted from the poor cost accounting procedures which were dismissed as "only desk work" from the very beginning of the project. Furthermore, the costs couldn't be properly assigned to the individual facilities, especially to facilities with an integrated basic design. A sophisticated computer-based accounting system failed and had to be replaced by a conventional manual system. As a matter of fact, the final cost statement was delayed for months and compelled the project owners to reschedule the liquidation of the project company.

2. Basic Design

Most of the Olympic facilities are located in a suburban area of Munich (called "Oberwiesenfeld"), which was designed by two architect teams. The guiding principles (see introduction) and the technical goals served as a framework for the design.

The basic designs of the cycling stadium, the press center, and the tent-shaped roof caused problems which severely affected the overall performance. Initially, the cycling competitions were to take place in a reconstructed facility. When cost estimates for its adaptation reached €6 m, the project owners decided to construct a new facility with estimated costs of €3.5-4 m. In the end, actual costs amounted to €8.5 m. Until December 1970, the project management planned to accommodate the media in a makeshift building. The late decision for a new building caused extraordinary time pressure.

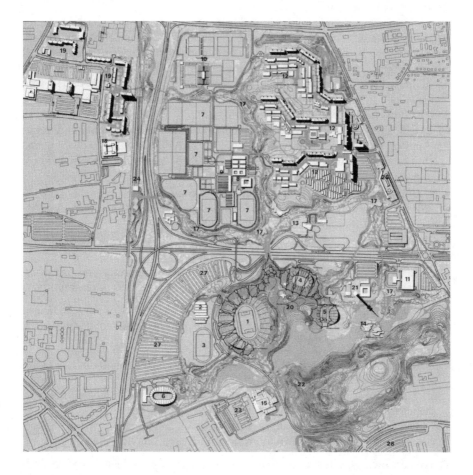

(1) **Olympic Stadium**; (2) Warm-Up Hall; (3) Warm-Up Site; (4) **Main Sport Hall**; (5) **Swimming Hall**; (6) **Cycling Stadium**; (7) **Multifunctional Area**; (8) DOZ (Deutsches Olympiazentrum); (9) Volleyball Hall; (10) Hockey Stadium; (11) **Wrestling Hall**; (12) **Olympic Village**; (13) North Restaurant; (14) Lake Restaurant; (15) South Restaurant; (16) Tavern; (17) Kiosks; (18) **Press Center**; (19) Press Buildings; (20) Center (Coubertin-Platz); (21) Television Tower; (22) Olympiaberg; (23) OBG (Olympia Baugesellschaft mbH); (24) Train Station; (25) Subway Station; (26) Tram U-Turn; (27) Non-Public Parking Lot; (28) Bus Parking; (29) OK (Organisationskomitee)

Fig. 46. The Locations of the Facilities of the Olympic Games in Munich (Facilities in bold letters are the Subject of our Study)

As mentioned above, the ambitious design of the *tent-shaped roof* turned out to be the biggest problem. The architects designed a huge roof to cover three key facilities (Olympic stadium, swimming hall, and main sport hall). This integrated solution increased the already high complexity of the basic design and caused substantial problems because the constructional difficulties with the tent-shaped roof immediately affected other facilities. Another mistake was to underestimate the innovative design of the tent-shaped roof. In the beginning, project owners as well as high ranking experts perceived only a minor difference from "existing", "traditional" designs and were committed to a "more modern", "unusual" design with "some risks". In the planning and construction phase, however, the extraordinary design of this facility became painfully obvious:

- Architects could not provide a detailed technical description of the method of construction. Therefore, it was impossible to develop a sound evaluation, and orders to the construction companies had to be made on the basis of cost prices.
- Static calculations for the net construction proved incorrect.
- Finding a roofing material which was translucent as well as non-flammable seemed almost impossible from a technical point of view.
- It took 140 days instead of the planned 10 to construct the network of ropes, a key element of the tent-shaped roof.
- The costs of the facility exploded. Owing to the cost increase and time pressure, the eastern part of the roof of the Olympic stadium was never built.

Members of the board – some of them enthusiastic supporters of the tent-shaped roof design at the beginning – felt misled and poorly informed (Grün 1975a, pp.46, 54):

> "The fact that the revised static calculations would increase costs from €18.5m to €210m should have been announced immediately."
> "If I had foreseen the cost explosion, I would never have accepted the tent-shaped roof."
> "If the board had known about the cost explosion and the construction difficulties, it would have demanded a more feasible design from the beginning."

The project owners failed to revise the initial decision for the tent-shaped roof design even after constructional difficulties had become obvious. Insisting on the decision was justified by some formal reasons, such as the contractual rights of the architects to realize their design. Finally, time pressure was decisive for not changing the design; project owners doubted that enough time was left to develop alternative designs. This – at least partly "self-made" – time pressure resulted in hasty evaluation procedures and an unfavorable position in the contract negotiations with construction companies.

But the Olympic Games in Munich also present lessons for the *successful management* of the basic design: The decision-making process regarding the Olympic village started with 57 (!) alternative designs. The planning architect developed a procedure which enabled the board to select the "optimal" alternative step by step. Board members appreciated this procedure because it was not only transparent and saved time but also reassured them of having made the right decision.

3. Socio-Political Environment

The Olympic Summer Games 1972 in Munich experienced broad support from the socio-political environment. It was a matter of pride and prestige to present a new and peaceful Germany. The Games, therefore, received extraordinary attention from the public and the project owners to such an extent that they overshadowed other projects like the Munich Hospital (see case O).

Public attention was a strong driving force which greatly influenced the goal formulation. Costs and even substantial cost overruns were considered an investment that would serve national interests. The planning architects were able to implement their unusual tent-shaped roof design even in the face of dramatic cost explosions because he appealed successfully to national pride and self-esteem. Controlling the influence of the planning architects and of the socio-political environment was impeded by staffing the board with high-ranking politicians who were extremely sensitive to public opinion. This sensitivity underwent significant changes during the project. In the beginning, the board hardly noticed budget overruns amounting to millions of euros. After the cost explosion of the tent-shaped roof had shocked the public, even comparatively small amounts had to be publicly justified, and in the final phase of the project the board showed a strong determination to adhere to an absolute cost limit of €675 m.

Furthermore, the socio-political environment exercised pressure on the project management to engage local contractors and experts even when they were not the best qualified.

4. Management Structure and Management Capacity

We will concentrate on (1) the fundamental organizational design, on (2) the board structure of the project company "OBG", on (3) the integration of external experts and users, and on (4) problems of recruitment and turnover.

(1) Unlike other Olympic Games such as Lake Placid, in Munich the responsibility for the initial operation (the Games, including test events and art programs) was separated from the responsibility for planning, financing, and constructing the facilities. Therefore, two separate companies were set up: the Organizing Committee ("Organisationskomitee, OK", Fig. 47) and the Olympic Construction Company ("Olympia Baugesellschaft mbH, OBG", Fig. 48).

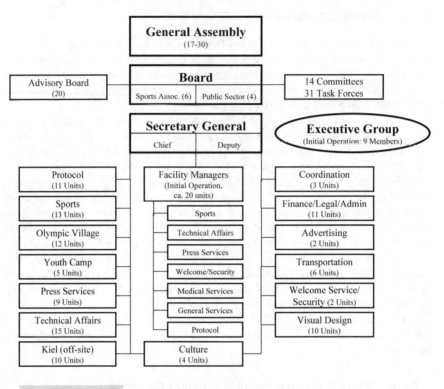

Fig. 47. Organizational Structure of the Organizing Committee (OK) of the Olympic Games in Munich

The OK was chaired by 63-year-old Herbert Kunze. He was extraordinarily experienced in Olympic affairs due to his former position as "Chef de Mission" of the German Olympic team. His deputy, Hermann Reichart, served in the State Ministry of Finance. The OK employed more than 500 employees (1972), one-third of them recruited from the public and two-thirds from the private sector. In the course of the Games up to 40,000 additional volunteers and members of the German Federal Armed Forces (performing a broad variety of functions such as ticket inspectors and sports physicians) constituted the workforce of the OK.

The OBG had about 120 employees (1971). Initially, two vice presidents heading the engineering and the commercial department, respectively, shared power. After severe internal problems and problems with the board, 64-year-old Carl Mertz took over as general manager in 1969. He had gained project management experience by successfully managing the German pavilion at the Word Fair in Brussels in 1958.

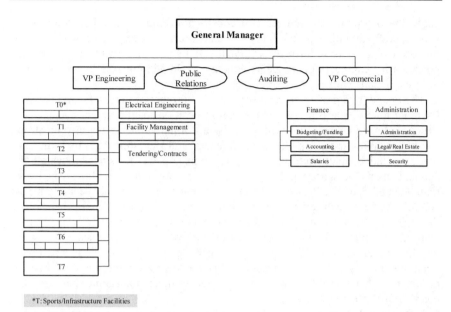

*T: Sports/Infrastructure Facilities

Fig. 48. Organizational Structure of the Olympic Construction Company (OBG)

The (public) project owners realized that a project management embedded in the public administration would fail and, therefore, decided to set up a separate project company in the fall of 1966. The *delayed establishment of the OBG* in July 1967 caused additional time pressure on the project.

The fundamental organizational design suffered from the *shared responsibility* of the OK and the OBG and from OBG's intention to manage the facilities without general contractors. The OK was responsible for defining the space and functional requirements and for initial operation, whereas the OBG was responsible for planning, financing and constructing the facilities. In the final phase of the project their cooperation was so inefficient that even special procedures ("urgent letters") did not speed up the communication process. The OBG had to coordinate about 20 planning architects, 100 construction engineering offices, 20 state and federal offices, and 80 construction and equipment companies, not to mention external auditors, savings commissions, numerous planning experts, and the media.

A different type of organizational structure providing for integrated responsibility for initial operation and for the planning and completion of facilities along with the appointment of *general contractors* would have been more effective, especially regarding the constraints in recruiting highly skilled staff (see later). The basketball hall, the only facility managed by a general contractor, showed exceptional levels of achievement concerning all goal dimensions.

(2) Full *authority of project managers* is fundamental for effective project management. As shown in Fig. 48, project managers were appointed for specific facilities. Their authority, however, was impaired by other project participants, espe-

cially the board, its committees (for construction and for administration & finance), and planning experts. The communication between project managers and the board had to pass through several hierarchical levels (team manager, vice president for engineering, and general manager). In addition, there was also some turnover of staff with negative effects on the project.

The *board* (comprising 20 representatives of project owners, OK, and the state Olympic lottery, see Fig. 36) held a central position in the project management structure. Its influence was based not only on formal authority but also on strong and high-ranking members like mayors, federal and state ministers. Its formal authority included, apart from supervising top management, decisions on overall and annual budgets, on space and functional requirements, and on facilities which cost more than €2.5 m. The board met more than twenty times in its six years' term, the committees for construction and for administration & finance more than fourty times. These frequent meetings reflect the board's commitment to bear the ultimate responsibility. Quoting a member of the board: "If we don't deal with a matter like this seriously, we'll sooner or later meet again in front of the federal investigation commission" or "The responsibility for the main issue, the cost increase of the tent-shaped roof, is not borne by the project management but by the board."(Grün 1975a, p.16)

Unfortunately, the board was not able to live up to its own commitment because it lacked specific expertise in sports functions and technical affairs. This weakness was aggravated by the project owners' preference to appoint high-ranking politicians as their representatives. Apart from their lack of specific experience and their sensitivity towards public opinion and local interests, the politicians impeded the decision-making process for several reasons:

- Politicians were often unable to attend important board meetings and thus delayed decisions crucial for the progress of the project.
- The prominence of the politicians encouraged senior managers of the project company to submit to the board issues which actually did not need its approval, in order to shift responsibility.
- As the project developed, top management assumed more and more responsibility and occasionally even bypassed the board's approval by establishing a separate budget item called "contingencies", in order to offset overruns by savings of project costs. This budget item at times amounted to as much as €50 m! The board and its committees were upset: "The construction committee has neither been informed nor approached, not even when crucial problems needed to be discussed ... giving the impression that the construction committee is a troublesome and superfluous appendix which impedes the workflow and the decision-making process. In four months' time, there will be nothing left for us to decide (Grün 1975a, p.30)."
- The committees of the board (for construction and for administration & finance) more or less successfully assisted the board and acted as troubleshooter. Yet, some deficiencies have to be mentioned: Overlapping responsibilities of the committees caused extra work and fostered the tendency of the committees to reject responsibility; it also contributed to the dominance of technical goals.

Summing up, the board's influence was weak despite its remarkable formal authority and its prominent and influential members. Quoting a somewhat frustrated board member: "Of course, I am aware that ultimately the board has no alternative but to approve cost overruns because of the time pressure. Considering the taxpayers' and the parliament's reaction, however, a version has to be found, which indicates the board's effort to keep control over the costs (Grün 1975a, p.35)."

> Project management power should rest with the top executives and not with the board.
> Splitting the responsibility for technical (construction) and financial goal achievement is not appropriate because the goals are mutually interrelated.
> Politicians are not the best suited to fill top positions in project companies.

(3) External experts like architects and engineering offices often have a strong influence on the formulation of goals without being responsible for their actual achievement. *Architects* act as a driving force because they often pursue design interests rather than economic ones. They also may gain financially when the construction volume increases. The architects of the main facilities in Munich were able to enforce their tent-shaped roof design even in the face of extreme cost overruns. In the early project phases the committee members explicitly praised the architects for defending their design, the cooperation was said to be smooth and effective, and the project management permitted substantial delays in the implementation of the architects' plans. With continuous difficulties in the construction of the tent-shaped roof, the project owners' dissatisfaction kept growing: "Again and again it has been said that all requirements have been met in an unprecedented manner. In fact, we are more or less compelled to chase after the plans of the architect" (Grün 1975a, p.43). Finally, the architects and the project owners took their financial dispute to court.

Additional deficiencies were due to weak cooperation between planning architects and *engineering offices* responsible for construction supervision. Joint responsibility for planning and completion would have been favorable, especially as the project owners and project management had only limited technical experience.

A remarkable number of *external planning experts* were engaged in order to solve difficult technical problems and to advise the board in the case of conflicting opinions. Unfortunately, but not surprisingly, experts' advice also differed. One expert, for example, concluded that the tent-shaped roof design would lower construction costs and would be more cost efficient in operation than traditional designs. A frustrated board member was surprised "... that any expert could make detailed estimates, although no experience was available for this kind of construction" (Grün 1975a, p.46). Delays in the decision-making process and high fees were the only measurable and incontrovertible effects of the experts' engagement.

Employ *internal* experts to have a countervailing power to external experts and to ensure a balance of authority and responsibility.

Some difficulties in goal formulation and in managing goal change resulted from the project owners' preference for procedures common in routine undertakings in the public sector. These require that tenders are not to be started until planning has been completed. Such procedures are inadequate in the case of MOEs under time pressure because substantial uncertainties cannot be reduced in time or arise only in the course of completion. A member of the board complained: "It is frustrating, in general, that the OBG has to make decisions without substantial inputs from the planning" (Grün 1975a, p.49). In order to achieve feasible technical solutions and to obtain reliable cost estimates, a "joint responsibility pact" between project management, planning experts, and construction companies would be appropriate. Such a procedure would have mobilized substantial engineering capacity during the planning phase, impeded changes of the space and functional requirements, and lowered costs. However, when submitted to the board it failed to get its approval.

Representatives of sports associations and permanent users also had to be integrated into the project management structure. *Sports associations* aimed at high standards of the facilities in terms of user-friendliness and functionality. They had no formal authority and responsibility in the project management structure of the OBG but were supposed to submit their requirements through the OK which held seats on the board. This arrangement was to prevent willful actions by the diverse sports associations and to ensure a fair consideration of all requirements. It failed because sports associations often bypassed the formal lines of authority and presented their requirements straight to the project management (see Fig. 41). Furthermore, sports associations often delayed decisions on the specification of requirements, and their negotiations with the OK were tough and time consuming. We, therefore, believe that the integration of sports representatives into the project teams of the OBG would have been more favorable for the project.

Seven representatives of the *permanent users* were subject to our analysis: the State of Bavaria, the City of Munich, the City of Augsburg, the Bavarian Shooting Association, the Munich Fair Company, the Olympic Park Company (owned by the City of Munich), and the Students' Association of the Munich University. All of them had less influence on the project management than the sports associations. Their level of activity (documented in the files of our analysis) was only about one third of the level of the sports associations. Furthermore, in ten out of fifteen facilities, the permanent users were not involved in the planning process. Some of them were only nominated in the late phases of the project. Owing to the inadequate involvement of the permanent users in the management structure, priority was given to the goals of completion and initial operation. Consequently, permanent operation & maintenance experienced a less favorable goal achievement. The project management underestimated the problems of this phase and overestimated the financial resources of the permanent users.

A final coordination problem refers to auditing and savings activities. Internal, city, state and federal *audit offices* were engaged to investigate the orderliness and cost efficiency of planning, bidding, and construction procedures. Some of these audit activities were too bureaucratic and too unspecific, and did not sufficiently reflect the unique requirements of project auditing and project controlling. In addition, much of the project management capacity was tied up with analyzing and commenting on audit reports.

Savings commissions were established after heavy cost overruns, especially of the large facilities. The commissions' ad-hoc activity could not curb the cost increases, a further proof that external cost control cannot make up for insufficient cost control by the project management.

(4) The decision makers on the board did not have sufficient technical experience to evaluate technical goals and consequently were unable to control the driving forces by means of technical arguments. The project owners' intention to separate the management of the Games from the public administration proved difficult to implement because the board's salary policy was derived from the standards of the public administration and *impeded recruiting highly skilled project staff*. Many successful managers from private firms refused to join the project company, especially because salaries in the private sector were higher due to the economic boom in Germany at that time. As employees' salaries accounted for only a small fraction of the total project costs the recruitment of more highly skilled personnel from the private sector would have been justified in order to improve goal achievement. Some staff members of the OBG who had worked for the project owners faced conflicting interests between their current and their former employer, who could possibly be their future employer again! Finally, it should be mentioned that no efforts were made to improve the staff's performance by special training programs.

The board's authority, experience, and its cooperation with the top management were impeded by a *turnover of board members* that usually followed changes in the political landscape. The federal representatives faced excessive turnover, whereas the state (of Bavaria) members of the board experienced only a low turnover rate due to the steady power of the ruling conservative party in Bavaria.

IV.   Interdependence of Success Factors and Goal Achievement

Many problems of the Olympic Games in Munich resulted from an unbalanced initial goal framework. The technical goals were far too ambitious compared to the limited time available for their achievement and to the initial cost limits (see [4] in Table 21). The initial imbalance was further aggravated by strong driving forces represented by project owners, sports associations, architects, and the sociopolitical environment sensitive to arguments like national pride and prestige.

In the face of invariable time goals and early budget overruns, project owners and project management should have made substantial efforts to rebalance the framework by reformulating the technical goals. Initial overoptimism, lack of technical expertise, and confidence in conventional decision-making procedures prevented project owners and project management from taking the necessary corrective actions in time. When the full extent of the technical difficulties with the basic design became obvious, project management did not believe in the possibility of developing alternative basic designs within a limited time period. For them, the point of no return had already been reached.

The call for a "frozen zone" [7] once construction had started [8] was disregarded. The first strong feedback regarding goal achievement was not taken as chance to balance the goal framework. Owing to cost overruns the socio-political environment was mobilized [11][14]. With some delay, project owners made a final decision on the basic design and on financial goals [12][13][15]. The responsibilities in the top management of the project company were split (engineering vs. commercial). By nominating a general manager and reducing the board's influence [10] the management capacity improved substantially.

GF: Goal Formulation & Change					SE: Socio-Political Environment	
BD: Basic Design					GA: Goal Achievement	
MS: Management Structure/Capacity						

#	Date	GF	BD	MS	SE	GA	Event
[1]	1966-04-26					■	IOC awards the Games to Munich
[2]	1966-07-03			■			Olympic Organization Committee (OK) is established
[3]	1966-fall			■			project owners decide to establish a project company
[4]	1966-12	■					project owners state a cost limit of €260 m
[5]	1967-07-10			■			project company (OBG) is established
[6]	1967-10-13			■			decision on the basic design (architects' design)
[7]	1968	■	■			■	call for a "frozen zone" to prevent further changes of technical goals and basic designs
[8]	1968-03					■	start of construction
[9]	1968-03			■			establishment of a savings commission
[10]	1969-06-10			■			Carl Mertz is nominated as general manager
[11]	1969-07-15				■	■	auditing because of cost explosion (tent-shaped roof)
[12]	1969-08-18	■	■				final decision on the tent-shaped roof and on a cost price contract
[13]	1969-11					■	new cost estimate amounts to €575 m
[14]	1969-12-17				■		extended external auditing (all facilities
[15]	1969-end	■					an ultimate cost limit is set (€675 m)
[16]	1972-05-26					■	opening of the Olympic stadium
[17]	1972-07					■	pre-Olympic test events
[18]	1972-08-26 to 1972-09-11					■	Olympic Summer Games; terrorist attack and hostage taking (1972-09-05)
[19]	1972-09-16					■	handing over of facilities to permanent users starts
[20]	1974-01-01			■			liquidation of the project company (OBG)

Table 21. Interdependence of Success Factors and Goal Achievement in the Case of the Olympic Games in Munich

M. The Olympic Winter Games 1980 in Lake Placid

No internal files of the project owners were available to analyze this case. We had to rely on reports of the Lake Placid Olympic Organizing Committee (LPOOC) to the IOC, on a consultants report, on newspapers and journals.[25] An on site visit and interviews with representatives of the permanent users offered the opportunity to get to know the post-Olympic shape of the facilities and how tourism industry in Lake Placid has gained from the Olympics.

I.   Characteristics of the Winter Games

Lake Placid, the host city of the XIII. Olympic Winter Games 1980, is part of the County of North Elba in the north-eastern part of New York State. The village with its 3,000 inhabitants lies 530m above sea-level in the heart of the Adirondack State Park, famous for its beauty and wilderness. The village was described as an isolated small world with narrow streets and a single traffic light. Lake Placid's economy is based on the tourism industry with unemployment rising up to 20% in the low season. Therefore, the predominant motivation to host the Games was an economic one.

Lake Placid has a long tradition in winter sports events. The village already hosted the III. Olympic Winter Games in 1932 but was rejected several times to host the Games by the National (USOC) and International Olympic Committee (IOC) prior to the award in 1974.

With the award of the Olympic Games Lake Placid was obliged to provide all necessary *facilities* for the sports and cultural events and for the ceremonies as well as infrastructure (housing, transportation, energy, and communication systems). Furthermore, the events themselves had to be organized. The plans for the facilities and events were based on the assumption of 1,800 athletes and coaches and a maximum of 52,000 spectators per day. These numbers did not include the officials and journalists. About 80 different events had to be organized, in particular

- 32 competitions in 8 disciplines,
- victory ceremonies,
- opening and closing ceremonies.

Sports facilities had to be prepared for the following competitions:
- Alpine Skiing: downhill, slalom, giant slalom;
- Nordic Skiing: ski jump, cross country, biathlon;
- ice sports: hockey, figure skating, speed skating;
- bobsled and luge.

---

[25] See LPOOC (1980); for additional references and more details see Grün (1988)

The facilities included cooling systems for skating, snow making equipment for the ski runs, and timing services. Furthermore, Lake Placid had to provide housing for athletes and coaches. An adequate infrastructure required:

- accommodation for officials, journalists, and spectators;
- roads and parking facilities;
- transportation systems (buses etc.);
- communications network;
- media center;
- security systems for athletes, spectators, and for the facilities;
- office space for the LPOOC and IOC headquarters.

From the very beginning Lake Placid showed *clear preference for permanent operation* rather than for completion and for initial operation. Their driving motivation was to revive tourism. Another characteristic of Lake Placid was the hosts' *preference for athletes and other members of the Olympic family* and their minor awareness of the interests of the spectators. This attitude provoked ironic-cynical remarks like: "Probably that is why the Games survive; the athletes and officials, and journalists like them" (Time, 1980-02-25).

Concerning *financial goals* the hosts were very much aware that the whole history of the Olympics is losing money. They were eager to avoid losses, especially since the previous Winter Games in Sapporo (Japan) and Innsbruck (Austria) showed poor financial results. In the following sections we also question the hosts' ability to bring the Games "back into perspective" (NYT, 1980-02-10) as they promised.

II.   Achievement of Goals

Similar to other Olympic Games analyzed in the course of our research, the Olympic Games in Lake Placid have shown rather satisfactory results. In the following section we will present details on the achievement of technical, time, and financial goals. The nature of this type of MOE requires separate evaluations of the goal achievement for completion, for initial, and for permanent operation & maintenance.

1. Technical Goals

Completion goals refer to the Olympic facilities (sports, housing, and infrastructure). We do not have separate ratings for every *sports facility* like in Munich. Overall the facilities were rated as "world-class standard". Extraordinary results such as world records in several speed skating competitions confirm this evaluation.

Housing for the athletes was criticized as substandard and – due to its strict security measures – as depressing: "If the housing for Olympic athletes looks suspiciously like a prison, it's because it soon will be one. The Lake Placid organizers came up with this unusual kind of lodging out of justifiable concerns about security" (Fortune, 1980-01-14). Indeed, the buildings for the athletes were designed to be a prison after the Games.

Due to the hosts' preference for the Olympic family, *housing for spectators* was neglected. Hotels and private rooms in or nearby the village were reserved to the Olympic family which amounted to about 28,000 athletes, coaches, officials, journalists, and volunteers (some of them even used trailers). The accommodation facilities spread over an area of 20 square miles around Lake Placid reaching from Albany, N.Y., to Montreal, Canada. A journalist, therefore, recommended to visit Lake Placid during the test events and to watch the actual Games on television.

The *initial operation*, especially the organization of the events was praised. Lake Placid's experience with winter sports events, the extensive tests, and the intensive training of the service staff paid off. However, *attendance of athletes and spectators* fell short of the planned numbers: 1,400 instead of 1,800 athletes from 37 nations and 25,000 instead of 50,000 spectators per day. One reason for the low number of athletes was the boycott of the eastern bloc countries in retaliation for President Carter's boycott of the Olympic Summer Games in Moscow in 1980. Some disciplines were carried out with almost no spectators at all (e.g. only 400 spectators watched the 30 km cross country ski event). All in all capacity utilization (spectators per event) was rather disappointing due to extreme low temperatures at the time of the Games.

The *transportation system* caused substantial difficulties which led to a great loss of the overall positive performance of the Games. According to some of the commentators, the breakdown of the transportation system did not come as a surprise. A masterplan of the State of New York in 1975 should ensure sufficient transportation capacity. After the media initiated a discussion on the narrow access roads to Lake Placid, the LPPOC developed a five-level computer-based transportation concept for the different participants (athletes, coaches, officials, journalists, sponsors, and spectators). Only one (!) of the five levels was intended for the spectators. The organizers prepared huge parking lots for private cars at the outskirts of Lake Placid and a shuttle service to the various sports facilities. After a test operation in 1979 they promised a full, safe, prompt, scheduled, and rapid transportation system. The results of further improvements were a ten-level transportation system and additional restrictions for all but official cars.

Whereas the transportation system for athletes and officials worked well during the Games the system for spectators and journalists collapsed. First difficulties were reported on the February 11th, 1980 when a strike of the drivers resulted in a shortage of buses for the shuttle service. The disastrous situation lasted for several days. Finally, the governor of New York called a limited state of emergency and a new transportation management system was introduced by a professional bus company to solve the problem. The break down not only caused long waiting time for spectators in extremely unfair weather conditions but also some injuries. Speakers of the LPOOC explicitly underlined their a priori preference for the Olympic family after the transportation disaster: "We never did say we were putting on the Olympic Games for spectators or for the press. We said the athletes would be No. 1 and every one else should be No. 2" (Sport Illustrated 52, 1980-02-25). Of course, this preference was subject to harsh criticism:

- "Never in the history of arithmetics was a No. 2 more widely separated from a No. 1" and
- The Games were great, but the buses were a bust and the organizers ornery" (Sport Illustrated 52, 1980-02-25).
- "Lake Placid's logistics tended toward the existential" and
- "Bring your own balloon" (Time, 1980-02-25).
- "The only real amateurs here are the ones who organized the Games ..." (US. News and World Report, 1980-03-03).

The president of the LPOOC (Rev. J. Bernard Fell) even submitted the idea of banning the spectators from future Olympic Games (Sport Illustrated 52, 1980-02-25). In 1985 under similar circumstances Marc Hodler, the former president of the Fédération Internationale de Ski (FIS), remarked: "Ski run is not a discipline for spectators but for competitors" (Die Presse, Vienna, 1985-06-20), paving the way for the TV Games.

The *permanent operation* of Olympic sports facilities does not always have to be successful. In Squaw Valley, which hosted the Winter Games in 1960, for example, most of the facilities were torn down or are now in poor condition. The Lake Placid hosts never denied their strong focus on the permanent operation: "What you see here has been designed with the years after the Olympics in mind ... There are no white elephants here" (Spurney in NYT, 1980-02-10). After the adaptation of the Olympic sports facilities for permanent operation Lake Placid was able to strengthen its good reputation for summer and winter tourism ("Winter Sports Capital of the World"). It offers lodging capacity in about 50 hotels and inns, facilities for water sports, tennis, golf, and hiking. Special attractions are linked to its Olympic facilities: The Olympic center (for figure skating and ice hockey competitions), the Sheffield Speed Skating Oval, the bobsled and luge runs, the ski trails, the biathlon facilities, and the Whiteface Mountain Alpine Ski Center with snow making equipment offer a variety of utilization for training and competition purposes. Some of them are run as official training center of the United States Olympic Committee. The center can host great events like revues, conventions, fairs, and tournaments. Some sports facilities have even become known as landmarks, especially the 90 meter ski jump tower with a glass-enclosed elevator. The company managing the permanent operation of the sports facilities records 60,000 visitors and 40,000 cross country skiers per year.

A special aspect of permanent operation was Lake Placid's consideration to bid for the 1992 Olympic Games (finally awarded to Albertville, France) and its plan to rotate the Games between Lake Placid, Innsbruck (Austria), Sapporo (Japan), and Sarajevo (former Yugoslavia).

2. Time Goals

The construction work on the Olympic facilities started in 1977 more than two years after the Games were awarded to Lake Placid. This delayed start caused some doubts about their on-time completion. The completion was impeded by serious adversities:

- The village has a respectable distance to the next industrial center.
- 14 different construction sites cover an area of 20 square miles.
- The ski jumps, the bobsled and the luge run, and the cooling system of the speed skate oval caused technical problems or construction failures. The ski jumps and the luge run had to be redesigned. The latter additionally showed heavy cost overruns.
- Unfavorable weather conditions during the winter season affected progress of construction.
- In order to avoid time overruns, the hosts signed a no-strike agreement with the unions.
- The construction progress of the Olympic center and the ski jumps suffered from delayed delivery caused by the bankruptcy of the steel supplier.

In the end, all facilities were finished early enough to allow for extended test events. The hosts voiced their pride with the slogan "Welcome World, We're Ready".

No special time goals were reported for *permanent operation*. Efforts to use the Olympic facilities for national and international world-class competitions as well as for a national Olympic training center started in May 1980 only a few months after the end of the Games. The split ownership of the Olympic facilities proved to be disadvantageous for permanent operation, especially for the establishment of an Olympic training center. Therefore, efforts concentrated on a new management structure for the permanent operation (see section III.4).

3. Financial Goals

The actual *costs for completion and initial operation* amounted to $178m (1980, see **Table 23**). Media reports even indicated total costs of up to $220 m, including $100m state funds. The following table shows the breakdown of the actual costs:

	Relative (%)
Sports Facilities (New Buildings)	39.7
Sports Facilities (Adaptations)	6.6
Infrastructure	20.6
Project Management	4.6
Administration/Initial Operation	28.5
Total	100.0

Table 22. Costs for Completion and for Initial Operation of the Olympic Games in Lake Placid

Ticket sales, public and private (sponsor) funds, and revenues from licenses and TV rights only covered one third of the total costs. The ticket sale was unexpectedly low (fewer spectators, high ticket prices, chaotic ticket distribution). A direct mail fundraising campaign failed. Several potential sponsors refused their support for fear of cost overruns and an unprofessional organization of the Games.

The remaining two thirds of the costs – especially for new buildings, for adaptations, and for the infrastructure – were covered by federal (49%) and state funds (19%). The federal funds rose from $28 m, which President Ford was willing to spend in 1976 (NYT, 1976-05-08), to about $80 m, by far the largest financial contribution to the Games. State funds initially amounted to $10m (NYT, 1974-11-08) and rose to more than $30 m. This sum also included funds to adapt the facilities for the permanent operation.

The evaluation of the cost overrun for completion and initial operation has to consider the different cost estimates and different assumptions underlying the actual costs. The cost estimates were adjusted for inflation to consider the time lag between the date of the estimate and the start of construction:

An overrun of 76% of the estimated costs (adjusted for inflation) is a good performance compared to other MOEs in general and to other Olympic Games in particular. The figures in Table 23 indicate a remarkably high cost overrun for completion. This may be explained by the fact that the first estimate for the completion costs was made before the Games have been awarded to Lake Placid ($22m in 1973) and that it was subject to deliberate overoptimism in order to prevent critical discussions concerning the costs of the Games.

It should be mentioned that the hosts of the Games made every effort to market the Games to broadcasting companies, sponsors, and to general public (remember the direct mailing campaign). A well staffed marketing division was established. Some critics, therefore, accused the Lake Placid Games of being the most widely merchandised event ever held. Although the Lake Placid hosts could not avoid a deficit, they paved the way for a turnaround in the history of the Games. Only four years later the Olympic Summer Games in Los Angeles finished with more than $200m profit. The hosts of the Calgary Games received $325m for the TV rights. Compared to those sums the $21m TV revenues for the Lake Placid Games are quite modest.

The achievement of the financial goals of *permanent operation & maintenance* should be measured with the hosts' explicit will not to be burdened with financial obligations of post-Olympic use. In the months following the Games the financial transactions to settle the completion phase mingled with the efforts to ensure the financial base for permanent operation. The LPOOC faced increasing debts, especially to contractors, that had accumulated in the completion phase. Efforts to substantially reduce the debts by selling equipment and souvenirs failed. Therefore, the hosts pressed state and federal government for further financial aid. Eventually after tough negotiations the federal senate approved financial aid and some sports facilities were sold to the State of New York. The revenues were used to lower the debts.

Early studies on the costs of permanent operation predicts state subsidies of $1m p.a. "for many years" besides $42m already spent on the Games (NYT, 1980-03-05). The financial situation became more transparent after a report of a consulting firm was presented to the state government in fall 1980. The report predicted costs of about $2m for adapting the Olympic facilities to permanent use. A significant part of adaptation costs had to be spent on reinstalling equipment which had to be removed after initial operation. All facilities except the ski jumps would cause losses in permanent operation. The bobsled and luge runs were found to make the biggest deficit. This deficit could only be reduced by either operating the bobsled and luge on one run by "mothballing" the runs, or by transferring the facilities to other post-Olympic users.

The further development confirmed the consultants' expectations regarding additional revenues from the Olympic facilities: The media reported a notable revival of the local economy ("business has never been better"), including the creation of new jobs. Nevertheless, the permanent operation burdens the local and the New York State tax payers (reports stated an amount of $3.5m state subsidies per year, NYT, 1981-05-26).

4. Overall Performance

In the hosts' view the Olympic Games in Lake Placid were a huge success promoting the local business especially tourism industry ("Lake Placid will never again see anything as great"). The Lake Placid residents are still proud of "their" performance and unanimously reject the criticism of "outsiders", even in the face of obvious failures like the breakdown of the transportation system. Our evaluation takes a more selective approach as we analyze the performance on the different goal dimensions:

Starting with the *technical goals*, performance regarding *completion was high*, except housing facilities for athletes and for spectators. Performance regarding *initial operation was excellent* from the athletes' point of view but rather inadequate for spectators considering the breakdown of the transportation system. Finally, the Games proved favorable for the Olympic family but unfavorable for the spectators.

Regarding *time goals*, performance of completion and initial operation was high. Performance of permanent operation was adequate considering the difficulties of setting up the management structure as well as the financial base for permanent operation & maintenance.

Performance of *financial goals* for completion and initial operation was inadequate but not disastrous, whereas the financial performance of the permanent operation was sufficient considering both the positive effects on the local economy and the continuous state subsidies.

III.   Success Factors

1. Formulation and Change of Goals

Our analysis of formulation and change of *technical goals* will concentrate on completion and initial operation as no explicit goals were formulated for permanent operation & maintenance (apart from the intention to rigorously avoid post-Olympic ruins).

The formulation of technical *goals for completion* is predetermined by the rules of the IOC and the international sports associations as far as the disciplines and the standards of the facilities are concerned. This predetermination may facilitate the formulation of goals but does not prevent their *change* as the following discussion will demonstrate.

Lake Placid experienced several driving forces for enlargement of technical goals, e.g. increasing numbers of athletes (expected), additional changes required by international sports associations after the test events, as well as sites and buildings claimed by local residents and institutions as "compensation" for the temporary use of their facilities.

Apart from other project participants project owners themselves were responsible for enlargement of technical goals. Important facilities (like parking lots) were forgotten at the beginning and the initial assumption that the 1932 facilities (left over from the Olympics held in Lake Placid) would still meet the needs vanished: "Then people thought, let's do it right; let's do refrigeration; let's make a good facility, a great one. You just walk on up the ladder" (Spurney in Engineering News-Record, 1979-02-22). When Spurney, the general manager, made this statement in 1979, the process of goal enlargement had already gone too far to be stopped.

Due to the strict regulations of the IOC and the international sports associations there were *no major changes of the goals for initial operation.* Unfortunately, the spectators' interests were not subject to these regulations. Otherwise the breakdown of the spectators' transportation system might have been prevented.

Besides the a priori preference of the hosts for the Olympic family there were some unfavorable goal changes that affected the transportation system. According to the report of a state investigation committee in April 1980 the weakness of the transportation system was caused by saving measures of the hosts: The Canadian bus company (its drivers went on strike during the Games) was chosen because it had offered the lowest price and the initial number of 450 busses was reduced to 300 buses.

Formulation of time goals was determined by the invariable date of the Games, which also included the requirement for intensive test events during and after the final phase of completion.

Our comments on *formulation and change of financial goals* start with a figure of the cost estimates:

Date of Estimate	Estimated Costs (m$)	Estimated by	Remarks
1973-10	22	J.B. Fell (member of the bid committee)	construction and adaptation costs of the sports facilities
1975-05	97	LPOOC	excluding administrative expenses
1977-05	58	N.N.	budget for buildings
1977-07	100	chairman of LPOOC	cost limit
1977-08	90	N.N.	budget for buildings
1978-09	150-200	N.N.	
1979-02	150	LPOOC	increase by one third compared to the estimate of the EDA and Congress (remark by the general manager), federal obligation amounts to $73.2 m
1979-04	168	LPOOC	costs of the facilities will probably increase by $18 m
1979-06	190	AP	six times the initial estimate
1979-10	146	LPOOC	"costs to date"
1979-11/12	150	N.N.	
1980-01	150	LPOOC	general manager
1980-02	150-200	N.N.	
1980-02	178	N.N.	total costs
1980-06	156	N.N.	

Table 23. Cost Estimates for Completion and for Initial Operation of the Olympic Games in Lake Placid 1980

We assume that the hosts adapted an overoptimistic attitude regarding the early cost estimates in order not to endanger the bid for the Olympic Games. Furthermore, there is some evidence that the hosts were more cautious on those parts of the basic design which they would be funding (costs of the Olympic events, the project management and administration) than on those which would be funded by state or federal sources. Assuming the figure in 1975 ($97 m) as a first reasonable estimate, covering all important parts of the MOE, its increase to about $178m in 1980 as well as the failed direct mailing campaign opened investigations. Finally, additional funds from the state and the federal government were granted.

The most important reasons for the cost increases and the final cost overrun that were quoted are:
- additional adaptation work on existing facilities;
- environmental protection measures;
- provision of parking facilities;
- compensation for local property owners;
- corrections of insufficient planning and unreliable cost estimates;

- inflation;
- innovative character of some facilities;
- unforeseeable events.

Some of the reasons are closely related to the enlargement of technical goals which we described earlier. The incompleteness of cost estimates (especially regarding infrastructural facilities) is linked to the hosts' initial intention to draw up an optimistic rather than a pessimistic budget for the Games.

2. Basic Design

The following map shows the location of the sites in the Lake Placid area. 14 different construction sites were spread over an area of 20 square miles.

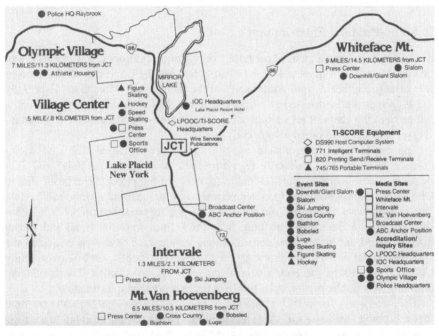

Fig. 49. Location of the Facilities for the Lake Placid Olympic Games

The facilities for the ski jumps, for hockey and figure skating, the luge run, and the Olympic village had to be built. Other facilities, some of them built for the Games in 1932, had to be adapted (alpine ski runs, cross country trails, biathlon, speed skating, bobsled run, facilities for ceremonies, roads and parking lots, broadcast and media center, LPOOC and IOC headquarters). Adaptation work included retracking of runs, installing new equipment (e.g. snow and ice making and time keeping), and temporary installation of spectators seats (esp. for ceremonies).

Most of the *victory ceremonies* were to be held at a site on Mirror Lake providing a capacity of 10,000 spectators. A temporary stadium was planned for the opening ceremony which would turn into a local stadium once the Games were over. Its capacity of 15,000 spectators had to be increased by 5,000 during the planning process.

Initially, the *Olympic village* should have been an adapted building. But in the life of the project, the hosts decided to establish a new building which would serve as a prison in permanent operation. Further, location of the ski jumps had to be changed, which caused substantial replanning for this facility.

Despite this changes we have to mention that the decentralized location of the facilities reduced the complexity and that the rules and regulations of the IOC and the international sports associations, as well as the engagement of a general contractor for the construction work had a substantial and – to some extent – stabilizing impact on the basic design.

3. Socio-Political Environment

The Games in Lake Placid experienced only minor environmental impacts. Opposing statements were based on the assumption that the Games would have negative effects on "beauty and wilderness" of the Adirondack Mountains. Especially the ski jumps were criticized as "sight pollution". Although these arguments could not prevent the Games they caused some interventions – and subsequently cost increases – from environmental agencies.

The residents of Lake Placid were a strong driving force from the socio-political environment, especially regarding their "commercial attitude" and their demand to dominate the decision-making process of the project. The hosts' aim to benefit from the Lake Placid Games resulted in a remarkable *commercialization*. The Games were told to be "run for and by a private organization" (NYT, 1980-04-13). Yet the chances of profiting from the Games were not equal and consequently greed and resentment spread among residents. Those who criticized the commercialization of the Games asked for rigorous public control over future Games. Considering the poor financial outcome of past Games – most of them dominated by public organizers – this demand is more than questionable.[26]

The strong *involvement of residents in project decision-making* calls to mind that according to the rules of the IOC Olympic Games are not awarded to a nation or a state but to a village or an area. Lake Placid, therefore, insisted on a local majority in the management committees. Furthermore, the committee meetings were open to the general public. This measure increased the local influence on decision-making and the border between "formal" and "informal" authority blurred (for details see next section). Lake Placid successfully strengthened its influence in order to safeguard the interests of the village and the business community. Measures which supposedly were advantageous for the village were fostered, e.g. improvement of infrastructure or sports facilities with the prospect of a successful perma-

---

[26] For a market oriented view of special events like Olympics see Catherwood/Van Kirk 1992, Crompton 1995, Spilling 1996, Teigland 1996, Jeanrenaud 1999, Preuss 1999.

nent operation. Other interests – e.g. those of spectators – were considered to be of less importance. The contribution of federal and state government frequently seemed to be limited to the provision of necessary funds.

The Lake Placid hosts showed remarkable skills in manipulating the socio-political environment. In order to gain advantages for the village they insisted on Lake Placid's leading role as hosting village. In case of larger problems (like deficits) they successfully appealed to state and federal administration for help: "It's a matter of national pride, national spirit" (Newsweek, 1980-06-30). The mobilization of about 6,700 volunteers and the no-strike agreement with the unions (1977) are other indications for their efforts to manage the socio-political environment.

4. Management Structure and Management Capacity

Our analysis starts with managerial aspects of completion and initial operation. The management of permanent operation is discussed separately.

The *management structure until 1974* (award of the Games) consisted of different institutions. The Department of Environmental Conservation (ENCON) was responsible for the Whiteface Mountain Alpine Ski Center and the cross country and bobsled area at Mountain Van Hoevenberg. Some of these facilities had already been used for the Games in 1932.

The Lake Placid bid commission was formed to present the bid at the IOC session in October 1974 in Vienna. A Methodist minister (chairman), a New York State senator, a representative of the region (the winner of two gold medals at the 1932 Games), a consultant, a local sports coordinator (later president of the LPOOC), and the mayor of Lake Placid were members of the commission. A special state commission supported the bid commission.

After the award the LPOOC was responsible for the project management of the Games (see Fig. 50).

The board of directors consisted of 48 honorary members and 30 non-voting members. 13 members of the board were nominated for the executive committee, representing the United States Olympic Committee (USOC), the IOC, the State of New York, the county, and the village. From 1978 on all divisions of the LPOOC reported to the general manager. Two important members of the board, the legal consultant and the chief fund raiser resigned in 1978 and 1979, respectively.

The construction and initial operation were integrated in one project company. At the Olympic Games in Munich these two functions were managed separately. The integrated approach was feasible because the hosts delegated management of construction work to a general contractor with sufficient prequalification who competed successfully against 17 other bidders. The construction company's "supermanager" with the assistance of 19 project managers was in charge of 1,800 employees. Professional planning and completion procedures were employed to finish the construction despite severe time pressure.

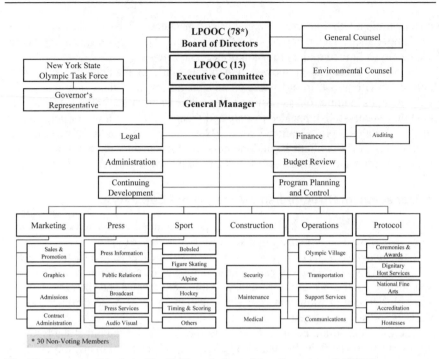

Fig. 50. Structure of the Lake Placid Olympic Organizing Committee (LPOOC)

We have already mentioned the important role of the marketing division for fund raising, a rather innovative function in the history of the Games. The transportation division failed to manage the transport of spectators. This crisis was mastered by employing a management team from a professional bus company (see above).

The project *management capacity* suffered from the recruitment policy and the initial lack of top management authority. The *recruitment policy* favored Lake Placid residents. Local residents which gained commercial profit from the Games (e.g. hotel owners, real estate agents) held influential positions. The chairman of the LPOOC (Roland M. MacKenzie) was a retired post officer and an enthusiastic winter sports-man. He had been a part of Lake Placid's Olympic ambitions since 1962. When he died in 1978, a Methodist minister (J. Fell) was appointed chairman following lengthy discussions and an interregnum under former ski jumper and sports commentator Art Devlin. The local managers were described as "nearby good ol'boys, who are not likely to make waves" (Skiing 1979, p.60). The managerial qualification of these insiders has frequently been doubted: "A small group of Lake Placid's proud citizenry is staging the event, in much the same way local civic clubs put on car washes or bake sales" (Fortune, 1980-01-14). Contrasting to Lake Placid, other Olympic Games, such as Squaw Valley (1960) and Los Angeles (1984) were known for their professional recruiting procedures.

Another weakness of the management structure owed to the fact that sessions of the board were open to the public until 1978. The discussions – some of them very controversial and noisy – quasi took place "on the street": "When we decide something, any one of our neighbors can come up to us on the street and tell us we're crazy. They wouldn't do that to a stranger" (Fortune, 1980-01-14).

The initial *lack of top management authority* rooted in the hosts' preference for collective decision-making. The board was overstressed with details because nobody was responsible for day-to-day decisions. In October 1978 the board nominated Peter L. Spurney for the position of general manager, a civil engineer and a successful trouble shooter in large events. His nomination followed a consultant's recommendation (the consultant being Spurney himself!), lengthy debates, and substantial pressure from federal and state representatives on the board. The nomination came late, considering the beginning of the Games only about one year ahead. His status of "a stranger" caused additional problems. He strengthened his position by appointing an experienced finance manager and a marketing manager whom he knew from former joint engagements. As the construction activities were already too advanced for significant changes, he concentrated his saving efforts on the costs of project management and the initial operation: Spurney ordered a hiring stop and decided in all purchases over $3,000. His saving measures were successful with regard to labor costs. The cut in costs for the transportation system clearly proved dysfunctional (see above). The measures, however encouraged his opponents. Although he undoubtedly contributed to the success of the Lake Placid Games, Spurney was never accepted as "saver of the Games" but remained "a stranger" all along.

The Olympic Games in Lake Placid may serve as a model case for analyzing the change of management structure in the transition of completion and initial operation to permanent operation. The set up of the *management structure for permanent operation* was impeded by the split ownership of the Olympic facilities. A consultant, therefore, recommended transferring the ownership to a single owner (Olympic Regional Development Authority, ORDA) in two steps.

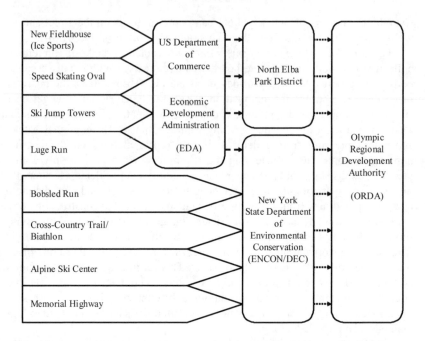

Fig. 51. Actual and Planned Ownership of the Olympic Facilities after the Lake Placid Games (1980)

ORDA was established in October 1982 following intensive negotiations concerning state and county subsidies, as well as the residents' access to the facilities. Its nominal capital was raised by the Olympic lottery and the estimated value of its assets was $70 m. At that time Lake Placid was accredited as official Olympic Training Center of the United States.

IV.   Interdependence of Success Factors and Goal Achievement

The success of the Lake Placid Games (in particular the high performance regarding permanent operation) as well as failures in completion (cost overrun) and initial operation (inefficient services for spectators) can be derived from formulation and change of goals and from management structure and capacity. The success factors socio-political environment and basic design have been of minor importance (see [5] and [8] in Table 24). The influence of *socio-political environment* 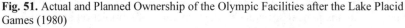 was closely linked to the management structure which allowed for an "informal" involvement of Lake Placid residents in decision-making until 1978 [3]. The dominance of local residents caused some problems [17]. They were partly offset by the *management structure/capacity* that provided for the engagement of an experienced general contractor and compensated for the initial lack of a professional top management. The necessary changes that would remedy these deficiencies were enforced by continuous budget overruns. One reason for the disastrous transportation system was the effort of the new management to set up a cost limit.

The *basic design* caused no major additional effects: The MOE was neither burdened with a high a priori complexity of the design nor did it change substantially in the life of the project [9][16].

Goal formulation and goal change as well as management structure/capacity were not only influenced by driving forces endangering goal achievement, but also by constraining forces facilitating its achievement.

Strong *driving forces* were the residents' interest in successful permanent operation and the organizers' preference for the athletes and other members of the Olympic family.

- Facilities and systems suitable for permanent operation were planned more carefully than those with less significance for permanent operation (like transportation facilities).

- Housing and transportation service for athletes, coaches, and officials was much more effective than services for spectators.

- Cases of conflicting interests between residents and athletes were settled in favor of residents. The suitability of the Olympic village as a prison after the Games, therefore, was more important than to provide athletes housing with all conveniences during initial operation [14].

The structure of the decision-making committees eased the development of these driving forces. Residents held the majority on the committees as well as on the project management staff. With the IOC, the representatives of the international sports associations and even with the personal ambitions of some residents, the sports interests had a number of strong custodians. Spectators' interests lacked an equally strong representation. Preference for local representatives without adequate experience [13] may explain some of the management failures, like the breakdown of the transportation system for spectators and journalists. We should keep in mind, however, that the same constellation which caused some failures in completion and initial operation was suitable regarding permanent operation & maintenance.

The financial goals failed to serve as a constraining force [10]. State and federal government had only one representative on the board of the LPOOC despite their large subsidies. A stronger state and federal influence on the decision-making process and more awareness of the financial implications of the hosts' local interests could have limited the enlargement of the technical goals and therefore the increases of costs. The weak representation of financial aspects in management structure as well as substantial increases in state and federal subsidies [23][24] ultimately favored the dominance of technical over financial goals. At the beginning – when the organizers promised to bring the Games back into perspective – it was the other way round. Therefore, the following statement of the general manager must be seen as a justification not as an intention: "Projects like these don't have economics as their foundation. To me, the production of the event, the translation of the idea within limited resources, is the ultimate challenge" (Fortune, 1980-01-14). This statement can also be interpreted as Spurney's confession, that his nomination and his saving measures came too late to establish a reasonable balance between the technical and the financial goals [12].

The driving forces caused some failures but no disaster due to the presence of *constraining forces*. The most effective constraint was the time limit set by the date of the Olympic Games. The initial time pressure (the period between the award and the actual event was less than six years) was intensified when sports officials in 1977 predicted Lake Placid's withdrawal from the Games due to severe delays in construction [6]. A second important constraint was created when the hosts decided to delegate construction management to a general contractor. His authority, based on the terms of the contract and his experience in the construction of sports facilities [11], functioned as a filter for changes. It enabled the project company to concentrate on other important project matters. By delegating work to external participants management capacity was implicitly increased. Summing up, only minor reformulation of the goal framework was necessary and the consistency of the basic design was relatively high.

GF: Goal Formulation & Change   SE: Socio-Political Environment
BD: Basic Design   GA: Goal Achievement
MS: Management Structure/Capacity

#	Date	GF	BD	MS	SE	GA	Event
[1]	1974-10-23					■	IOC awards the Games to Lake Placid, after the withdrawal of the other competitors (Banff, Vancouver, Oslo, Chamonix, Garmisch-Partenkirchen)
[2]	1974-12-11			■			LPOOC is established
[3]	1974-76				■		committee meetings are open to the public until summer 1978
[4]	1976					■	start of the planning activities
[5]	1976-11				■		warnings about environmental damage caused by the facilities of the Winter Games
[6]	1977-01					■	President of the FIS predicts Lake Placid's withdrawal from the Games, as the start of construction has been severely delayed
[7]	1977-04					■	the foundation-stone of the Games is laid by the son of President Carter; start of completion
[8]	1977-05				■		LPOOC, the project management, and the contractors sign a no-strike agreement with the local unions
[9]	1977		■				the consistency of the basic design is endangered (jump towers, athletes' housing)
[10]	1977-78					■	budget overruns cause special investigations
[11]	1978-08					■	construction activities are at full stretch at seven sites and go off without any notable problems
[12]	1978-10	■		■			nomination of Spurney as general manager; efforts of the new management to limit costs
[13]	1978-12-13			■			the President of the LPOOC (Mac Kenzie) dies at the age of 75; Art Devlin and later on J. Bernard Fell succeed him in office
[14]	1978-79					■	the standard of the athletes' housing and the transportation facilities become subject to criticism
[15]	1979-02					■	bankruptcy of the steel contractor causes serious time pressure

GF: Goal Formulation & Change BD: Basic Design MS: Management Structure/Capacity				SE: Socio-Political Environment GA: Goal Achievement		
#	Date	GF	BD	MS	SE	GA	Event
[16]	1979-04					■	doubts about the security of the new facilities for spectators and athletes arise
[17]	1979-08				■		Lake Placid is seized by the "Olympic fever", including greed and tensions in community life
[18]	1979-10					■	construction of the main facilities almost completed
[19]	1979-12					■	doubts about the tax-based funding of post-Olympic operation & maintenance of facilities arise
[20]	1980-01				■	■	lasting discussions on quality and reliability of design/construction/ structure of facilities and rumors about corrupt contractors; Americans fear retaliation for boycotting the Summer Games in Moscow 1980; concerns about lack of snow
[21]	1980-02-04				■	■	discussions concerning Taiwan's admission to the Games; security of the alpine events endangered
[22]	1980-02-13 until 1980-02-24					■	XIII. Olympic Winter Games with 32 competitions in 8 disciplines
[23]	1980-02				■	■	state and federal government refuse responsibility for maintenance of Olympic facilities
[24]	1981-07				■	■	state and federal government undertake measures to support Lake Placid.

Table 24. Interdependence of Success Factors and Goal Achievement in the Case of the Olympic Games in Lake Placid

N. The University Hospital Vienna

This MOE is considered to have been a disaster. It has been one of the most intensively discussed topics in the Austrian media for years. As a resident of Vienna and contemporary witness I had the chance to observe the development of this MOE for decades. Detailed auditing reports by city and federal accounting offices have been additional and highly reliable sources for our analysis.[27]

I. Characteristics of the Vienna Hospital

The old Vienna Hospital was built under Emperor Franz Josef II (1780-1792). The first segment of the pavilion-type hospital was finished in 1784 (after the adaptation of already existing buildings), the second segment in 1788. The plan to build a new hospital dates back to the end of the 19th century. At that time, especially the older section of the hospital suffered from outdated technical standards, which not only impaired the patients' treatment and the quality of nursing but also the image of the Vienna School of Medicine, being one of the most highly reputed schools in the world at the beginning of the 20th century. The new hospital was to put an end to this appalling situation (Wyklicky/Skopec 1984).

The Vienna Hospital is one of several hospitals in Europe which were planned in the 1950s (beside Aachen, Berlin-Steglitz, Munich, all in Germany). It was intended to be the most modern hospital in terms of technological standards. According to media reports, it turned out to be one of the "biggest scandals of the Second Republic of Austria". This harsh judgment in media reports stems from the corruption which was revealed in the early 1980s and led to a series of investigations, parliamentary debates, law suits, and even to the resignation of federal ministers.

From an economic point of view, it was not the corruption (which amounted to less than 0.5% of the costs of €3.1 bn, but the numerous and severe failures, bedeviling the undertaking from its very beginning, which caused the real scandal. The Vienna Hospital, therefore, may serve as a good example of the mismanagement of an MOE and as verification of Murphy's law.

II. Achievement of Goals

1. Technical Goals

Due to numerous and substantial goal changes (see later) the evaluation of goal achievement is rather complicated. The vagueness of the initial goals of the MOE was manifested by a statement of a journalist who said that "the only thing we

---

[27] Kontrollamt (1980, 1981); Rechnungshof (1980, 1989, 1995, 2003); for details and additional references see Grün (1981a, 1981b, 1983).

know for sure is that they are not going to build a tunnel but a hospital" (Die Presse, Vienna, 1976-05-26).

The Vienna Hospital was designed to meet the highest technical standards. For this "hospital of the superlatives" only the best should be good enough, and the project owners explicitly and implicitly committed the project management to perfectionism. The users took this exceptional opportunity to call for the highest technological standards and all doubts were dismissed by the argument of ensuring the very best of health care.

In the end, the goal of building the "most modern hospital in Europe" has not been achieved. Experts claim that due to the long planning and completion phases the technical standards were outdated by the time the hospital went into operation. Apart from the standards of equipment, the block-type design has been subject to criticism: "Nowadays such a monster would not be built any more" (Kurier, Vienna, 1980-02-24). The state of the art expertise for hospitals calls for a limit of 1,500 beds.

After a rather modest beginning, the demands grew rapidly and peaked in the goal to build the "biggest hospital in Europe". This quantitative completion goal was achieved notwithstanding the question whether several mid-sized hospitals would have been more advantageous than one huge hospital. As a matter of fact, the Vienna Hospital shows remarkable dimensions (figures of 2002)[28]:

- approx. 2,200 beds (only 1-, 2-, 3-bed rooms)
- 57 departments and institutes, respectively
- 83 standard care units
- 51 operating theatres
- 95,000 in-patients p.a.
- 428,000 out-patients p.a.
- 4,000 students
- 9,100 staff members
- 345,000 square meters of usable floor space
- 3.6m cubic meters of building volume.

The start-up operation was delayed as new regulations from public authorities had to be met, and even several standstills of operation were ordered by these authorities. The huge dimensions of the hospital cause extremely long distances for staff members and patients. In 1991 up to 20% of the beds could not be used due to the lack of nurses and medical-technical staff. Hospital operation also suffers from coordination problems between federal and city project owners. Due to schedule overruns medical equipment was outdated when permanent operation started and had to be partially replaced.

Despite these failures, the hospital is highly reputed for its hospital services, teaching and research activities meeting outstanding international standards.

[28] Allgemeines Krankenhaus Wien (2003)

2. Time Goals

The development of the Vienna Hospital is a long record of countless estimates regarding the date of completion, most of which had to be corrected within a short period of time (see Fig. 10). Considering the first release of funds in 1955 (for the reconstruction of one clinical department) as the start of the MOE, the official start of the full operation in the hospital building was in 1994, with a few facilities finished in 1995. A construction period of 40 years is enormous even when considering the ambitious goals of the undertaking. The initial completion date (estimated to be between 1970 and 1975) was missed by 20 (!) years.

To determine the achievement of time goals we chose the same time basis as for the cost goals (i.e. 1972). At that time, a completion period of 9 years was estimated. Given the actual completion date of the hospital in 1994, the schedule overrun is 144% (22 instead of 9 years). Other calculations based on more optimistic completion dates result in even worse overruns. Based on a rather pessimistic estimate made in 1971 with a completion date in 1985, the schedule overrun is still 64%.

The unbelievable schedule overruns raise a series of questions: How did the users justify increasing their requirements knowing that these claims would delay the date of completion and would make them stay much longer in the old facility with its "unacceptable" standards. Another question may refer to the rather short period of time between the first activities of detailed planning (1960) and the start of construction (1964). These almost parallel planning and construction activities may indicate insufficient time for reliable planning and a tendency to plan from hand to mouth.

3. Financial Goals

Just like time goals, financial goals were missed drastically. The cost overrun of the completion costs is about 710%. This calculation is adjusted for inflation and based on an initial cost estimate of €0.33 billion in 1972 when construction of the central building was started and on €3.09 billion of actual costs in 1994.

No substantial efforts were made to estimate the costs for operation & maintenance in the first place. Figures drawn from past experience have been discussed. A rule of thumb which predicts operation costs per annum to be one quarter of the completion costs has proved quite reliable: In 1994, operation & maintenance costs amounted to €0.61 billion and were expected to exceed €0.73 billion. We have no precise information on the additional operation costs for the old hospital, which had to be run in parallel to make up for the delayed completion of the new hospital. The necessary maintenance costs which were incurred during the construction periods alone are quite impressive: They come close to the early estimates for the whole new hospital.

The Austrian Federal Accounting Office criticized the project owners for the underachievement of the financial goals. Compared to national and international standards for university hospitals the ratios are extremely unfavorable: €872 per cubic meter, €1.49m per bed, an extremely low number of beds per net square meters, and high treatment costs per in-patient (about €9,400 in 1994 and about 8,100 in 2002).

4. Overall Performance

The overall goal achievement of the Vienna Hospital is highly insufficient. The achievement of technical goals was partly a success (overachievement of 157 % regarding the usable floor space) and partly a failure (underachievement of 12 % regarding the number of beds). The time and financial goals were missed drastically.

Apart from usable floor space and bed capacity, the volume (cubic meters) of the hospital is another criterion by which to measure the achievement of technical goals. In fact, the volume increased by about 265%. The square-meters-per-bed-ratio is 161 for the Vienna Hospital compared to 80 and 93 for the Munich and Innsbruck Hospitals respectively. It is hard to tell whether this ratio indicates comfort or extravagance. A huge volume may be beneficial to planning architects or contractors, if they have a cost-plus contract or to users and patients who may appreciate a spacious building. For project owners a mere increase in volume can hardly be seen as a success. In addition, the bulky hospital dominates and disfigures the unique skyline of Vienna.

A special benefit of the Vienna Hospital, though not an intended one, was a rising skepticism concerning giant projects with public ownership and the ability of politicians to successfully perform or even to control project management. A striking example of the highly optimistic and even naive attitude of the politicians is a statement by the Federal Secretary of Finance made in 1980 who called for "a quick, cost-efficient completion of the hospital, considering all user demands" (Die Presse, Vienna, 1980-03-29). Later, MOEs like the Expo 1995 failed to obtain the approval of the Vienna residents. The case of the Vienna Hospital has since been discussed as a warning example of the risks of mismanagement.

III.   Success Factors

1. Formulation and Change of Goals

The technical goals of the Vienna Hospital were its most significant weakness, not only regarding their vague and open-ended formulation from the beginning but also their incompleteness and their almost endless changes. The goal to build the "most modern hospital" and (later on) the "largest hospital in Europe" created and encouraged many driving forces from the very beginning. Only determined project owners and a strong and experienced project management would have been able to control these forces. The Vienna Hospital had neither of the two as will be demonstrated later.

Goal formulation was incomplete as it focused only on completion, and detailed planning of operation & maintenance was not started until the most crucial decisions on the design of the hospital had been made. It is remarkable, therefore, that, instead of serious planning efforts for permanent operation, early discussions in 1961 (!) focused on the alternative use of the facilities and sites of the old hospital.

The significant *changes of technical goals* – an additional weakness of the Vienna Hospital – are shown in the following figure.

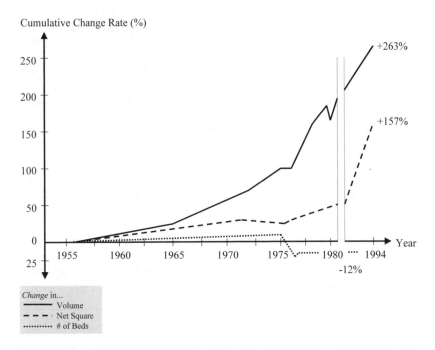

Fig. 52. Changes of Technical Goals of the Vienna Hospital in Volume (Cubic Meters), Usable Floor Space (Square Meters), and Number of Beds

The figure shows a continuous increase in volume (263%) and usable floor space (157%) while the bed capacity decreased by about 12%. The ratio of volume to usable floor space, already criticized by experts in the earlier phases of the project, kept deteriorating.

The users were identified as driving forces for the enlargement of technical goals, asking for more laboratory facilities, more beds for private patients and intensive-care units, more room for staff members, and sufficient space to be reserved for unforeseeable developments. Politicians, representing the project owners, did not oppose but even supported goal enlargements by urging project management to meet users' requirements. They also failed to define a clear deadline for goal changes. Several unsuccessful efforts were made to stop goal changes. Quoting a former Minister of Health who said in 1962 (!): "Now construction starts in any case - the basic design will not be changed even in the face of new medical developments" (Neues Österreich, Vienna, 1962-12-14). Unfortunately, the politicians involved held diverging views. The mayor of Vienna, e.g., stated in 1979: "I commit myself to ensuring the most modern medical and techni-cal equipment of the Vienna Hospital" (Arbeiter-Zeitung, Vienna, 1979-04-22).

Changing the time goals for the Vienna Hospital reflects the different levels of aspiration and the changes of technical goals. Estimates regarding the dates of completion for the hospital are illustrated in Fig. 10.

For a period of about 20 years (1960-1980) the answer to the question when the hospital would be completed was: "In ten years from now". These estimates were not only optimistic but unprofessional. They were optimistic because the esti-mated completion time was not extended according to (substantial) enlargements of the technical goals and unprofessional because they were not adjusted for the experiences gained during the completion phase. Another sign of lacking profes-sionalism was the assumption that a two-step instead of a one-step completion would reduce the completion time and avoid delayed decisions which were thought to cause setbacks in completion.

Due to continuous rescheduling, time goals could not serve as guidelines for project participants. Obviously, the project owners and project management did not use time goals as an instrument to influence the activities of project partici-pants. The absence of time pressure encouraged the fatalistic attitude that the hos-pital would never be finished and that the participants (e.g. users) would never see the completion of the hospital.

Considering the process of formulation and change of technical and time goals, the *number and variety of statements on financial goals* is not surprising. There were even cost estimates from early planning phases which covered only parts of the actual basic design:

Date of Estimate	Estimated Costs (m€)	Estimated by	Remarks
1955	44	Mayor of Vienna	for one clinical department
1958	51-58	project owner	
1959	109	NN	for completion step one
1962	73	Mayor of Vienna	
1963	254	experts	
1964	>145	trade minister	
1965	327	planning experts	
1968	291-363	construction commission	
1970	291	NN	
1971	363	NN	

Table 25. Early Cost Estimates for the Vienna Hospital

To ensure a meaningful analysis, we start with a cost estimate made in 1972, when the fundamental decisions on the basic design had been made: construction of the entire hospital in block-type design and in one completion step. The estimates cover about 80% of the central and the annexed buildings excluding the required funds (see Fig. 11).

The cost estimates show an increasing tendency, peaking in estimates made by the opposition party in 1975 (€2.1 bn) and by a planning expert in 1979 (€2.2 bn). The jump from 1974 to 1975 reflects the establishment of the project company (see later) which aimed at realistic estimates when it assumed responsibility for the project in 1975.

We have to remind ourselves that realistic cost estimates for MOEs with high rates of innovation and complexity and with long completion periods face extreme difficulties, especially when figures drawn from comparable undertakings are not available for benchmarking. This inherent handicap, however, cannot serve as an excuse for an obvious lack of realism. The change of the completion mode (two-step instead of one-step completion) and of the block-type design (two blocks instead of one) as well as a rather explosive increase in the construction volume since 1976 did not lead to the necessary upward correction of the cost estimates; the changes were wrongly expected to even lower the costs.

Other striking deficiencies of the cost estimates were their *incompleteness* (e.g. regarding the medical and EDP equipment or the project management costs), their *inconsistency* (within two days three different cost estimates were reported in the media, ranging from €1.8 billion to €2.7 billion), and the *lack of learning transfer* from previous cost estimates. The actual costs of a minor but already completed facility exceeded estimated costs by about 80 % (the time schedule overrun was about 100 %). Although this facility was repeatedly declared to serve as a test unit for the remaining facilities, the cost estimates for the hospital building were not sufficiently corrected.

Finally, it should be mentioned that the project owners and project management failed to define an ultimate cost limit. Several "limits" like a statement by the project owners in 1979 (7 years after the start of construction of the central building), had no effect. The fact that neither the project management nor the project owners kept to their own limits did not encourage other project participants to do otherwise.

2. Basic Design

The Vienna Hospital is located downtown close to the old hospital. The Vienna Hospital has a block-type design which was unanimously favored in the 1950s. The hospital building consists of a main body with 11 floors, designated for diagnostics and treatment (including surgery units), class rooms, and libraries. The two tower-blocks rise above the main body, each block 13 floors, for standard and intensive care. The annexed buildings are used for staff housing, for a nursing school, pediatrics and psychiatric departments, a neurosurgery department, additional research units, a school for medical technical assistants, admission and service facilities, administration, underground parking, and public transportation. Gradually, the annexed buildings increased in number and size thus turning the original block-type design more and more into the old pavilion type.

The two-block solution is favorable in principle. The huge volume of the blocks, however, caused lighting problems as major parts of the buildings have only artificial light. Additional light-shafts had to be constructed afterwards in order to correct this deficiency.

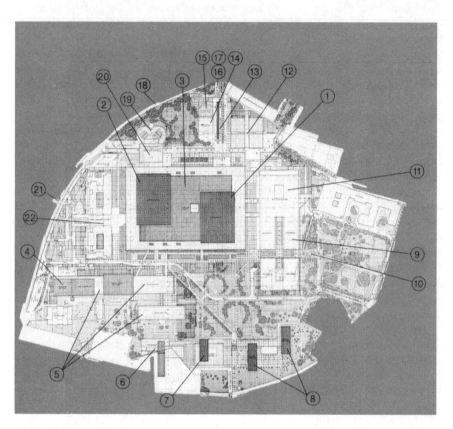

(1) East Tower; (2) West Tower; (3) Low Building; (4) Neurosurgery; (5) Pediatric Clinic/Psychiatry; (6) Technical Assistants' School; (7) Nurses' Training School and Boarding School; (8) Staff Residential; (9) Medical Research; (10) Entrance for Handicapped; (11) Catering; (12) Technical Supply; (13) Tunnel Exit; (14) Fire Department; (15) Medical Gas Center; (16) Exit to Main Drive; (17) Underground Parking Lot; (18) Main Drive; (19) Rescue Vehicle Lot; (20) Skywalk to Subway; (21) Entrance Hall

Fig. 53. Design of the Vienna Hospital

The initial plans aimed at a *step-by-step* replacement of the old hospital by the new one, starting with one clinic (surgery). In 1957, the project owners decided on a two-step construction with the first step providing 1,000-1,200 beds. The decision in 1965 to finish the hospital in one step only was based on cost saving arguments and – still more important – on the users' interest in the replacement of the entire old hospital.

This change of plan had substantial consequences since it increased the complexity. Chances of learning transfer from the first completion step to the second as well as the opportunity of partial completion in the face of serious impediments were thus missed. Furthermore, permanent operation became more difficult due to administrative and technological centralization.

A special dilemma resulted from continuing planning because of changes of technical goals due to project owners' commitment to upgrade technical standards and to take into account even "unforeseeable" developments. Consequently, planning architects tried to ensure maximum flexibility. While project management took credit for this flexibility, users obviously misinterpreted it as an implicit invitation to demand further changes. It is not surprising, therefore, that about 30,000 (!) replanning activities had taken place by 1980.

According to latest reports, the federal accounting office predicts 2007 to be the official end of the construction phase, due to continuous requirements by the users causing further enlargements and adaptations of the facilities.

3. Socio-Political Environment

The Vienna Hospital experienced all kinds of influences from the socio-political environment right from the project start until 1983. The influence was due to the mission of the project to improve health care delivery. This missionary spirit may have caused users to demand further enlargements and the highest technical standards and politicians to approve almost all user demands.

The public ownership (federal and city) of the MOE meant strong involvement of politicians from both government and opposition parties. Political influence affected the recruitment policy of senior project managers, and close ties to the ruling parties were sometimes preferred to managerial expertise. Furthermore, local and national contractors were favored. Public influence was a serious handicap for project management from the very beginning, as neither the persons involved nor the timing or the intensity of the influence were under control. This may be illustrated by some examples:

- Even after the project company had assumed responsibility for the Vienna Hospital, almost every politician from the ruling as well as from the opposition parties claimed to be involved in the MOE. The great number and variety of estimates as well as the continuous and increasing user demands reflected their involvement.

- The media encouraged this informal but nevertheless effective self-involvement hoping to attract public attention. The topics were, therefore, often chosen by the criterion of public attractiveness. Consequently, not the obvious lack of professional management but corruption was considered to be "the real scandal". Public misinterpretations impeded quick and radical changes in the project management.

- The timing of this political influence reflected the then current political situations rather than requirements of the project. When elections were coming up, attacks by the opposition and defensive responses by the ruling parties (representing the project owners) increased.

- The intensity of the influence of the socio-political environment also depended significantly on other public affairs. After a long period of intense public attention to the Vienna Hospital from 1980 to 1983, other developments or scandals (like the so-called wine scandal, the anti-Waldheim campaign, the violation of Austria's neutrality by weapons exports) dominated the headlines. When the former opposition party joined the government in 1986, its members refrained from calling the coalition partner to account in order to prevent serious internal governmental tensions.

After frauds committed by the project management were uncovered and experts articulated serious doubts about the feasibility of the whole undertaking, public commitment was replaced by severe criticism resulting in a series of investigations and the establishment of a concurrent auditing system. In this period, responding to public discussions and investigations became a dominant concern for the project management. Almost all project management capacity was thereby absorbed and greatly impeded routine project activities.

The public attitude would not have shifted without serious failures of the project management. This shift obviously limited the strategic options of project owners and project management. The recommendation by a high-ranking state official to break off the project in 1974 was ignored by the project owners because they believed its termination to be politically unviable. They did not even consider the possibility of a referendum which was employed in similarly precarious situations, like opening the only Austrian nuclear power plant (Zwentendorf) or hosting the Expo 1995 in Vienna.

4. Management Structure and Management Capacity

The management structure and capacity was crucial for the near failure of the Vienna Hospital. The management structure of this MOE went through many organizational designs, most of which were inadequate in view of complexity and duration of the undertaking (see Fig. 35).

The presence of two project owners (federal and city governments) – both claiming influence on the project – as well as the size of the undertaking would have required the early *establishment* of a project company, thus separating MOE-activities from the routine processes in its parent organizations. Yet 20 years and a remarkable number of unsuccessful committees had to pass before this essential measure of professional project management was taken in 1975.

The following two figures show the management structures before and after the *establishment* of the Vienna Hospital project company (AKPE):

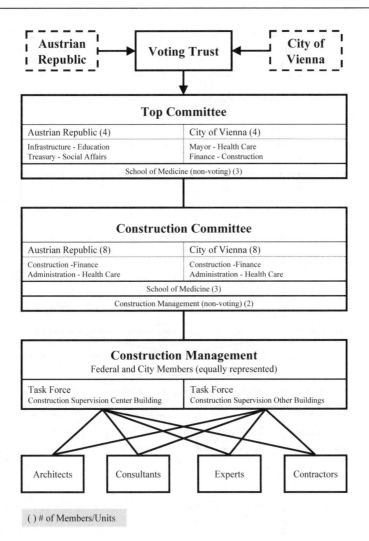

Fig. 54. Management Structure of the Vienna Hospital prior to the Establishment of the Project Company (AKPE) on 1975-09-09

Overburdened top politicians trusted in their ability to control project developments by means of occasional committee meetings. Some of the senior staff members did not even work full-time on the project.

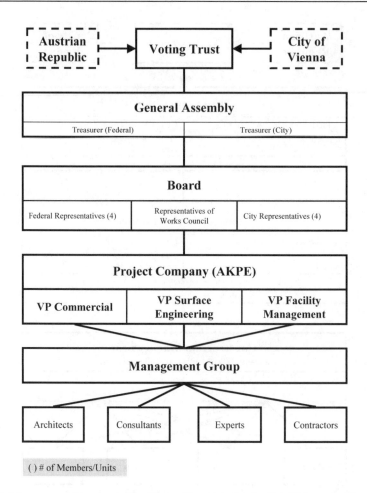

Fig. 55. Management Structure of the Vienna Hospital after the Establishment of the Project Company (AKPE) on 1975-09-09

The separation of the project management from the parent organizations of the project owners was delayed but finally dictated by time pressure resulting from increasing problems. The separation was not only delayed but also inadequate due to various and close institutional and personal links to the public administration (see later). It took another 6 years (from 1975 to 1981), however, to define the tasks and responsibilities of the project company by a formal agreement.

Fig. 56 shows the organizational structure of the project company about 6 years after its establishment:

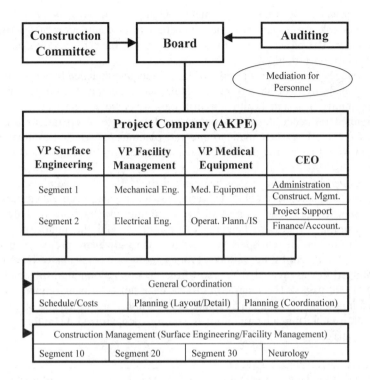

Fig. 56. The Project Company of the Vienna Hospital (AKPE) 1981

The project company was designed as a matrix type, comprising the responsibility lines for facilities including facility management and medical equipment and functions ("general coordination", construction management etc.).

The new company with about 215 employees resulted from a merger of the project company (AKPE) and a company responsible for the coordination of planning architects and contractors (Arbeitsgemeinschaft Projektmanagement Allgemeines Krankenhaus Wien, APAK). Insufficient communication between the AKPE and the APAK was the prime reason for the merger. The chief executive officer had a remarkable span of control. He was a close friend of the chairman of the board, who acted as a "grey eminence" until he resigned in 1982.

The project company which finally took over in 1982 was a subsidiary of a state-owned Austrian steel company (VOEST-ALPINE), specializing in medical technology (VAMED, VOEST-ALPINE Medizintechnik GmbH). Once again, the project owners had to act under substantial time pressure. Their position during the establishment of the new project company was rather weak. The new project company started without distinctive technical and time goals, and the financial risks remained with the project owners as VAMED insisted on a cost plus contract.

Another weakness of the management structure was its *focus on completion*. In order to enable a smooth and quick transition from completion to operation & maintenance, the project company structure should have been extended by departments for operation procedures.

The *integration of users* did not ensure an adequate balance between authority and responsibility. The faculty of medicine had a dominant influence from the very beginning. The state health administration was involved early enough but had only limited influence despite its important future role in operation & maintenance. No real efforts were made to integrate planning experts and contractors in a way that would have provided for early warnings against unrealistic technical solutions.

A *concurrent auditing system* was established after basic administrative and managerial standards like public tendering procedures had been disregarded. The system was set up to end a phase of hectic ad-hoc investigations by federal and city accounting offices, parliamentary committees, and the public prosecutor. Concurrent instead of retrospective auditing was to safeguard project owners' interests and to prevent further failures. From a short-term perspective, a remarkable control overkill was created. The report from the city accounting office had a volume of 1,000 pages! The long-term effects were not convincing either. Auditing delayed important planning and completion decisions, often focusing on minor issues with a rather bureaucratic attitude, and thus jeopardized the authority of the project management.

> The lesson to be learnt is that inconsistencies in the framework of goals and insufficient power and expertise of the project management can not be compensated by means of auditing.

The *turnover of staff* of the project management was exceptionally high and lasted until the early 1980s. More than ten general managers/vice presidents and twenty members of the board worked for the project company. The *turnover* of the representatives of the project owners on various committees was even worse: five mayors, seven city council members (for health, finance, and construction), and 23 federal ministers (for health, finance, construction, science) were involved in the period from 1954 until 1984.

There are various reasons for this remarkably high rate of *turnover*. As the project owners nominated high-ranking politicians for the committees, changes in government (which are almost unavoidable in the case of long-term projects) led to *turnover*. Changes in the project management structure and insufficient performance by project managers caused further *turnover*.

High rates of *turnover* are bound to have negative impacts on the progress of projects. Important decisions are likely to be delayed until the new management has become familiar with the situation. In addition, a substantial loss of know-how has to be taken into account if positions are not handed over properly as in 1975 when the project company took over the construction supervision office.

Owing to continuous changes in the management structure, the *turnover* of executive managers, the split authority between project management and the concurrent auditing system, and the misfit of authority and responsibility, the *sense of responsibility* decreased more and more:

- Newcomers were almost invited to blame their failures on the difficulties faced at the time of their nomination.
- Countless planning experts with remarkable influence on crucial decisions but no responsibility were engaged for enormous fees (amounting to almost the initial cost estimates for the Vienna Hospital).
- Users ceaselessly demanded the enlargement and upgrading of the technical goals. It does sound rather provocative, if a very prominent member of the medical faculty who favored the block-type design in the 1950s, stated 25 years later: "Once the hospital is finished, we'll try to remedy its defects by building pavilions on the site of the old hospital" (Die Presse, Vienna, 1980-03-22/23).

By the time the politicians realized the mismatch of authority and responsibility and their role in this unfavorable situation, they proclaimed their *political responsibility* diverting the evaluation of their management performance to the ballot box. This conception of responsibility cannot be accepted from a managerial point of view as project issues are mixed up with completely different issues of politics.

Appropriate management structures are not sufficient for project success. Additional efforts are necessary to ensure an adequate *management capacity* in terms of quantity and quality. Project management was *severely understaffed* (about 100 employees in 1980). Substantial parts of the additional management capacity provided by the coordination company (APAK, about 115 employees), were lost due to cooperation gaps between the two companies. They corresponded by mail although they shared the same building! Organizational units had to be established to make up for this capacity deficit, e.g. a unit for the planning of operation procedures (Arbeitsgemeinschaft Betriebsorganisation, ABO).

Another quantitative aspect of management capacity refers to the number and variety of other MOEs which have to be controlled and staffed by the project owners. The project owners of the Vienna Hospital were also involved in the Vienna International Center (UNO-City), the development of the Danube Island, the Vienna subway system, the reconstruction of a suburban commuting line, and several bridges across the river Danube. Being involved in too many MOEs overtaxes not only the financial but also the management capacity of project owners.

Concerning the *qualitative aspects of management capacity* the project owners of the Vienna Hospital favored executive managers whom they could presumably control, e.g. managers with close ties to the ruling parties. In 1976, one year after his nomination, a vice president of the project company stated: "I can imagine that the project company (AKPE) will build other hospitals after having finished the Vienna Hospital, because of its experience" (Die Presse, Vienna, 1976-10-19). The manager was dismissed after the company's crisis in 1980. His outstanding self-confidence may tell us more about the capability of the project management than a detailed record of its trials and errors.

The project owners also preferred managers with experience in public administration. This attitude dominated the recruitment policy for about 20 years and was preserved even after acts of frauds by vice presidents were uncovered in 1980. A former top manager and other senior managers of the federal accounting office were nominated for executive management positions in the MOE but could not achieve the necessary turnaround.

IV.   Interdependence of Success Factors and Goal Achievement

The case of the Vienna Hospital tells us that feedback from goal achievement is no guarantee for prompt and adequate reaction. Sometimes project owners and project management prefer blind flights to using navigation systems.

The history of this MOE can be divided into two periods. During the first period, until 1973/74, the hospital faced an almost unlimited change of technical goals and basic design even after the (early) start of the completion phase (see [8]-[11] in Table 26). The management structure was completely disorganized (overlapping responsibilities, part-time project managers and politicians, insufficient separation from the parent organizations, and insufficient management capacity, [4]) but no significant influence by the socio-political environment was noticeable.

The second period started after the call for a complete stop of the MOE in 1974 (two years after the construction of the hospital building started) by a high-ranking representative of the project owners was ignored [15]. A project company was established, burdened with initial deficiencies like shared responsibility of three vice presidents [18]. Yet, the new project management was unable to stop the continuous changes and to enforce cost limits [24][26]. The uncovering of corruption caused a strong involvement of the socio-political environment [27] and two more changes in the management structure [29][31].

Hence, the outcome of the project is not very surprising: Overachievement of the technical goals but substantial financial and schedule overruns. We have every reason to believe that an *exaggerated initial overoptimism* – almost on the verge of negligence – was the source of the disaster. This overoptimism affected all three goal dimensions. A rather modest beginning, i.e. the intention to rebuild only one clinical department [1], and later on, to construct the whole hospital in two steps [3], may have supported the initial optimism. The question arises why no warning signals flashed when the technical goal was changed to build "the largest and most modern hospital in Europe".

The answer is quite simple. Neither the time nor the financial goals were properly defined by the project owners nor were they regarded as limitations on further demands by project participants (especially users). As all users' demands aimed at increasing the standard of health care they were, therefore, popular. Nobody, especially not the politicians, would have dared to fight against this popular aspect.

The users – mainly represented by prominent members of the faculty of medicine – may exculpate themselves by their intention to go for "the best" in the common interest and by their limited managerial and economic know-how. But why did the project management not intervene? Actually, the project management was unable to intervene effectively as it lacked authority. Again, the source of its weakness was the initial overoptimism, including the assumption that committees staffed with leading politicians and managers with administrative experience would be capable of managing MOEs. Obviously, the users did not accept the authority of the project management: They often bypassed it by addressing their demands directly to the politicians, thus performing a kind of "back-door demanding".

Due to the lack of effective barriers, the driving forces kept the fateful loop going (enlargement of technical goals → delay of completion → adaptation of technical standards due to delays → etc. etc.). This loop could not even be interrupted by the already mentioned call for an immediate project stop. This recommendation was rejected by the argument that a holdup would not be politically viable. There may have been other – even more important – reasons for rejecting the idea. A postponement would have revealed the disastrous state of the project. The politicians involved were afraid of being held responsible for this failure. In addition to this already unfavorable situation, the socio-political environment became aware of the MOE failure and caused further upheavals.

The fact that the project finally disappeared from the daily headlines was due to other scandals and to a substantial economic crisis that shook the whole of the Austrian nationalized industries. This loss of attention facilitated the installation of a new project company which successfully prevented further interventions by politicians, thus neutralizing the users' most powerful allies. In our opinion, it was neither the increasing insight of the project owners nor improved managerial performance that prevented further harm to the Vienna Hospital, but the changed conditions in the socio-political environment. It should be mentioned, however, that the project company is engaged until 2007 to manage further adaptations required by users [32].

GF: Goal Formulation & Change						SE: Socio-Political Environment
BD: Basic Design						GA: Goal Achievement
MS: Management Structure/Capacity						

#	Date	GF	BD	MS	SE	GA	Event
[1]	1955-08	■					federal government approves the funds required for reconstruction of one clinical department
[2]	1957	■	■				decision on block-type design and a downtown location
[3]	1957-07		■	■			establishment of federal/city voting trust and of top committee, decision on two-step completion with 1,000-1,200 beds in step I
[4]	1959-01			■			establishment of committees for construction supervision and construction
[5]	1959/60		■				decision on basic design
[6]	1961/62	■	■				efforts to stop ongoing changes even in the face of new medical-technical developments and call for immediate start of construction
[7]	1962-04/05	■		■			establishment of partnership for construction (ARGE AKH); city government approves first step of completion
[8]	1963		■				decision on block-type design (flat building with one block
[9]	1964-07					■	start of construction of housing facilities for staff
[10]	1965-06	■	■				decision on one-step completion
[11]	1966	■	■				replacement of one-block design by a two-block one for financial reasons
[12]	1967-06					■	start of construction of pediatric and psychiatric departments
[13]	1968-02					■	housing facilities go into operation
[14]	1972-06					■	start of construction of central building
[15]	1974	■				■	high-ranking state official recommends stop of MOE
[16]	1974-fall					■	psychiatric department goes into operation
[17]	1975-summer					■	pediatric department goes into operation
[18]	1975-09			■			establishment of project company (AKPE) following ongoing changes of management structure since 1955
[19]	1976-03					■	new project management orders status report by external consultants.

GF: Goal Formulation & Change				SE: Socio-Political Environment		
BD: Basic Design				GA: Goal Achievement		
MS: Management Structure/Capacity						

#	Date	GF	BD	MS	SE	GA	Event
[20]	1976			■			establishment of project company for coordination of planning architects and contractors (APAK)
[21]	1976-10 until 1977-01		■				decision on basic design of central building and annexed buildings
[22]	1978		■				decision on enlargement of basic design by annexed buildings
[23]	1979-03				■		start of federal and city public auditing
[24]	1979-07	■					first(!) and "ultimate" cost limit: €1.42 billion (adjusted for 1976)
[25]	1979		■				project management guarantees flexibility of basic design
[26]	1979	■	■				decision on enlargement of pediatric department; project owners press for cost saving measures
[27]	1980-spring			■	■		uncovering corruption, engagement of accounting offices, parliament and courts; dismissal of senior project management
[28]	1980-09			■			establishment of concurrent auditing system
[29]	1981-04			■			project company changes legal form; merger of two project companies
[30]	1981					■	completed buildings show serious deficiencies in performance
[31]	1982-06	■		■			new project company takes over (VAMED); obligation to prepare a status report and realistic cost and time estimates by end of 1983
[32]	1982 until 2007		■				continuous changes/enlargements of the basic design, managed by the project company (VAMED)
[33]	1991-02					■	start of operation in central building
[34]	1994-06					■	official start of full operation
[35]	1995	■	■				last clinic (gynecology) moved into the new hospital after adaptation

Table 26. Interdependence of Success Factors and Goal Achievement in the Case of the Vienna Hospital

O. The University Hospital Munich

As mentioned earlier, a couple of huge university hospitals in block-type design were started in the 1950s. Munich was chosen for a case study because of the remarkable differences in performance from the Vienna Hospital. Politicians involved in the Vienna Hospital even chose it as a model when the Vienna Hospital experienced serious setbacks. Furthermore, it seemed attractive to investigate how the same project owner (State of Bavaria) handled different MOEs (University Hospital and Olympic Games, see case L). The Munich Hospital is well-documented by authors representing different perspectives, ranging from project owners to planning architects, and users.[29]

I.   Characteristics of the Munich Hospital

The Munich Hospital is one of the largest hospitals in Europe built after World War II. The hospital is located 8 km outside of the city in Großhadern. The project owners are the State of Bavaria and the Federal Republic of Germany. Like the Vienna Hospital the Munich Hospital was started in the 1950s following early discussions on a peripheral facility in 1937. This similarity and the threefold objective of nursing, medical teaching, and research, as well as the same block-type building encourages a comparison of the two. While the Vienna Hospital turned out to be a disaster long before its completion, the Munich Hospital received a rather positive evaluation and in the project owners' opinion created new standards for such undertakings.

II.   Achievement of Goals

The following evaluation of the achievement of technical, time, and financial goals as well as of overall performance will provide explanations for the success of this MOE.

1. Technical Goals

The Munich Hospital shows remarkable dimensions (figures from 2002)[30]:
- 1,400 beds (rooms with 1, 2, or 3 beds; 500 spare beds)
- 23 clinics or departments
- 24 operating theatres
- 45,500 in-patients p.a.
- 192,600 out-patients p.a.
- 1,600 students

---

[29] See Goerke (1974) and (1977); for details and additional references see also Grün (1985)

[30] Klinikum Großhadern (2003)

- 3,700 staff members
- 125,000 square meters of usable floor space
- 1.2m cubic meters of building volume.

The following statements indicate a good performance concerning the achievement of the technical goals:

- The Munich Hospital is said to be one of the leading hospitals in Germany.
- The block-type building has proven satisfactory because the different clinical departments are well integrated without giving up their independence.
- The crucial point for the size of hospitals which is assumed to be 1,500 beds has not been exceeded substantially.
- A suburban location instead of downtown has proven favorable.
- Bed capacity utilization is high.

Beside these positive aspects there are important negative ones of goal achievement:

- The planned capacity had to be reduced by 1,000 beds and four clinical departments.
- The reduction of capacity necessitated the continued operation of the old city hospital which was intended to be closed. Therefore, the new and the old hospital in two different locations had to be operated in parallel.
- Due to this reduction, major parts of the remaining hospital capacity in Munich suffer from insufficient technical standards. The initial plan of completely replacing the old hospital and having a single location for the Munich Hospital is still under discussion.
- A two-block instead of the actual one-block design would have been more favorable for permanent operation.
- The hospital is well equipped for intensive-care but not for rehabilitation.

2. Time Goals

Due to a decision in 1966 the first completion step was scheduled to be finished in 1974, the second step in 1980. The planned completion period of 13 years could be adhered to despite the long time horizon (more than 20 years including preliminary planning).

There is strong evidence that time goals were taken as serious deadlines and not just as rough guidelines. A comparison with the Vienna Hospital demonstrates the remarkable performance of the Munich Hospital in achieving completion goals: Whereas the ratio of planning to completion time for the Munich Hospital is about 1:1 (1952-1966 and 1966-1980), the same ratio for the Vienna Hospital is about 1:2.3 (1955-1967 and 1967-1994).

The achievement of the time goals was encouraged by the users' strong commitment to operate the new hospital as soon as possible. The two step completion mode made this possible.

3. Financial Goals

Financial goals were almost met at the Munich Hospital. The relevant figures and dates of the *estimated costs for completion* are listed below:

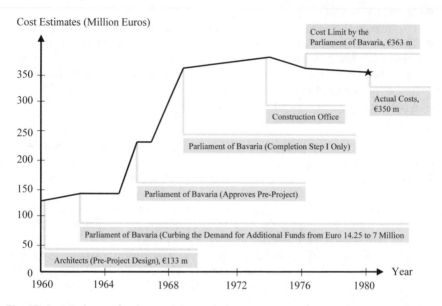

Fig. 57. Cost Estimates for the Munich Hospital (Completion Including Sites, Excluding Medical Equipment)

The *actual costs* for completion (excluding sites) were €350m (costs including sites and medical equipment were approx. €500 m). After adjusting the figures of the first cost estimate (1960) and the actual figures (1980) for inflation, cost overrun is only 34%. This must be seen as outstanding performance compared to other MOEs in general, and to university hospitals in particular.

The achievement of the financial goals is even more impressive when based on the estimate of €230m in 1966 (*before* start of construction). According to this calculation there is a relative *cost saving* from 5% (adjusted for inflation). These results are evidence of the statements by top executives of the Munich Hospital that the actual costs did not exceed the planned costs.

For a more detailed discussion of the achievement of financial goals we compare the costs per bed in the Munich Hospital to those in the Vienna Hospital. The numbers are €250,000 for Munich compared to €1,200,000 for Vienna! This remarkable difference cannot be explained away by aspects of construction efficiency alone. It reflects different profiles of utilization: While 52% of the usable floor space of the Munich Hospital are designated for nursing, 19% for diagnostics, and 29% for research facilities, the corresponding figures for the hospital in Vienna indicate that most of the floor space is dedicated to research and teaching purposes. We assume, therefore, that the project owners and project management of the hospital in Munich successfully defended their interests concerning nursing and diagnostic activities against the research interests of the faculty of medicine of the Munich University.

Our results also indicate a strong commitment to the financial goals by both the project owners and the project management. They seemed to favor a design-to-cost concept instead of adjusting costs to design.

We do not have reliable evaluations of the achievement of the financial goals for *permanent operation,* because there were no explicit cost estimates available. Some statements indicate, however, that the goal achievement was less successful in this respect:

- Due to increasing labor costs during the start-up of the hospital, operating costs were thought to be "still too high" after the first completion phase in 1977.
- Operating costs increased because of high nursing standards (rooms with only one, two, or three beds).
- A comprehensive calculation of operation costs would also have to include additional costs resulting from the parallel operation of the old (downtown) and the new (peripheral) university hospital.

4. Overall Performance

Our findings on goal achievement by the Munich Hospital may be summarized as follows:

Time goals and financial goals were fully or almost fully achieved whereas technical goals were somewhat missed. In greater detail:

- The planned dates of completion for the first and the second step were met exactly.
- The figures for the achievement of the financial goals range from cost savings of 5% to cost overruns of up to 34%.
- The achievement rates of technical goals vary depending on the base of calculation. We calculated a deficiency rate ranging from 20% (based on the number of medical research units) to 37% (based on the number of beds).

The remarkable overall performance was due to the balanced framework of technical, time, and financial goals which in turn was due to the awareness of the project owners and the project management of the importance not only of their formulation but also of their achievement.

III.   Success Factors

1. Formulation and Change of Goals

Unlike with other MOEs, the formulation and change of goals were not a weakness but a strength of the Munich Hospital. The relative stability of the goal framework is a key success factor of this MOE.

In particular, the *technical goals* showed sufficient consistency although the project owners (represented by the State of Bavaria) required the hospital to keep up with the latest technical standards in all stages of planning and completion. This goal, which was unlimited in general, enforced various changes during planning and even minor reconstruction work during completion. The most significant changes aimed at reducing instead of enlarging the initial technical goals (as reported by a couple of other MOEs). The initial idea to replace the entire old (downtown) hospital stepwise by the new hospital was dismissed as early as 1964 for budgetary reasons. Consequently, not one (new) but two (old and new) hospitals had to be operated in parallel. In 1966/67, the decision on a second major reduction was made concerning 5 surgical units and 1 unit for X-ray diagnosis.

Fig. 58 shows the change in bed capacity which represents a reliable measure for technical goals:

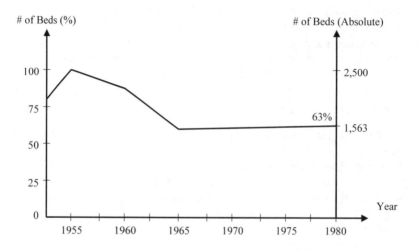

Fig. 58. Change of Technical Goals (Bed Capacity) of the Munich Hospital

Despite the demand for the latest technical standard, the project owners and project management did not insist on "perfect solutions" – in contrast with the Vienna Hospital. Examples of simple ("old fashioned") solutions are:

- Brick walls (non-removable) were built instead of expensive self-supporting walls. This measure did not significantly weaken flexibility for necessary changes: A gynecological clinic could be replaced by an eye clinic at low costs and without technical difficulties.
- For cost and energy saving reasons, aluminum sidings and small-sized windows were installed.
- Project management relied on traditional pick-up and delivery systems instead of a sophisticated and expensive internal transportation system and an automatic waste disposal plant.

The planning architects were very much aware of the consequences of goal changes – especially changes of time goals – upon overall goal achievement. Change was managed quite efficiently in the case of this MOE. Flexibility in the planning and completion phase allowed for indispensable changes without jeopardizing key issues of the project. This controlled flexibility was based on and enforced by the deadlines for the project determined in 1966.

2. Basic Design

The design of the Munich Hospital is characterized by a large block-type hospital and several annexed buildings (see Fig. 56). Two other hospitals in Germany (Berlin-Steglitz and Hanover) were designed in the same way. The Munich Hospital includes a block foundation with various sections for surgery, diagnosis and treatment, administration and management, and class rooms. The block on top of the foundation has 17 floors. Annexed buildings house the various departments, services, a cafeteria and staff housing, as well as a nursing school.

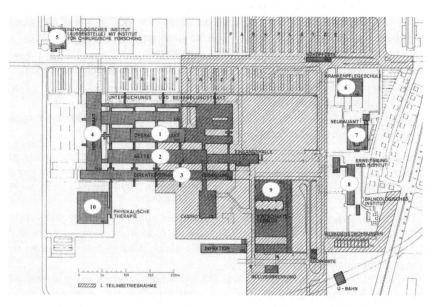

(1) Surgical Theatre; (2) Bedding; (3) Head Office; (4) Lecture Auditorium; (5) Institute of Pathology; (6) Nurse's Training School; (7) Building Authority; (8) Institute of Internal Medicine; (9) Offices and Service Rooms; (10) Institute of Physical Therapy

Fig. 59. Basic Design of the Munich Hospital

The decision on the block-type design was made in the early phases of the project. The arguments in favor of this design were:
- Short distances between various in-house divisions, especially diagnosis, treatment, nursing, teaching, research, and administration.
- It facilitates the cooperation between pre-clinical and clinical departments and partly offsets the disadvantages of ongoing specialization in the field of medicine.

- It allows for a better use of the expensive medical and logistic equipment.
- It facilitates the adaptation of bed capacity to the changing demands of various departments.

Whereas some media criticized the block-type hospital to be a "mammoth building" and a "huge health factory", users' experience in the case of the Munich Hospital was positive. They would even favor this type, if the decision on the basic design had to be made again but would insist, that the boundary of 1,500 beds should not be surpassed. Furthermore, a two-block design would be preferred for logistic reasons. The one-block design causes continual transportation problems because it permanently exceeds elevator capacity. The entrance zone is said to be another weakness of the hospital. The main lobby was reduced by 800 square meters in favor of several decentralized entrances. The reduction of the entrance area was intended to minimize the danger of infections and to shorten internal distances, but the outcome did not prove favorable.

The location of the hospital – besides the block-type design – was the second crucial decision on the basic design. The hospital was built on the outskirts of Munich instead of downtown for the following reasons:

- fewer constraints on the basic design which meant more planning flexibility;
- better conditions to meet environmental requirements;
- improved standards of living for patients;
- better chances to establish a national medical competence hospital by integrating additional medical departments in the future.

Both decisions have proven to be the right choice in the project owners' and users' experience. The only constraint was the insufficient integration into the public transportation system. Opening a new subway line in 1994 remedied this weakness.

Due to rather limited changes of technical goals only minor adaptations of the basic design were necessary. Even a substantial reduction in capacity could be managed without redesigning the basic design, which in its essential elements had been determined in 1964.

The stability of the basic design was mainly achieved by its *strict breakdown*. The total project (approved in 1966) was broken down into 9 separate construction stages and 2 completion steps (1974 and 1980) in order to reduce the initial complexity of the MOE and to better control the undertaking with regard to the achievement of time and cost goals. In addition, adaptations to new medical and constructional trends as well as the experience transfer from preceeding to succeeding project activities were facilitated.

For future projects, the planning architects and project management of this MOE recommend the splitting of completion into at least two steps. More steps would have been favorable in order to reduce the time lag between completion and operation.

They also recommended starting with those project segments which require the highest technical standards (e.g. intensive-care units). This procedure is well known in production planning and is supposed to guarantee on-time completion by dealing with the most time-consuming project activities first. Experience from learning processes, however, favors gradually increasing the level of complexity.

3. Socio-Political Environment

The Munich Hospital was not substantially affected by the socio-political environment. Neither serious failures in the achievement of goals nor doubtful activities of the project management (like corruption) provoked interventions. The objective of the MOE (an increase in regional health standards) served as a protective cloak. Some architects assume that the Munich Hospital was even overshadowed by the 1972 Olympic Games in Munich which absorbed the attention of the socio-political environment. The Games were awarded to Munich in 1966 and paralleled early completion phases of the university hospital. The project management of the university hospital recognized the Games as a "... capricious child, cared for with extravagant and forbearing love" (Eichberger/Schlempp 1977, p.61). We suppose that the presumed neglect by the socio-political environment was an advantage for this MOE.

> The case supports our assertion that project failures attract the involvement of the socio-political environment; project success can at least reduce the probability of its interference.

4. Management Structure and Management Capacity

Despite its size, the Munich Hospital was not managed by a project company. This may be explained by the fact that the State of Bavaria acted as the only project owner. The Federal Republic of Germany, which had to provide a substantial part of the funds, delegated most of its rights to the Bavarian State thus enabling a simpler management structure. A construction office established in 1967 guaranteed sufficient autonomy for the project management.

The following chart shows the different institutions forming the management structure.

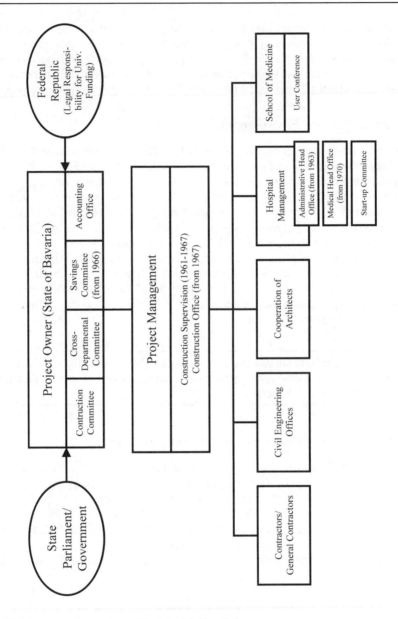

Fig. 60. Management Structure of the Munich Hospital

The *project owner* (State of Bavaria) concentrated on milestone-decisions like the approval of the requirement specifications. Its most important intervention after the start of the project was the decision (1964) to reduce the capacity of the hospital by almost 40%. The project owners established a concurrent auditing system in order to safeguard their interests. The state accounting office had been involved since the early phases of the project. Symptoms of control overkill – as experienced in the case of the Vienna Hospital – were not reported.

The *project management* was carried out by state offices. An office for construction supervision was established in 1961. Responsibility for the project management was delegated to the construction office in 1967. For a short period of time, a civil engineering office was responsible for the construction supervision. This organizational measure proved unsuccessful as the fees for the office were high and cooperation between project management and planning experts was severely impaired. Procurement of the medical equipment was initially delegated to the administration of the university. This delegation had to be withdrawn when the adaptation of the medical equipment to the construction progress proved to be insufficient.

The *integration of planning experts* did not raise serious problems. The architects formed a special cooperation unit separated from project management. This separation was rated to be the best solution, considering the size of the project as well as the long planning and completion period.

The responsibility for project segments requiring less than two years for completion (e.g. the project management office, the nursing school, housing for maintenance staff, support buildings) was shifted to *general contractors*. This solution is advisable for small-sized segments after planning is completed and only marginal interdependencies with other segments are to be considered.

The *integration of users* was ensured by the early establishment of a permanent "user conference" which had already proven effective for another hospital in Germany (Berlin-Steglitz). Only potential users of the university hospital had influence on project decisions. This restriction created real awareness, as all decisionmakers faced the danger of suffering from their ill advice. A side effect of user integration was the early sensibility of project management to operation & maintenance issues.

Planning the operation start-up was delegated to a special committee. Its functions included analyzing and designing operation procedures, designing job descriptions, and calculating the necessary work force in the various phases of operation. The committee's proposals had to be approved by the users' representatives. Despite early recruitment and sophisticated training of the staff, the project experienced difficulties in the start-up phase.

The common failure of insufficient *project management capacity* could be averted in the case of this MOE. In order to meet the deadlines for completion, the size of the project management team was adapted to the growing workload during the phase of detailed planning. Similar adaptations were reported from the administration of the university, from planning experts' teams, and from engineering offices.

The risk of delayed decision-making caused by overstressed top politicians was avoided by appointing special commissions. These were staffed with middle management representatives and had widespread responsibilities beyond the competences of various state departments.

The concern for sufficient management capacity was remarkable not only from a quantitative but also from a qualitative point of view. The *recruitment policy* aimed at hiring managers experienced in construction *and* operation of medical facilities. In the administrative head office, e.g., which served as an interface with the users, some managers were experienced in the fields of both medicine and management. Due to highly skilled project managers and the absence of notable failures, the problem of staff *turnover* did not arise.

IV.   Interdependence of Success Factors and Goal Achievement

The *socio-political environment* did not significantly influence this MOE because it focused its attention on another MOE (the 1972 Olympic Games in Munich). An additional reason for the lack of intervention was the absence of significant failures. Thus the project management's task was facilitated immensely, because this success factor, which has often troubled MOEs, did not have to be worried about.

The *management structure and capacity* were not the source of success but served as a catalyst for the performance of other success factors. Not a project company but a separate state construction office was established in 1967 (see [21] in Table 27) succeeding the office for construction supervision founded in 1961 [10]. The project management was not fully separated from the project owner but no negative effects on the success of the project were reported because there was only one project owner (State of Bavaria) who could influence the project management's decisions. Responsibilities of the various decision-making units were clearly defined and the integration of users as well as of experts worked well. Project management promoted the interests of project owners and prevented other project participants (users, contractors, planning experts) from maximizing their interests. The staffing of the project management positions corresponded to the increasing workload during the planning and completion process. The recruitment focused on skilled personnel.

We assume that the basic design as well as the formulation and change of goals are the crucial success factors of the Munich Hospital. At the beginning, the *basic design* showed high complexity as the project owners intended to centralize most of the diagnosis, treatment, nursing, teaching, and research facilities in a single block-type building [2][5]. Despite its complexity, the consistency of the basic design was great because the fundamental and crucial decisions (block-type, peripheral location) had been made early and were not changed during the life of the project. The early and undisputed decision to break down the MOE into several segments for stepwise completion and operation (initially four, later on two steps), offered the chance to reduce the inherent complexity of the technical goals without withdrawing from or redesigning the undertaking [4][17].

Despite the early fixation on the block-type design the *goal formulation/change* preceded and determined the basic design. The process of the formulation and change of goals can be divided into two quite different phases: The first phase was dominated by technical goals whereas financial and time goals were not regarded as crucial topics. This attitude changed in the early 1960s when increasing user demands [11] forced the project owners to require a substantial reduction in technical goals [12].

Since 1964 the forces to stabilize or even to reduce technical goals dominated the driving forces [14]. Financial and time goals were fixed in 1966 [17][18]. Financial goals did not experience substantial changes. An absolute cost limit of €363m was set by project owners in 1976 [31] and could be met. The time goals were never seriously questioned and could be met as well [27][34].

The goal formulation process showed a *sense of realism as well as of strength*: Sense of realism because the imbalance of the initial goal system was recognized and technical goals were reduced; strength because project owners forced other project participants to accept the limits of funds and the deadlines for replanning activities. The users were not allowed to make unlimited changes and nobody compelled project management to settle for a compromise with users as happened to the project management of the Vienna Hospital. From 1966 onwards, half-way through the total duration of the project, the goal system of the Munich Hospital was balanced and stable.

A sense of realism, strength of the project owners as well as an experienced project management would not have been sufficient without *strong driving forces towards early completion*. These forces were initiated by formally involving those users who would personally be affected by a schedule overrun.

GF: Goal Formulation & Change   SE: Socio-Political Environment
BD: Basic Design   GA: Goal Achievement
MS: Management Structure/Capacity

#	Date	GF	BD	MS	SE	GA	Event
[1]	1952	■					project owner orders a master plan
[2]	1953-02		■				recommendation of block-type design
[3]	1954-07		■				invitation for preliminary study: 2,000 beds, downtown location (reconstruction/enlargement of the old hospital) or peripheral location with stepwise start-up of departments
[4]	1955-05	■					jury decision: block-type design, 2,500 beds, peripheral location, 4 completion steps; faculty of medicine approves
[5]	1955-08	■					project owner approves jury decision
[6]	1959-04			■			contract with planning architects (preliminary study) and planning expert (specification of requirements) is signed
[7]	1958/59		■				specifying requirements
[8]	1959-07		■				presentation of preliminary design: 2 zones, 5 complexes, €133 m
[9]	1961-03		■				project owner approves preliminary design
[10]	1961			■			establishment of construction supervision office
[11]	1962	■					improvement of preliminary design: new technical requirements, faculty of medicine demands more usable floor space
[12]	1963-05	■				■	project owners cut user demands (less volume, less floor space) and limit total costs; planning activity suspended
[13]	1963			■			establishment of administrative head office
[14]	1964-02	■					project owner orders continued planning for the first completion phase (about 75% of the initial size, 500 beds fewer); second completion step (4 clinics and 1 aftercare-unit with about 500 beds) postponed
[15]	1964-03	■					decision on service buildings (housing facilities for nurses)
[16]	1964-09/10	■					presentation and approval of the "September 1964" study: reduced volume; some units are moved from the central to annexed buildings

GF: Goal Formulation & Change						SE: Socio-Political Environment
BD: Basic Design						GA: Goal Achievement
MS: Management Structure/Capacity						
#	Date	GF	BD	MS	SE	GA	Event
[17]	1966-07	■					presentation and approval of new design study: Costs €230 m, 1,500 beds, 120,000 square meters usable floor space, ultimate stop for 3 out of 4 completion phases; 9 independent stages of completion; two start-ups: conservative departments (1974), operation departments (1980); two locations for the school of medicine
[18]	1966			■			establishment of a savings commission
[19]	1966/67	■					cutback of 5 surgery units and 1 unit for X-ray diagnostics, reduction of the main lobby (by 800 square meters)
[20]	1967					■	preliminary phase completed: 1 building for 3 departments, nursing school, construction office
[21]	1967			■			establishment of construction office and faculty construction commission
[22]	1967 (end)					■	release of the second planning and completion phase
[23]	1967/68					■	construction of block is started
[24]	1970			■			medical office established
[25]	1973-10					■	housing for staff members completed
[26]	1974		■				replacement of the eye clinic approved
[27]	1974-07	■				■	completion of step 1 (eastside): Staff housing, service buildings, block (600 beds), parts of the diagnostics and treatment section, 5 surgery units, conservative departments, 3 medical departments, and neurology; actual cost estimate: €375 m
[28]	1974-fall					■	opening of 4 clinics and departments, bed sections
[29]	1975-06	■				■	reduction of job positions (due to high operations costs); functional instead of group nursing
[30]	1975/76	■					enlargement of bed capacity, transfer of a clinical department to the new hospital
[31]	1976	■					project owners approve funds (€245 m) and state a cost limit of €363m
[32]	1976-11					■	end of the first start-up
[33]	1977					■	second start-up of operation
[34]	1980					■	full operation

Table 27. Interdependence of Success Factors and Goal Achievement in the Case of the Munich Hospital

P.   The Large Energy Converter Growian

J. Hauschildt/J. Pulczynski[31]

GROWIAN is an acronym consisting of the abbreviations of "Große Windener-gie-Anlage" (large wind energy converter). The authors had access to the files of the project company responsible for construction and permanent operation of the MOE (GROWIAN GmbH). In-depth interviews with experts from a preceding project company focused on early phases of the project, especially on the process of goal formulation.[32]

I.   *Characteristics of GROWIAN*

This project was aimed at testing the generation of electric energy from natural movements of air on a large scale. The public discussion following the energy crisis of 1973 and 1974 revived the demand for non-fossil energy sources. This discussion was furthermore enhanced by the criticism of nuclear energy. From a political point of view, the utilization of solar and wind energy seemed advisable; moreover, it seemed economically interesting. The construction of a wind energy converter which would exceed all its preceding projects in size was to be a revolutionary step establishing a technological edge. The research on wind energy did not start before the 1970s, though: It was possible to fall back on the works executed by Albert Betz in the 1920s as well as on designs by Hermann Honnef and Franz Kleinhens from the 1930s. After World War II Ulrich Hütter constructed and installed two minor wind energy converters. The wind energy converter W34 (100 kW) built by Hütter may have brought a large amount of practical experience, the important knowledge of local wind conditions and the design of a considerably larger wind energy converter, however, were still missing. In order to eliminate all these uncertainties the construction and implementation of GROWIAN was embedded into a series of sub-projects, which in part preceded the actual construction of GROWIAN and partly were carried out simultaneously. Due to the considerable political interest in the utilization of wind energy GROWIAN was almost entirely financed by the German Federal Ministry of Research and Technology.

The original idea of GROWIAN was born in 1976. The actual construction began in Kaiser-Wilhelm-Koog, Schleswig-Holstein, Germany, in January 1980. On October 1, 1982 the plant was put into operation for the first time, although the official phase of construction had not been completed. Construction ended in 1987 officially. Only a few months later, GROWIAN was stopped; and in the following year it was torn down.

---

[31] Both University of Kiel (Germany)
[32] The case is elaborated in Pulczynskis Dissertation (1991); see also Endres et al. (1988), Reinhold/Scholz (1988).

From an external point of view, this project can obviously not be rated as a success, but is a clear failure. The aim of the following case study is to identify the causes of this failure. We should mention, however, that in 1994 another wind energy converter with moderately reduced dimensions (AEOLUS II) located in Wilhelmshaven, Germany, performed a successful one-year test period. The project AEOLUS is proof that wind energy converters can produce megawatts of electricity even with low wind (less than 6 meters per second). No doubt that this success has been facilitated by the experience gained through GROWIAN.

II.   *Achievement of Goals*

1. Technical Goals

The GROWIAN project was determined by various technical goals: Goals of construction, goals of permanent operation, and scientific goals.

The superordinate *goals of construction*, essentially supported by the representatives of the political system, were described as follows in the Federal Research Reports of 1979:

- saving resources and preserving the natural living conditions;
- improving the information based on the chances and risks of technologies in general.

These intentions had already been expressed in a study on non-fossil and non-nuclear sources of primary energy (Armbrust et al. 1976, pp.44):

- "The technology of wind energy converters has been very well developed, and the future is not likely to bring up any new epoch-making principles. All recently observed physical and technical principles have already been suggested in such a form or in a different way. Considering the advantages and disadvantages of the single plant, the designs show an evident preference for a high-speed machine with a horizontal arbor to other designs. For a large-scale energy supply it represents the only practicable conception."
- "For testing several solutions on site it is absolutely necessary to build a test plant. For further development within the Federal Republic of Germany a 1 MW plant with a horizontal arbor and also a diameter of 80 meters can be considered as a starting point, as the W34/100 has already provided detailed operational results and experience to the Studiengesellschaft Windkraft e.V."
- "The next stage of development could then be a large plant with a diameter of 113 meters (10,000 square meters of rotor surface in the wind), the installed power of which depends on the site of installation, i.e. between 3 and 6 MW. From a technical point of view, large plants with a diameter of 160 meters or even 200 meters are also practicable. Their installed power per square meter of rotor surface may exceed 300 W/square meters, as in these altitudes the wind speed may be very high and relatively stable."

The goals of construction of this plant were almost achieved. However, to construct the rotor blades as planned turned out to be impossible. This led to considerable goal changes and finally caused the failure of the entire project.

Concerning the *goals of permanent operation* the wind energy converter was to operate for three years, so that all necessary information could be collected. At the same time, the electric energy was to be fed into the public supply grid in order to gain experience of how reliable the supply with wind energy could be.

The goals of permanent operation were clearly missed. Instead of operating for three years the actual operation lasted only 420 hours, i.e. 17.5 days, caused by a system overload, as will be shown in detail.

Looking at the *scientific goals*, GROWIAN was embedded in 13 sub-projects. The first group of these projects referred to meteorological measurements, especially wind measurements in high altitude and under special consideration of the site of the plant (near the coast of the Federal Republic of Germany). A second group of sub-projects aimed at examining the vibrational behavior of the whole system, especially considering the use of large rotor blades. A third group was to estimate the technical and economic feasibility.

According to the judgment of the experts concerned, most of the scientific goals could be achieved.

2. Time Goals

The entire unit was supposed to be handed over after a 32 months' construction and test period. In fact, the official handing over was constantly delayed. Not only was the start of construction delayed by 8 months, but there were also various technical problems which became evident only during the test phase of the plant and which eventually delayed the handing over by a total of 55 months. Table 28 indicates the disregarding of the deadlines. It becomes evident that particularly the phase of implementation, dragging on from January 1983 to February 1987, was subject to these essential delays.

Project/ Project Stage	Planning Stage	Starting Point	Termi- nation	Duration in Months	Deviation in Months		
					Start	Termi- nation	Dura- tion
Construction	Jan. 79	79-04-01	81-12-01	32.0			
GROWIAN	Jan. 80	80-01-01	82-08-01	31.0	9.0	8.0	-1.0
	Actual	80-01-08	87-02-28	86.0	0.0	55.0	+55.0
Start of	Jan. 79	79-10-01					
Construction	Jan. 80	81-01-81			16.0		
Works	Actual	81-05-15			3.5		
Components	Jan. 79	80-06-01	81-06-30	13.0			
Assembly	Jan. 80	81-05-15	82-03-14	10.0	11.5	8.5	-3.0
	Actual	82-03-15	83-02-10	11.0	10.0	11.0	+1.0
Rotor Blade	Jan. 79	82-04-15	81-05-14	1.0			
Assembly	Jan. 80	81-11-01	81-11-30	1.0	6.5	6.5	0.0
	Actual	82-08-15	82-10-03	1.5	9.5	10.0	+0.5
Excavation of	Jan. 79	81-05-21	81-05-31	0.3			
Power House	Jan. 80	82-02-05	82-02-14	0.3	8.5	8.5	0.0
Foundation	Actual	82-10-04	82-10-20	0.5	8.0	8.2	+0.2
Initial	Jan. 79	81-07-01	81-09-30	3.0			
Operation	Jan. 80	82-03-15	82-06-14	3.0	8.5	8.5	0.0
	Actual	83-01-25	87-02-28	49.0	10.3	56.5	+46.0
Test	Jan. 79	81-10-01	81-11-30	2.0			
	Jan. 80	82-06-15	82-07-31	1.5	8.5	8.0	-0.5
	Actual						
Delivery	Jan. 79	81-12-01					
of the	Jan. 80	82-08-01			8.0		
Property	Actual						
Operation of	Jan. 79						
GROWIAN	Jan. 80	82-08-01	85-07-31	36.0			
	Actual	83-03-15	87-05-08	49.5	7.5	21.0	+13.5

Table 28. Achievement of the Time Goals in the Case of GROWIAN

3. Financial Goals

The project was supported by the Federal Ministry of Research and Technology (BMFT) with a budget of €19.5 m. Table 29 shows the cost overruns of the GROWIAN project. In fact, the construction costs amounted to €26.7m exceeding the planned budget by 12%. The operation costs had initially been estimated at €2.1m but finally amounted to about €3 m. This is an overrun of 19% (both figures adjusted for inflation).

| Project | Date | Cost Object* | | | | Total* | Change of Total Cost |
		BMFT	GRO-WIAN GmBH	Invest-ment Allow-ance	Revenues from Sale of Elec-tricity		
Construc-	79-11-14	19.5	0.4			19.9	
tion	82-07-15	24.0	0.4	2.2		26.6	33.8%
GROWIAN	85-07-22	22.4	0.4	3.8		26.6	0.0%
	87-02-28						
	Approved	22.4	0.5	3.8		26.7	0.4%
	Settled	22.4	0.5	3.8		26.7	0.1%
Operation	79-11-14	1.4	0.7			2.1	
GROWIAN	82-07-15	1.8	0.7			2.6	24.4%
	83-03-18	1.4	0.7		0.500	2.6	0.0%
	87-06-30	1.9	0.7		0.016	2.6	0.0%
	87-08-11	2.3	0.7		0.016	3.0	15.0%

* Figures in m €

Table 29. Achievement of the Financial Goals in the Case of GROWIAN

4. Overall Performance

Summing up, there is no doubt that the GROWIAN project was a failure.

- It was a technical failure: The experts were not yet ready to tackle the innovative technical challenges of such a large plant. There were several components which had not been worked out thoroughly.
- This technical failure made it impossible to achieve the planned goals of permanent operation.
- It cannot be denied that this project has brought about considerable scientific and technological experience which has been used for follow-up plants. The meteorological results were so encouraging that a large wind park was set up on the former GROWIAN site.
- The technical problems and the variety of modifications to the original design resulted in a considerable time overrun.
- The cost overrun correlates with the failure to adhere to the time limits.

III.   Success Factors

1. Formulation and Change of Goals

The process of goal formulation can be illustrated as an *interaction of the political, scientific, and private-sector systems*. The representatives of the political system were especially those of the Federal Government or of subordinate national institutions, especially of the nuclear research plant in Jülich (KFA). The scientific system was mainly represented by professors of engineering. The private-sector system consisted of the suppliers to the wind energy converter on the one hand and, on the other hand, of the public utilities supposed to run the wind energy converter during the permanent operation. A relatively great simplification allows a circular representation of the common interests pursued by these three systems, located approximately in the middle of all interests.

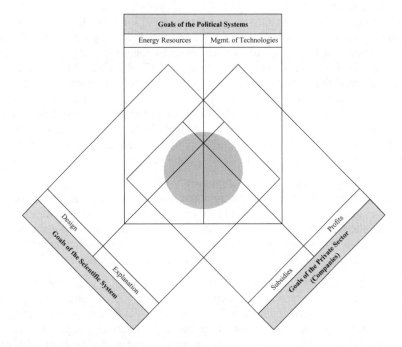

Fig. 61. Interaction of the Political, Scientific, and Private-Sector Systems in the Goal Formulation Process of GROWIAN

In the beginning, the Federal government pursued goals relating to energy generation as well as to technological policies. The weight eventually shifted to the latter.

From a scientific point of view, there were two interests in the beginning. The scientists intended to improve their knowledge of rotor blade dynamics, of vibrational behavior of the system as a whole, of the controller action under different wind speed conditions, etc. ("interest to explain"). On the other hand, they were interested in applying existing technological knowledge, which had been gathered on much smaller plants, to a large plant ("interest to design").

The two interests of the engineering companies who were supposed to construct the wind energy converter were – in our view – mainly of a financial nature: First, to receive subsidies and, second, to increase their profits by regular business and by follow-up orders.

In the following, the operating companies will be considered only indirectly under the aspect of social policies. They only partly realized their interests, as the permanent operation of the plant never occurred.

During the process of goal formulation, the different interests of the interacting partners were transformed into project goals. In this context, the performance goal had to be specified in full detail. The corresponding technical sub-goals determined the specification of duties and charges. This reduced the degree of freedom of goal formulation.

The goal formulation process started between 1973 and 1974. During this time, the energy crisis triggered off a search for new sources of energy. The utilization of wind energy at that time was overshadowed by the government's research policy in the field of nuclear power. However, in 1973 the Federal Government already indicated that it would examine further "new and environmentally friendly sources of energy including solar or geothermal energy (among others)". In autumn 1974 this energy program was continued demanding for the first time the development of new energies for large-scale technical exploitation. It was not until December 1977 that wind energy became explicitly mentioned in the German parliament printed matter (Bundestagsdrucksache 1977).

> "Activities to develop ways of tapping 'new' sources of energy are focusing primarily on the use of solar energy, but also on the exploitation of wind as well as geothermal energy. The objective of the development activities is to increase the share of these sources of energy to an extent which is economically exploitable and profitable. If necessary, the Federal Government will financially support the market entry of projects exploiting 'new' energies."

This official statement of objectives was pronounced one year after the actual goals had been determined. The decisive event in the goal formulation process was a discussion of experts on June 11, 1976. This was Scientists' Day. They enthusiastically supported the idea of constructing a relatively large wind energy converter. Their technical specifications were very detailed. The most influential expert suggested building a wind energy converter with two rotor blades in a composite manner, providing the rotor system with a swing hub and giving the plant a capacity of 1 to 3 MW. The result of the discussion was summed up by the chairman as follows (source: unpublished minutes): His overall impression was that it was perfectly feasible, from a technological point of view, to construct a large wind energy converter with an output of 1-3 MW, and that the problems which were still to be expected could be solved. After this discussion, the various components of the converter could already be specified in a fairly detailed way. He had learned that it was desirable for the rotor to be built in a composite manner, to have two blades and a swing hub, and to be constructed as a high-speed engine and with a control system as designed by Prof. Hütter. The gear unit was to have a fixed ratio. The generator, he said, was to be a synchronous generator (50 Hz) for feeding the electricity into the national grid. The conception of the tower would depend on the overall system opted for.

The scientists' most important impact on the decision was the choice to build the rotor blades in a composite manner. It was made clear that a wind energy converter of the size discussed would have to be realized exclusively from composite materials.

2. Basic Design

In the subsequent invitation for tenders, sent to 16 companies, the goals were defined as follows:

1. Output: A value between 2 and 3 MW, if the annual average wind speed (measured approx. 10 meters above the ground) is about 5 meters/sec. Constant number of rotor revolutions at rated power, regulation according to Hütter.
2. Construction principle: horizontal arbor, high tip-speed ratio.
3. Components:

Rotor:	Two blades, composite construction, swing hub.
Tower:	For the conception of the tower (lattice tower, steel tube mast, reinforced concrete tower), one important aspect besides operation and construction costs and technical aspects, is the optical impression (the planned wind park would consist of 100 towers!).
Generator:	Synchronous generator, 50 Hz, for feeding the electricity into the power supply system.
Gear unit:	Fixed ratio.

The invitation asked for developed plans meaning a further restriction of the goals: The rotor would have to consist of two blades constructed in a composite manner. This was a clear fixation of the basic design. The capacity should be between 2 and 3 MW; the exact figure was left unspecified leaving room for negotiation. So far, nothing had been said about the height of the tower and the diameter of the rotor. Apart from the fact that the design would have to meet optical requirements, there were still remarkable degrees of freedom in specifying the basic design.

When the technical alternatives were presented for the first time, the diameter of the rotor was declared to be the main problem. Three alternatives were discussed: 80, 100, and 113 meters. At this point the government representatives made the most important decision. Although the experts preferred a rotor with a diameter of 80 meters, the representatives of the political system insisted on the larger alternative of 100.4 meters. In the most flexible formulation this variable would have been left open ("... the biggest diameter possible"). A monovalent fixation would still be flexible ("... a diameter of at least 80 meters"). Instead, the most rigid form of determination was chosen. This fixation anticipated the subsequent decision, i.e. the height of the tower. It was fixed at 96.6 meters thus determining the height of the hub to be 102.1 meters above the ground (see Fig. 62).

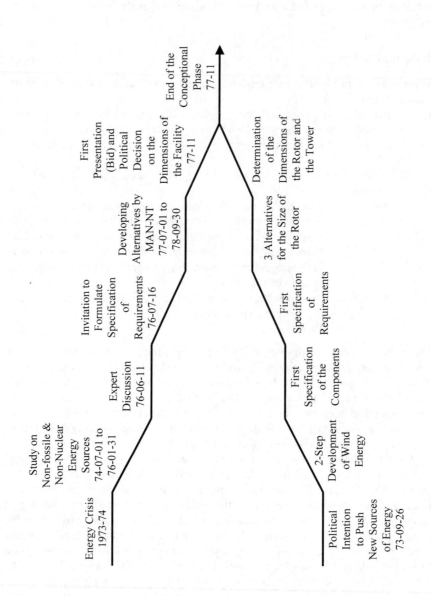

Fig. 62. Formulation of Goals and Basic Design in the Case of GROWIAN

In order to make the dimensions of the project more comprehensible the promotors of the project used a comparison which strongly influenced the discussion: The tower plus the radius of the rotor were higher than the cathedral of Cologne (see Fig. 63).

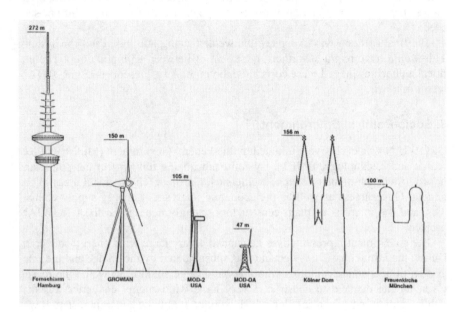

Fig. 63. The Size of GROWIAN in Comparison to Selected Buildings

Although the basic design seemed to be clear by the end of the design phase, considerable problems arose during the following period:

- It was impossible to build the rotor blades exclusively from composite materials.
- In an initial attempt to solve this problem a "hybrid" construction was chosen, and an infrastructure of steel was inserted into the rotor blade. This steel frame was supposed to be 32 meters in length covering approximately 2/3 of the entire rotor blade.
- This approach was dropped because the problems of combining the steel with the composite material appeared too difficult to handle. Therefore, it was decided to build the rotor blades with an infrastructure made entirely of steel, only the covering consisting of composite materials. This was in turn the reason for an enormous increase in weight of the rotor blades by 2 tons and of the swing hub from 36 to 54 tons. The entire equipment of the machine room became increasingly heavy, finally weighing 420 tons instead of the planned 280 tons, an increase of 50%!

The increase in weight caused a number of "minor" technical problems. Just one example: The winches to heave the machine room, including the rotor, onto the tower had to be replaced entirely. The actual problem resulted from the fact that the swing hub could not cope with the heavy burden. Only a few days after the nominal load had been reached for the first time, the frame showed cracks. Although the engineers made great efforts to repair these cracks, they did not succeed.

The final solution was to replace the welded swing hub by a cast-iron system. This would have required further investment of between €5m and €6 m. The political authorities judged these costs to be too high. As a consequence, GROWIAN was torn down.

3. Socio-Political Environment

GROWIAN was exclusively initiated by the Federal Government (Ministry of Research and Technology, BMFT). By fully subsidizing this project the politicians hoped to win the industry over to tackle such a project. The political ideas of the Federal Government as well as the economic interests of energy supply companies, and the interests of plant constructors strongly determined the GROWIAN project.

The government representatives demanded a very large wind energy converter. During the initial phase, this demand was substantiated by the choice and the integration of academic promotors who favored a large solution as well. One reason given for the demand to construct a very large wind energy converter was that public opinion required a solution which would not only be a marginal step. It was said that under the then predominating conditions only a "big bang" would make sense and be justified. A second argument was the fact that in other countries wind energy converters with a rotor diameter of about 90 meters were planned. It was a question of demonstrating the international competitiveness of the Federal Republic of Germany. Hence, the project received a certain politically determined prestige. The aim was to make GROWIAN the world's largest energy converter. Various statements imply that the huge dimensions of the wind energy converter were the consequence of naming the project "GROWIAN" in the first place. It is even said that by choosing this handy and concise abbreviation, the government representatives determined the size of the plant.

The attitude of the public utilities towards wind energy converters tended to be negative. They argued that a performance of only 3 MW would hardly cover the so-called "current on contact" which flows when switches are thrown. Additionally, the unsteady wind conditions would lead to a destabilization of energy supply and therefore other forms of energy generation would have to be held in reserve. At that time the public utilities favored the construction of nuclear power plants whose contribution to the energy supply was considered to be far easier to calculate. Furthermore, they published feasibility studies to show that wind energy could not compete with nuclear energy. According to these studies, the investment in wind energy converters per kw would be about five times higher than investments in nuclear power plants.

This rather negative attitude shown by the public utilities in turn determined the attitude of the plant constructors. They feared that due to this negative attitude there would be no considerable market for wind energy converters. The attitude shown by the public utilities and the constructors resulted in the demand that this project should be promoted entirely by the Federal Government. In fact, in the life of the project the other parties concerned hardly made any financial contributions.

During the setting-up of GROWIAN the political composition of the Federal Government changed. Initially, this decisive event had no influence on the completion of the project. However, when the failure of the project became evident, the Federal Government lacked the necessary intention to make this project a success despite all obstacles.

4. Management Structure and Management Capacity

The GROWIAN project consisted of very distinct phases: First, there was the phase of goal formulation which was carried out mainly by politicians and scientists. The second phase was meant to transform these goals into technical solutions, and can also be called the conceptional or design phase. It was mainly supported by the engineering firms involved, i.e. Maschinenfabrik Augsburg-Nürnberg, Dept. New Technologies (MAN-NT). The third phase was the actual phase of construction to realize the technical goals. A company called GROWIAN GmbH was founded for the construction by three public utility firms. The fourth phase was supposed to be the permanent operation. However, for the reasons mentioned above this phase was never reached.

This strict differentiation of phases reflects the structure of the project management. The *first phase* was hardly structured at all. The nuclear research centre in Jülich (KFA) was responsible for the project management. They invited the experts to participate in the discussions and initiated the closed invitation to tender for the specification of requirements. After three tenders had been submitted, it was once again the KFA who awarded the contract to the MAN-NT. The KFA allowed one year for the preparation of detailed plans. Later it became evident that this period had been much too short.

During the *second phase*, a professional project management was established under the overall control of MAN-NT. Fig. 64 shows its structure. Notably this project structure included the Deutsche Forschungs- und Versuchsanstalt für Luft- und Raumfahrt e.V., DFVLR (German Research and Experimental Society for Aviation and Space Travel, today: German Research Society for Aviation and Space Travel). The task of the DFVLR was to construct the rotor blades from synthetic materials in a composite manner, reinforced by glass- and coal-fibres. When it became evident in the design phase that the rotor blades in the size demanded could not be built in a composite manner, the DFVLR left the project. The project management chose a company which was able to bring in its traditional strength in steel construction and thus determined the solution of the material problem.

In the *third phase*, a project company was founded for construction and permanent operation to assume the project management throughout its further course, including tests of the wind energy converter (see Fig. 65). The government representatives wanted several energy supply companies to participate in the project company in order to assure the acceptance by the potential users of this innovation at an early stage. For this purpose, the detailed plans were sent to all public utility companies in the Federal Republic of Germany, asking them for comments. Strikingly, there was hardly any reaction – a clear reflection of their negative attitude. Eventually, the electric power company of Hamburg, HEW, was won over to take on the overall control of the construction and permanent operation. Other firms were the electrical power companies of Schleswig-Holstein (Schleswag) and of the Rheinisch-Westphalian region (RWE).

The organizational structure of the project company was rather complex. It should be noted that the project management changed again: The two managing directors of the GROWIAN GmbH were nominated by HEW and Schleswag. MAN-NT no longer participated in the management. The evaluation of the files shows 513 different names from 219 different authorities, ministries, institutions, associations, clubs, institutes, companies, and departments during the construction phase. 131 individuals, specified by name and 47 non-specified groups are mentioned more than ten times. 80% of the actors concerned with the construction and the implementation of GROWIAN were from private-sector companies.

The management had to cope with considerable coordination problems. At least 17 specific persons were involved in this coordination activity. Therefore the management capacity can certainly be judged as sufficient. Yet, the frequent shift of project responsibility throughout the project caused substantial difficulties.

Science and practice are rich in the tradition of structuring a process into a (temporal) phase scheme. However, the idea of phases may mean an artificial splitting up single parts of the process. In the case of GROWIAN, the most negative consequence of the phase structure was the change of responsibility in the project management. As shown above, the various phases were dominated by different forces and also controlled by different teams. There was no continuity in personnel, and there was no permanent promotor of power, promotor by expertise, or a process-promotor responsible for the entire project throughout all phases.

As a consequence, each group concentrated only on favorable results of the phase it was responsible for and handed over the "achievements" of its phase to the following group. In turn, the follow-up group could always justify its mistakes or failures by pointing out that the actual decisions and assessments had already been determined during preceding phases, and that it could not be held responsible for these failures.

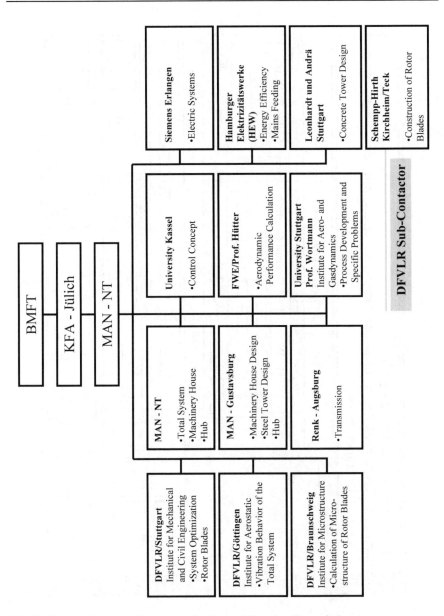

Fig. 64. Project Company Structure in the Case of Growian (Second Phase)

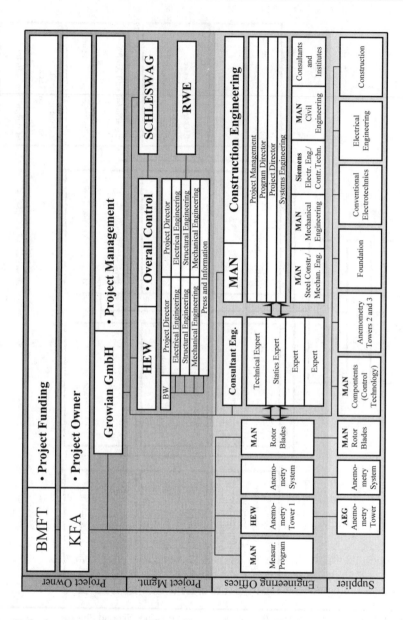

Fig. 65. Project Company Structure in the Case of Growian (Third Phase)

The question can be raised whether or not the relevant positions where adequately filled during the various phases. During the phase of goal determination the political will was passed on through the KFA. The scientists, who had a very strong influence in this phase were never more than an informal force. The handing-over of the project management to MAN-NT in the design phase was certainly the right decision. However, the fact that the DFVLR left the project though being responsible for a central element of the project, indicates their weak influence on the design process.

IV.   *Interdependence of Success Factors and Goal Achievement*

The case of GROWIAN is characterized by a remarkable involvement of the *socio-political environment* (including scientists) from the very beginning (see [1][2][3][5][10] in Table 30). Private industries refused to share project ownership and contented themselves with the role of contractors [7]. This attitude facilitated the politicians' drive for prestigious and risky technical goals (huge diameter of the rotor) as well as the fixation on specific technical solutions (rotor blades from composite material). The construction problems experienced with composite or hybrid materials offered the chance for a fundamental redesign of the project. The chance was missed by insisting on the original design, which finally failed and caused the tearing down of the plant after a few months of operation [28][30]. With private industries as participating project owners we suppose that the MOE would have taken a different course: The initial design would have been smaller in size and less risky. The plant would have been redesigned at least after the construction problem with the rotor blades became obvious. Even the continual changes of the project management might have been avoided by the closer involvement of experienced industrial partners [15][19].

The GROWIAN case demonstrates that clear goals do not necessarily guarantee the success of a project. As to GROWIAN, the deficiency in its goals was a *lack of flexibility*. The dimensions of the main features of the basic design, i.e. the height of the tower, the diameter of the rotor, the construction of the rotor blades, and the swing hub were fixed and therefore inflexible. They could either be fulfilled or not. There were too many strict conditions and it did not become evident which goal function should be optimized. With hindsight, it would have been more useful to define the height of the tower and the diameter of the rotor as variables [8], and not as rigid parameters.

Goals are based on preconditions, i.e. on assumptions about the context. If these preconditions turn out to be incorrect the decision-making process must be repeated. One of the central preconditions of this project was the assumption that rotor blades could be built in a composite manner. This assumption proved to be untenable. In this situation the experts had to find new alternatives and decided in favor of a steel construction [12]. Nobody ever thought of repeating the goal-formulation process. The overall success of the project was, therefore, put at risk despite the achievement of sub-goals.

In contrast to the fixed technical goals and the basic design, the time goals and the cost goals were flexible. The time goal was exceeded by about one and a half years, the cost goal by 34%. The fact that these goals were missed would perhaps have been tolerable if the technical goals (and above all the permanent operation goal) had been achieved. Concerning the cost goal, the cast-iron construction of the swing hub failed because the additionally required investment of €5m to €6m would have meant a cost overrun of 65%.

The goals were determined at a relatively early stage [6][9]. It may be true that for each activity the goals must be definitely fixed at some point or other. However, the case of GROWIAN raises the question at which point the goals should be fixed at the latest. This point was reached when it became evident that the rotor blades could not be built in a composite manner. Experts ought to be aware of goal flexibility and should adhere to it until irrevocable subsolutions, necessary for achieving all goals, have been realized.

Furthermore, the GROWIAN case has shown that goal flexibility is also a question of the power structure among the interacting partners. If one of the partners, in this case the Federal Government, argues that it would eventually bear all the costs, the conflict between a "desirable" and a "feasible" solution is one-sidedly fixed at "desirable". In the case of GROWIAN there was no efficient counter-force that could have ensured more goal flexibility. Only a financial engagement by the private companies would have forced the partners to critically check their goal system. The goal changes would then have been initiated by those with the highest degree of technical knowledge. In our case, however, the political representatives managed to push through their ideas [11] which were hardly based on technical arguments but on their interest in prestige and on other political arguments.

Innovative projects require flexibility. Rigid limits, unalterable goal preferences and inflexible time limits do not fit the uncertainties of technical alternatives and their features in unknown situations.

It certainly cannot be the desired result of a huge experiment to only know in the end that the achievement of the sub-goals in a fixed specific combination did not lead to a success.

After the failure had become evident, the ones responsible naturally tried to *justify their actions*. This can be observed especially in the re-interpretation of the initial goals, as shown in the next figure:

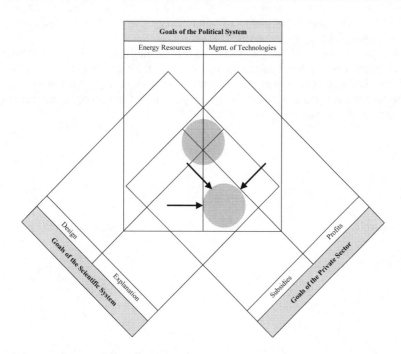

Fig. 66. Re-Interpretation of the Initial Goals by the Political, Scientific, and Private-Sector Systems after the Failure of GROWIAN

The representatives of the government gave up their economic goal to feed energy into the power supply grid and started to merely evaluate the technological and political implications of GROWIAN. The scientists focused on their "interest to explain" (see above) in contrast to the "interest to design". They regarded GROWIAN as a highly interesting experiment that provided a large amount of data [29]. The construction engineers claimed that GROWIAN had proven that such large plants can be built [26][27], that the electric energy generated can be fed into an existing power supply system without problems, that the planned performance had been reached, that there had been no environmental problems, that the global dynamics could be controlled, that the safety system was reliable, and that the control engineering operated excellently. All of the above were important details but did not make up the overall success of the plant, however. The private firms – although this was not publicly announced – could only have been interested in being subsidized, as there were no profits or follow-up orders to be expected.

With this failure in mind, the energy suppliers participating in the project did not have to choose between wind energy generation and other kinds of energy. Even more, this failure encouraged those forces in the energy sector who had spoken out against this technology. It was not until the accident in Chernobyl that the ideas of energy politics experienced a turnaround in favor of wind energy converters. In the following years plenty of wind energy converters were built with increased financial support by private companies.

Actually, already 25% of the energy supply of the State of Schleswig-Holstein are accounted for by wind energy converters and this rate is supposed to increase to 50%. The height of the newest generation of wind energy converters reaches 130m but residents are opposed to the "pollution" of the scenic coastline (Süddeutsche Zeitung, Munich, 2003-07-30).

GF: Goal Formulation & Change		SE: Socio-Political Environment			
BD: Basic Design		GA: Goal Achievement			
MS: Management Structure					

#	Date	GF	BD	MS	SE	GA	Events
[1]	1973-74				■		energy crisis
[2]	1974-09	■			■		Federal Energy Program demands the development of "new energies"
[3]	1974-1976	■					studies on "sources of energy for to-morrow?", funded by the Federal Ministry of Research and Technology
[4]	1976 begin			■			KFA appointed for project management
[5]	1976-06-11	■			■		scientists, energy experts, and politicians discuss the construction of a large wind energy converter
[6]	1976-07-16		■				invitation to tender for designing a large wind converter, 2-3 MW performance, rotor with two blades in composite manner
[7]	1977-06			■			MAN-NT appointed for engineering a large wind converter in detail
[8]	1977-11		■				presentation of technical alternatives: diameter of rotor: 80, 100, or 113 m
[9]	1977-11		■		■		political decision to build a large wind energy converter, rotor diameter 100.4 m, tower height 96.6 m
[10]	1977-12-19	■			■		printed matter No. 8/1357 of the German Bundestag mentions "exploitation of wind energy"
[11]	1977-07-01 to 1978-09-30		■				MAN-NT plans a large energy converter in detail under serious time pressure
[12]	1979-01		■			■	change of basic design: steel instead of hybrid material
[13]	1979-03		■				decision about location in Kaiser-Wilhelm-Koog, Schleswig-Holstein
[14]	1979-04-01	■					scheduled start of project completion
[15]	1980-01-08			■			establishment of the "GROWIAN GmbH" responsible for constructing and operation (shareholders: 3 public utilities)

GF: Goal Formulation & Change					SE: Socio-Political Environment	
BD: Basic Design					GA: Goal Achievement	
MS: Management Structure/Capacity						

#	Date	GF	BD	MS	SE	GA	Events
[16]	1980-01-08					■	actual start of project completion
[17]	1981-05-15					■	start of construction
[18]	1982-03-15					■	set up of tower and other components
[19]	1982 (first half)			■			MAN-NT withdraws from project
[20]	1982-08-15					■	set up of rotor blades
[21]	1982-10-01					■	test operation
[22]	1983-01					■	start of operation and test of performance, completion of research studies, technical improvements
[23]	1983-02-10					■	end of construction
[24]	1983-10-17					■	official start of operation
[25]	1984-03-29					■	start of full operation (3 MW)
[26]	1984-05-30 to 1985-11-07		■				modification of swing hub-frame
[27]	1986-04-11 to 1987-02-26		■				repairing cracks in the swing hub-frame
[28]	1987-05-08					■	official end of operation
[29]	1987-12-31					■	end of research program
[30]	1988 begin					■	GROWIAN was torn down

Table 30. Interdependence of Success Factors and Goal Achievement in the Case of GROWIAN

Part Five: Conclusion

Q. Lessons for the Future

By focusing on success factors, it is our intention to prevent MOE disasters in the future. This is a realistic aim due to the high risk inherent in every MOE and the rather limited current knowledge about MOEs. It is certainly worthwhile pursuing because we have witnessed remarkable differences in the level of goal achievement by MOEs. If the Vienna Hospital had been completed with the same performance as the Munich Hospital or if the level of performance of the hospitals had been equal to that of the Olympic Games, project owners (and tax-payers) would have benefited substantially. The lessons we can learn from our cases are various. Some cases have provided information on the "do's", others have clearly shown the "don'ts" of MOE management.

Our analysis is focused on the *position of project owners*. Addressing lessons to them is synonymous with a call for action. Project owners' responsibilities include more than initiating MOEs, their funding, establishing a project company, and recruiting some top managers. There are a lot of crucial events which require the full attention of project owners and their ability to make or influence key decisions.

The lessons are presented as recommendations based on the knowledge gained from the five cases. Standard tools of project management like network analysis are not subject to our discussion because we concentrate on *key issues*.

The lessons are divided into five parts. The first part deals with pre-start activities. The second part (minimax vs. maximin) calls for limiting risks as a guideline for the management of MOEs. The final three parts deal with specific topics of project management: cost management, reporting procedures, and controlling.

I.   Pre-Start Activities

In Part Three we pointed out that not only activities in the early phases of MOEs but also pre-start activities and decisions may predetermine MOE success. We furthermore assume that the technique of feasibility studies is employed to check the technical and financial settings of MOEs. Hence, we will concentrate on pre-start issues, which so far have been rather neglected in the current discussion of feasibility studies: the questioning of MOE initiatives and the evaluation of the management capacity of project owners.

1. Questioning MOE-Initiatives

Cases from our sample show that MOEs, once started, will be carried out even if troubles are foreseeable. Therefore, timely interventions have to be discussed. Questioning or fighting early initiatives seems to be easier than resisting a mature project specified by a framework of technical, financial and time goals.

Sometimes the MOE-initiative itself has to be seen as a driving force, often called a "mission". A good MOE-initiative should stand up to questioning, whereas a poor (too risky) initiative should be killed. Most investments in infrastructure like traffic or energy systems and university hospitals meet with positive public recognition because they are supposed to increase public welfare. Furthermore, one-shot events like the Olympic Games or world expositions ("Expos") are suitable to gain local, regional, or national reputation. They are, therefore, often linked to regional development programs, e.g. job creation by strengthening the tourism industry.

Although there is no simple rule telling us how and by whom the MOE-initiative is to be questioned, this pre-start activity is a must, because there is strong evidence that the demand forecast of MOEs is biased.[33] The best chances for serious questioning are given if potential project owners have to be convinced by the initiator of an MOE-initiative. Thus the intended MOE is subject to open discussions, particularly as to its benefits in terms of profit, economic opportunities and public prosperity vs. the risks in terms of technical failures, cost and schedule overruns, and even loss of reputation. The fact that no private investors can be found to share project ownership would be a serious early warning signal which should not be ignored as in the case of the large wind energy converter GROWIAN.

Questioning the MOE-initiative seems to be more difficult if the promotors of the initiative belong to the potential owners, e.g. representatives of city, state, or federal institutions. They have good chances to manipulate their parent organizations and public opinion. Only strong constraining forces like environmental matters or a mature public awareness are able to countervail the initiative. In the case of the World Exposition 1995, the Viennese citizens rejected the initiative in a plebiscite although the ruling parties and the lobby of the business community strongly recommended it. If promotors of MOE-initiatives have not only the formal authority but the resources for project ownership, questioning is very difficult and may even be dismissed as an unauthorized intervention.

A simple "no" to an MOE-initiative cannot be seen as a strong argument, especially if the MOE-initiative appeals to local, regional or national pride or prestige. It is advisable to understand the underlying motives of MOE proponents. Are they aiming at a special one-shot event (like the Olympic Games) or at a long-range development program initiated and executed by the MOE? In the case of the latter, a serious discussion may bring up less expensive and less risky alternatives to realize certain development programs.

In order to ensure questioning by individuals and institutions who are not identical with the promotors of the MOE-initiative, a formalized invitation for tenders for (shared) project ownership may be initiated. If potential project owners reject ownership but accept the role of contractor (see the case of GROWIAN), the initiative is likely to be too risky. Last but not least, the early and intensive involvement of the socio-political environment, often blamed for its destructive attitude to MOEs (remember the opposition to nuclear power plants) may be seen as a useful questioning procedure.

Questioning must fail if, intentionally or by chance the MOE-initiative substantially changes its dimension. In the case of the Vienna Hospital the initial initiative

---

[33] "Don't trust traffic forecasts, especially for rail" (Flyvberg et al. 2003, p.31)

of rebuilding just one clinical department was replaced by the initiative to rebuild the whole existing old hospital. Obviously, neither the project owners nor the public realized, that not only the size of the MOE but the underlying initiative had changed. If they had noticed this change, a restart of the MOE including a new discussion of the MOE-initiative might have prevented the disaster.

2. Assessing Project Management Capacity

The problem in question may be illustrated by an episode which could be observed during the *"Columbus"* research project, an empirical study of innovative decision-making in Germany in the 1960s. A medium-sized brewery experienced extraordinary delays in deciding on its first installation of EDP equipment. A detailed analysis showed that the brewery was actually engaged in two innovations. Beside the EDP installation, a decision on rebuilding the bottle cellar – one of the core facilities of a brewery – was pending. The capacity of senior management to analyze and to decide on both issues was limited. Only five decision-makers (two members of the executive board, two assistant managers, and a head clerk) were involved. Both decisions were delayed and problems increased until the company realized that their management capacity was simply too small to handle two complex decisions simultaneously. The management finally gave precedence to the bottle cellar and the decision on the EDP installation was postponed. After the completion of the first investment decision, and once the full management capacity was engaged in the EDP decision, the process experienced no further delays and could be finished in time.

Close observance of capacity restrictions is day-to-day work of the shop-floor management. These restrictions are often disregarded in complex decision-making processes and also in MOEs. Remember that the City of Vienna, while acting as a project owner to the university hospital, also operated some other huge MOEs: the Vienna International Center (UNO-City), the Conference Center, the subway and other public transportation projects, the Danube recreation area, as well as several bridges. Therefore, our primary concern refers to the *capacity of project owners*. If project owners take their role seriously, they not only have to contribute to the funding of the MOE but also to their management capacity. Individuals nominated to represent project owners in the project company should have enough authority to cover the whole range of interests of the project owners, thus preventing project management, contractors, or users benefiting from conflicting interests of project owners. The official representatives should also be the only ones to make public comments on the MOE in order to avoid contradictory information on MOE goals or goal achievement to the general public.

The project owners' capacity must be seen in relation to the capacity of other project participants. Furthermore, the extent of the delegation of project activities has to be considered. At the Games in Lake Placid delegating the construction responsibility to a general contractor proved to be a success. In the case of the Vienna Hospital, the delegation of the planning function to a special company (APAK) failed completely. Whereas the general contractor in Lake Placid had sufficient construction experience, the APAK in Vienna was overtaxed by the responsibility of coordinating the planning activities. Therefore, the availability of sufficient MOE management capacity has to be ensured *before* an MOE is started. If the capacity is not provided until the MOE is under way, this will inevitably cause delays and consequently other problems associated with long-term undertakings.

> The lesson for the future is that project owners have only limited MOE management capacity which cannot be enlarged within a short period of time.

If project owners intend to undertake several MOEs simultaneously, *multi-project-management procedures* will become necessary (King/Cleland 1988, pp.200; Archibald 1992, pp.136, Harrison 1992, pp.164; Nevison 2000; Hirzel 2002). They will have to define priorities, maximum overlapping rates of the different MOEs, and modes of allocation of resources. If the capacity of the project owners – including their option of delegation to a lead project owner or to external project participants (outsourcing) – does not meet the requirements of the MOE in question, adaptations will be unavoidable. One appropriate measure would be to postpone new MOEs until current MOEs are completed or newly established capacity is available. Another form of adaptation is to break the MOE down into manageable sub-projects.

II.   Minimax Versus Maximin

Minimax and maximin are well proven strategies. The maximin principle calls for *maxi*mizing the *mini*mum payoff. Conversely, the minimax principle calls for *mini*mizing the *maxi*mum loss. As MOEs are undertakings with high inherent risks and limited chances of an MOE payoff, we recommend strategies that minimize risk.

1. Limiting Risks

Looking at the results of our cases as well as the results of other studies, we realize that none of the MOEs was subject to unambitious technical goals. Quite the contrary, there were always enough driving forces to sustain or upgrade these goals. Most of the problems we observed were caused by excessive technical goals in terms of size, or quality standards, or both:

- All Olympic Games experienced an enlargement of the number of new and rebuilt facilities, of the infrastructure, and of the technical standards;
- all university hospitals and the wind energy converter GROWIAN were burdened with ambitious requirements regarding the volume and equipment of facilities (buildings, plants).

We, therefore, conclude that we are not dealing with a lack of innovative spirit or of readiness to take risk but rather with a lack of realism regarding the capability of project owners, project management, and other project participants as well as their insufficient patterns and techniques for limiting risks. Our aim cannot be to eliminate risks because risks are a characteristic of MOEs and anybody who intends to avoid risks is advised not to engage in MOEs.

> Starting MOEs is risky enough. Watch anything that is likely to increase the basic risks and ensure its containment![34]

In this context, the *Kiss-rule* is the only suitable advice for MOEs. Engineers may oppose this because they are afraid it may hinder technical progress. On the other hand, nothing is more detrimental to technical progress than failures owing to excessive technical goals and technical monsters produced to meet these goals.[35]

The following principles may help to make the concept of limiting risks more applicable to the management of MOEs:

(1) cut time,
(2) add responsibility,
(3) break down MOEs, and
(4) question optimism.

---

[34] "In reality, the world of megaproject preparation and implementation is a highly risky one where things happen only with a certain probability and rarely turn out as originally intended" (Flyvberg et al. 2003, p.6); they, therefore, ask for risk management plans (pp.81).

[35] The commission of inquiry into the cost of the Olympics in Montreal 1976, criticized the organizers for the Velodrome which they called "... an extravagant work out of all proportion to Olympic requirements and the post-Games needs of the City" (Malouf et al. 1980, Vol. II, p.344).

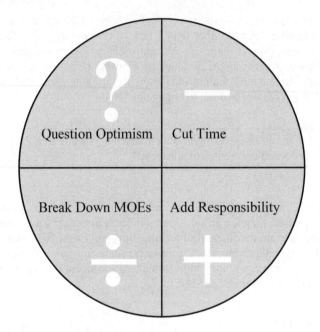

Fig. 67. Principles of Limiting Risks for MOEs

(1) The *"cut time principle"* is first on our list. Cutting time for project completion is likely to decrease the number of changes to technical goals and basic designs. Time pressure is undoubtedly the reason for a relatively good performance of the Olympic Games. Preventing changes has favorable effects on the complexity and consistency of technical goals and basic designs, even when strong driving forces are present (remember the influence of planning architects on the tent-shaped roof in Munich as well as on other facilities).

The cut time principle helps to prevent the mutually unbalancing of goal formulation and basic design. We have repeatedly shown that changes can trigger an extremely negative chain of reactions.

Time pressure may also help to enforce an early establishment of the project company and to accelerate the feed-back of actual as against planned goal achievement. Nevertheless, we have to take into account that time pressure may be misused as an argument to prevent the search for alternatives and the (necessary) reformulation of the basic design, as in the case of the tent-shaped roof (Olympic Games in Munich). In general, these negative effects are by far outweighed by the positive effects of time pressure on goal achievement.

Finally, it has proven easier to engage top managers for undertakings with a predetermined time schedule, such as the Olympic Games, than for undertakings of unlimited duration – another argument for the cut time principle.

(2) The *"add responsibility principle"* is geared to the driving forces just as the cut time-principle and is furthermore supposed to ensure the latter. The matching

of task, authority, and responsibility is a basic requirement in general and we have every reason to believe that it also holds true for MOEs. Nevertheless, in our sample individuals or institutions often influenced MOEs without having adequate responsibility. This applies especially to experts (like planning architects) and users. The point is not to exclude them (or their knowledge) from MOEs but to make them responsible for the consequences of their recommendations. There are several possibilities to generate responsibility:

- The responsibility of planning experts should be extended to cover the crucial events during the completion phase; other supplementary measures like success-based contracting may be employed too.
- The responsibility of users can be secured by their formal involvement in the project team and in the decision committees (e.g. on the boards of project companies).
- The decision to start or to continue MOEs should be based on the willingness of private investors (e.g. contractors) to participate in a public-private partnership with at least one third of the total funds needed (Flyvberg et al. 2003, pp.120).

We believe that the formal responsibility of experts for the success of MOEs in general and their (at least) factual responsibility for the consequences of their recommendations and decisions in particular will work against their attitude to shift risks at the project owners' expense.

The add responsibility principle refers not only to external project participants but also to the project management itself. Joint decision-making may be beneficial in the phases of information processing and evaluation of alternatives. The final decisions, however, should be made on the basis of the responsibility of individuals. There has to be one person who is responsible for the whole MOE. The absence of a general manager means a lack of management capacity. The preparations for the Games in Munich and Lake Placid improved significantly after a general manager had been appointed.

Individual responsibility is relevant for project ownership, too. Entrusting only one project owner with full responsibility for advising and controlling the project management has proved to be advantageous in the case of the Munich Hospital.

Turnover in the management positions may result in a loss of responsibility. The Vienna Hospital is a striking example of this problem. Some turnover was due to incompetent or corrupt managers, some resulted from the restructuring of the project management company necessitated by failures in the MOE process. The recruitment of highest skilled top managers is recommended in order to prevent turnover in top management positions and a shift of responsibility.

(3) The *"break down MOEs principle"* basically rules out the performance of huge and complex projects in a one-step mode. The MOE should be broken down in a way similar to large companies which operate successfully on the basis of organizational units like divisions. This breakdown makes for a better control of the various components of the project. There are various options available for breaking down an MOE (see Chapter H.III.2).

Breaking down MOEs must not be mistaken for opposition to large undertakings in general. The reason for project splitting is to increase the chance of successfully managing huge undertakings by concentrating on less complex sub-projects. Creating sub-projects can also be interpreted as a special means of complying with the cut time principle. Feed-back is received earlier and will be more reliable because actual data and not just estimates of goal achievement (which are always subject to disputes) are available. Last but not least, quick wins are much more likely to be achieved.

(4) The *"question optimism principle"* refers to the numerous examples of the bias towards overoptimism in MOEs (with regard to overcoming the difficulties of the technical goals, meeting the time schedule and the budget, and raising enough funds for MOEs). Generally speaking, the optimism is based on the assumption that the project risk is tolerable. This kind of optimism encourages project participants not only to take the initial risks (which are unavoidable) but also to shift the risks by enlarging the technical goals in quantity and quality in the life of the project.

In reality there is a variety of reasons for (over-)optimism: Buy-in strategies, insufficient knowledge, and long-established procedures, to mention just a few. As it seems almost impossible to destroy the roots of overoptimism, the only chance for project owners and project management to deal with this problem is to examine it thoroughly. We explicitly call for the questioning of optimism and not for its rejection. Suppressing optimism is not a suitable pattern for undertakings like MOEs since they always require some entrepreneurial spirit. In addition, rejections usually have to be justified more seriously than mere doubts, thus calling for an expertise which may not be available at that time.

The following questions are supposed to impede the enlargement of technical goals:
- Are the initial and additional requirements justified?
- Are alternative basic designs (less complex, cheaper) available?
- Can the basic design be broken down?
- What consequences for goal achievement have changes of the basic design?
- Are there other (pessimistic) opinions and estimates?
- How are other project owners performing; have they performed well?

If project owners get accustomed to questioning project management and project management practices questioning external participants, their answers and recommendations will be comprehensive (including optimistic, pessimistic, and even worst-case scenarios) and better justified.[36]

---

[36] An expert study on the Olympic Winter Games in Bern 2010 (Switzerland) predicts high risks of the Games especially concerning the financial goals and the long-term image effects (Arbeitsgemeinschaft 2002). Flyvberg et al. (2003, p.68) agree with this skepticism: "Even for a giant investment such as the Channel tunnel, five years after the tunnel's opening there were very few and very small impacts on the wider economy. The potential impacts on the directly affected regions were found to be mainly negative".

2. Learning in MOEs as a Tool for Limiting Risks

Many MOEs have experienced disasters because of the absence of learning transfers: Superprojects "... are so different from one another that no learning factor or experience curve can yet be applied to them" (Magee 1982, p.4)[37]. This phenomenon was one of the main reasons for our study. Before going into a more detailed analysis of this topic the various types of learning in MOEs have to be systemized (see Kotnour 1999).

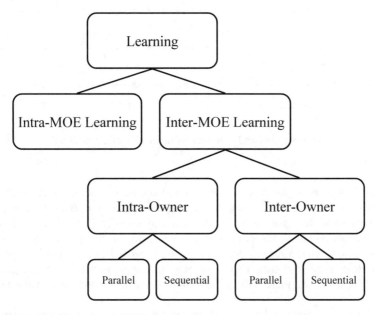

Fig. 68. Types of Learning in MOEs

(1) *Intra-MOE learning* refers to learning within a specific MOE. Although no comprehensive analysis of this topic was carried out in our study, there are several indicators of its effectiveness:

- The goal framework of the Munich Hospital was reformulated after technical goals had proven too ambitious compared to time and financial goals.
- Since joint decision-making had failed to work effectively, the position of a general manager was established at the Games in Munich and Lake Placid.
- Senior project management of the Munich Games realized that joint responsibility for planning and construction supervision, which was intended for some facilities, was more effective than divided responsibility (as in the case of the main facilities).

---

[37] Concerning cost underestimation and overrun, Flyvberg et al. (2003, p.16) state: "No learning seems to take place".

- Project owners and planning experts realized that more than two steps of completion would be favorable for university hospitals.

The NASA project "Mercury" is a very impressive example of intra-project learning (Swenson et al. 1966, pp.638, see Fig. 69):

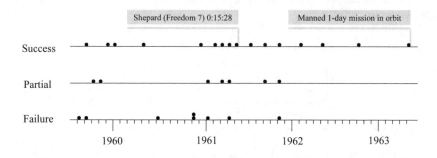

Fig. 69. Failure, Partial Success, and Full Success in the Life of the NASA Project "Mercury"

(2) Project owners and project management should not blindly rely on the effectiveness of intra-MOE learning but should also try to gain *inter-MOE experience*. Inter-MOE learning refers to the learning transfer from other MOEs. If MOEs are carried out by the same project owner, we call this process intra-owner learning. Inter-owner learning deals with MOEs carried out by different project owners. Both, intra- and inter- owner learning may apply to parallel and sequential MOEs. In most cases, there will be a combination of intra- and inter-owner learning.

Similar to intra-project learning, there are some cases of remarkable learning transfers as well as some notable examples of ignorance in inter-project learning, like repeatedly delaying the establishment of the project company or insisting on top managers from public authorities without adequate expertise.

Intra-owner learning in parallel MOEs was well represented in our study. Parallel, in this context, means that a project owner is engaged in two or more MOEs at the same time. The State of Bavaria, for example, was simultaneously engaged in the Olympic Games and in the Munich Hospital. The City of Vienna, one of the two project owners of the university hospital, was, at the same time, project owner of other MOEs (Vienna International Conference Center, the subway, the Danube recreation area, etc.). In all these cases no significant learning transfer from one MOE to the other could be detected. Maybe the project owners were not even aware of the chance to gain experience from simultaneous project ownership.

Our sample also enabled us to investigate *intra-owner learning in sequential MOEs*.

- Innsbruck (1964 and 1976) and Lake Placid (1932 and 1980) hosted the Olympic Games twice. Martinowsky (1987, pp.233), who analyzed the Innsbruck

Games, observed learning transfers regarding the achievement of technical and financial goals (i.e. limitation of initial technical goals, more reliable cost estimates, establishment of cost limits). The improvement of the post-Olympic (permanent) operation, though, was rather disappointing.

- The State government of Bavaria recognized the problem of having top politicians as representatives in project companies and excluded them from similar positions in the future.
- The experience gained from GROWIAN, which proved to be a failure, facilitated the successful construction of wind energy converters of moderately reduced dimensions like AEOLUS II (1994).
- The City government of Munich intended to draw on its experience from sequential projects, even though the MOEs were different in nature. The idea was to engage the project management and staff of the Olympic construction company (OBG) for planning and completing the new international airport in Munich. The intention failed because of extraordinary delays in the pre-project phase of the new airport caused by environmental opposition to the MOE.

Generally, we have observed that intra-owner learning transfer is very limited if MOEs differ significantly. The positive experience of the Austrian Federal and state authorities with project companies in the field of highway construction, for instance, could not be passed on to the Vienna Hospital.

Our sample included two cases of *inter-owner learning in parallel MOEs*: the Munich and Vienna Hospitals.

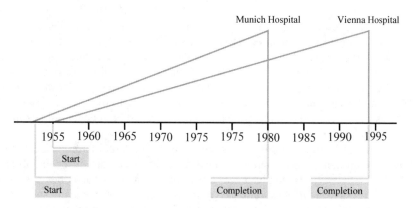

Fig. 70. Learning from Parallel MOEs (Inter-Owner Learning, Munich and Vienna Hospitals)

Both hospitals (as well as the hospital in Aachen, Germany) are block-type buildings but show noticeable differences in size, type of location, and socio-political environment. These differences may have impeded mutual observation and imitation. We do know that participants of the Vienna Hospital made some efforts to gain experience from the project management of the Munich Hospital. Since these efforts were made only after the big scandal in Vienna and were, furthermore, initiated by the opposition party, their effect was extremely limited.

Inter-owner learning in sequential MOEs offers better chances for learning transfer. Not only the continuous planning and completion process but also the overall (final) performances of previous MOEs can be observed and analyzed. Imitation is particularly feasible if MOE goals are identical or similar. The Olympic Games allow for this type of learning, with Innsbruck and Lake Placid offering the additional chance of intra-owner learning.

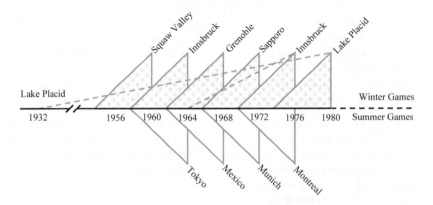

Fig. 71. Learning from Sequential MOEs (Inter-Owner Learning, Olympic Games)

Olympic Games are awarded six years before the actual event. This enables the hosts of Games to establish effective procedures for observing and analyzing all actions of their predecessors. In our cases, there were some explicit signs that suggested imitation. Delayed decisions at the Munich Games, for example, were justified by "waiting for developments in Mexico" (the hosting city of the Games in 1968), and board members were often found traveling to other Games sites. Owing to strict security measures, the Montreal Games suffered no causalities like the terror attack in Munich.

Additional learning is possible by studying the reports of former hosts to the IOC. Recommendations offered by hosts to their successors differ in substance. The Lake Placid hosts, for instance, dealt with a lot of minor issues concerning protocol affairs. Their most valuable (negative) experience, the insufficient expertise of the project management, however, was not mentioned in their reports.

By looking at the development of the Games, we can observe a change of their goals and their goal achievement. This may be interpreted as a learning process which, however, is not linear and continuous but erratic and selective like "pilgrim's steps" (two steps forward, one step back).

The Lake Placid hosts were fully aware of the fact that the whole history of the Olympics is losing money (see D.II.1). They reacted – in view of the negative results of the Games in Sapporo 1972 and Innsbruck 1976 – by inventing and introducing new funding methods. The marketing department tried different promotion methods, and the revenues from selling the TV rights made a remarkable contribution to the overall budget. Lake Placid certainly paved the way for following Olympic Games. The Los Angeles Games in 1984 and the Calgary Games in 1988 were the first to make the Olympic Games a profitable business.

Gradually, the long-established rule of technical overachievement and financial failure changed in favor of the financial goals. This resulted in the (temporary) underachievement of technical goals for the initial operation at the Games in Lake Placid with poor housing standards and disastrous transportation systems. Yet, the poor housing standards were compensated by avoiding "Olympic ruins" left behind by the Olympic Games in Mexico and Squaw Valley, for instance. Hosts of future Olympic Games will have to improve the balance of overall goal achievement with a special emphasis on high performances in technical as well as financial areas and the balance of initial and permanent operation.

III.   Benefits of Indirect Cost Management

There are two different options to influence project costs: the direct and the indirect cost management. Literature has focused on *direct cost management.* It calls for making reliable first estimates and for establishing effective *cost limits and target costing* from the beginning (for an overview see Kharbanda et al. 1987; Nicolini et al. 2000; Kerzner 2001, pp.813).

> "The most important point of all, we believe, is a realization of the profound significance of those first, early estimates of time and cost, especially when they are used for the authorization of funds. Those who authorize the money, whether it be a Board of Directors or a government department, inevitably look to and take those first figures as their standard of reference in all subsequent discussion. It is of no use saying later that 'it was only an estimate', that not enough time had been spent on development, that the scope had been changed" (Kharbanda/Stallworthy 1983, pp.257, see also p.236).

At the Games in Munich, an exact cost limit of €103m for the main Olympic facilities was established but not announced in the invitation for design bids. A prominent member of the project company board was right to ask how architects were supposed – without any target costs – to present a design which matched the estimated figure. Only a few years later, the same failure happened to the Games in Montreal because no constraint of time or money was placed on the architect (Malouf et al. 1980, p.326).

Another problem in this context are *poor cost reporting standards,* caused by the dominance of technical aspects in innovative undertakings and the tendency to label administrative procedures as secondary desk work. Flyvberg et al. (2003, p.20) come to the conclusion: "Don't trust cost estimates". The lack of comprehensive cost information (concerning estimated as well as actual costs) encourages the step-by-step enlargement of projects. The requirements of an effective direct cost management are:

- Cost reports should be available *at the time of occurrence* rather than at the date of completion. This requirement cannot be met without accurately formulating technical goals and basic designs and without accurately recording their changes (early establishment and regular update of cost reporting systems).
- *Comprehensive cost reporting* calls for considering all relevant cost items and events. Overhead costs (i.e. costs for site installation, project management, external consultants and experts, construction supervision, official approval procedures, etc.) are often forgotten in cost estimates. At the Munich Games overhead costs amounted to about 15% of construction costs. The requirement of comprehensive cost definition and reporting also includes the *costs of permanent operation*. The minimum requirement is to specify operation procedures and operation standards (e.g. service standards in a university hospital) which may serve as a basis for estimating the costs of operation & maintenance.
- The requirement of *realistic cost estimates* includes the development of pessimistic scenarios. The singularity of MOEs cannot be invoked as an excuse for ignoring the restricted likelihood of goal achievement. By combining the approach of limiting risks with the opportunities of learning transfer, MOE management can easily create scenarios of different goal achievements as a basis for realistic goal formulation.

Examples of different levels of achievement of financial goals are given in the following table:

Project	Average Cost Overrun	Comments
R&D Projects	50%	see Schröder 1980, p.647
Projects, Volume Less Than $1 bn	60%	see Morris 1982, p.158
Projects, Volume More Than $1 bn	150%	see Morris 1982, p.158
Nuclear Power Plants	184%	see Kharbanda/Stallworthy 1983, p.144, average of Figure 9.1
SST Aircraft "Concorde"	1,100%	see Kharbanda/Stallworthy 1983, pp.78

Table 31. Examples of Cost Overruns[38]

Knowledge about the range of cost overruns of past MOEs cannot justify poor or unreliable cost estimates or superficial cost management but can serve as information to project owners on the potential risks they are taking. It also justifies the permanent questioning of what has been done and what can be done to reduce risks. It is the responsibility of project management to make project owners aware of risks and to resist risky shift.

---

[38] Norris (1971) could not find an effect of R&D-project size on estimate accuracy. A survey of studies on cost overruns concerning military-systems projects is given by Rüssel (1992), pp.272.

There are some objections to direct cost management, though. Disregarding financial goals compared to other – in particular technical – goals, is the most serious objection. This disregard cannot be compensated by sophisticated accounting and recording procedures like PERT-cost, checklists, and benefit-cost-analyses but by a special management attitude which clearly expresses the willingness to influence costs. The design-to-cost concept (DTC) would be a first step in the right direction, but remains nothing more than an intention unless project management gears all its decisions (especially its decisions on technical goals) to this concept. Therefore, fixation of cost limits cannot be effective without the commitment of the project management to oppose to any enlargement of financial goals. This commitment must also appear credible to other project participants. If cost limits are repeatedly adjusted, project participants will probably have doubts about such a commitment.

The problems of direct cost management turn the attention to *indirect cost management.*[39] The underlying assumption of this measure is that ultimately nobody intends to increase costs. Cost increases are considered to be a consequence of changing other goals. Consequently, indirect cost management aims at concentrating on the determinants of cost increases ("cost drivers"), i.e. the enlargement of technical goals and the absence of time pressure.

Avoiding the enlargement of technical goals is one of the most challenging tasks of managing MOEs. If the initial technical goals call for the maximization of or adherence to up-to-date technical standards, or the adaptation to all users' requirements project management has to deal with a "built-in" enlargement. As repeatedly pointed out, even duly justified enlargements are crucial for MOEs with regard to schedule and cost overruns. Managing change is challenging but not impossible as we have learned from MOEs like the Apollo Program and the Munich Hospital. The following list of measures is based on lessons learnt from our empirical studies of MOEs:

- The first measure to prevent change is to fix and to declare an ultimate deadline for changes. Once this *"frozen zone"* has been reached, the reaction of project management to change requirements, in principle, should be "no".
- In the "frozen zone" the *burden of proof is shifted* to individuals and institutions demanding change. It is their responsibility to prove that the required change will not have negative effects on the overall performance of the MOE.
- *Change cannot be prevented by cost arguments alone.* Owing to technological progress many components of MOEs may improve their cost-benefit-relationship by offering the same or even improved performance at lower costs. However, such cost arguments do not always reflect the interdependence of MOE components. Due to this interdependence changes often cause replanning which may be extremely time consuming. Therefore, the widespread practice of replacing a more expensive component by a less expensive one should be treated with the greatest caution.
- In the case of the Apollo Program a separate *change control board* was established to ensure those changes which were necessary for project success and to

---

[39] "Cost cannot be controlled in isolation." (Kharbanda et al. 1987, pp 18)

prevent those which would be likely to cause MOE failures, especially schedule overruns (see Seamans/Ordway 1977, pp.290).

- The *drive for change can be reduced* by a strong and permanent involvement of users and other potential change proponents in the decision-making process. This involvement should be combined with transparent procedures of generating and selecting technological alternatives and their consequences in terms of time and costs. The Olympic village of the Games in Munich stands for successful selection as well as high transparency.
- It is important to *record* the individuals or institutions initiating changes of technical goals. Recording should include type, amount, date, and reasons for the required change together with comments by the project management. The project management should also be authorized by the project owners to make these requests known to the general public.

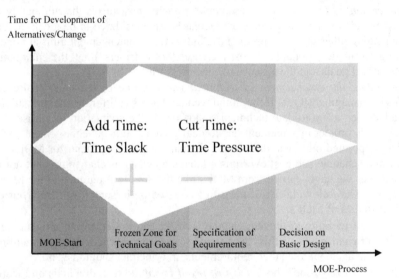

Fig. 72. Milestones in the Time Management Process

We doubt, however, that indirect cost management by means of restricting changes of the technical goals is sufficient. To be effective, it has to be combined with *time management measures*. Time management measures are much harder to oppose to than measures on a purely technical level, especially if project management and project owners lack technical expertise. Generating time pressure is one of the key problems of MOE management because it requires different attitudes in different phases of MOEs: In the beginning, project management has to provide sufficient time for developing alternatives to the basic design. After the decision on the basic design, further changes are to be prevented. This can be done by creating time pressure.

The Games in Munich are an example of unsuccessful time management resulting from inadequate "add time" and "cut time" approaches. In the initial phase of the project there was not enough time to generate alternative designs for the Olympic facilities. Some contractors (including architects) urged project management to make premature decisions on the design and to sign their contracts. Project management was not strong enough to resist this pressure, although critical voices called for more time to obtain further information on existing alternatives and to develop additional ones. After severe problems with the initial design occurred, there was no more time left (because of the fixed date of completion) to search for alternative solutions. The premature choice led to heavy cost overruns. In contrast to the early fixation of the basic design, requirement specifications were delayed, although project management pressed for fixing them in time. The first frozen zone, set for summer 1968, could not be adhered to because new studies and analyses were required. In particular, the Munich hosts wanted to wait for the Olympic Games in Mexico in 1968 to learn from these Games. In the case of GROWIAN project management – in a way similar to the Munich Games – allowed only one year for the first project phase. A longer period would have been necessary to thoroughly analyze the feasibility of the ambitious technical goals.

Traditional time management techniques offer very limited potential for the type of time control necessary for MOE success. At the Games in Munich a sophisticated network caused a lot of frustration among the members of the decision committee because planned and actual data rarely matched. A workable phase scheme for MOEs has to secure the early and close involvement of contractors in order to generate alternatives and sufficient time for decisions on technical goals, the basic designs, and the specification of user requirements. Furthermore, it should provide for loops in the initial decision process in order to allow for a reformulation of initial goals until the frozen zone begins.

Our knowledge of how to produce time pressure is still fairly limited because the prevailing traditional attitude seeks to avoid time pressure as it is assumed to increase costs. But even in the face of limited knowledge, a new attitude towards this important issue may be adopted. It includes opposition to all kinds of detours around the problem of time pressure. At the Vienna Hospital, for instance, the project management was actually proud to offer change options to users by means of "flexible planning": They provided "the most flexible planning" in order to continue the construction work and to meet all the unknown future requirements which had to be expected (Kurier, Vienna, 1978-12-07 and 1979-03-01). The price of this flexible planning was high. Completion costs were much higher compared to traditional procedures, and the duration of planning and completion was multiplied. Taking a formal approach, project owners are responsible to establish a tight system of time goals and to insist on their achievement. Obviously, it makes a notable difference whether time pressure is artificial and purely based on the interests and interventions of project owners or whether it is an inherent element of MOEs from the beginning as with Olympic Games. Close attention by project owners and project management to the time factor helps to generate time pressure. In addition, incentives for on time performance or penalties for schedule overruns may be included in the contracts.

Since basic techniques are not apt to create time pressure, additional management action is necessary. Based on the assumption of limited capability of the project management, measures with long-term or permanent effects on the driving forces of change are favorable. Time pressure can be created by *establishing competitive situations* (Murphy et al. 1974, pp.98, report negative effects of competitive situations). With at least three outstanding university hospitals under construction in Central Europe in the 1950s and 1960s (Aachen, Munich, Vienna), this was a unique chance for the project owners involved to encourage the project management and the participants to be the first to finish completion. But even without immediate competition, time pressure can be generated. President J.F. Kennedy, for example, announced that the "man-on-the-moon" project, started in the early 60s, would be completed within one decade. This challenge was effective in generating enough time pressure to achieve the time goal. Armstrong made his first step on the moon on the July 21, 1969.

IV.   Internal and External Reporting Systems

MOEs are subject to external and internal reporting for different reasons. External attention results from the great number of participants involved and from public ownership. MOE failures also attract the attention and the engagement of the socio-political environment. The importance of internal reporting systems is related to the size of the project which may impede the provision of sufficient and consistent information for all project participants, especially for project owners, contractors, and users. Therefore, reporting systems are not only a tool but also a separate field of project management activity. It is a crucial element due to its influence on the behavior of internal and external participants. Different reporting systems and techniques may be necessary for different groups of participants.

The Olympic Games in Munich as well as the Vienna Hospital have provided some insights into the problems of reporting. Our considerations focus on two major aspects:

- What should be reported? Is it preferable to report the optimistic or the pessimistic version?
- When should it be reported? Is it preferable to report at the earliest or the latest date possible?

The reporting approach should truthfully *reflect the basic risk* of MOEs. To promise that an MOE will be completed within a minimum period of time, at minimum costs, and with the highest technical standards is not only impossible but would raise questions as to the seriousness of the project management and project owners. MOEs require a cautious reporting attitude covering the whole range of expected project outcomes, including optimistic and pessimistic scenarios, especially in the early planning phases.

The reporting approach should be in line with the project management's capability *to influence the MOE activities and its goal achievement.* If, for instance, the time goal is fixed from the beginning and project owners have made a commitment to highly sophisticated technical goals, project management should not cause future disappointments by stating cost limits. In this case, project management should confine itself to goal achievement levels (ranges) and reporting activities which they are actually able and willing to answer for.

Project staff and project owners should be informed as early and as realistically as possible. The members of the project company board at the Games in Munich, for example, blamed project management not only for the cost overruns of the tent-shaped roof but also for belated and overoptimistic information. Delayed and incomplete reporting procedures can cause severe tensions in the relationship of project management and project owners and may result in poor performance and demotivation of project staff. There is some risk that reports addressed to representatives of project owners are misused for individual purposes or political issues. If problems like these occur, they ought to be discussed with the chief representatives of the project owners but cannot be used as a sweeping excuse for inadequate reporting procedures.

Information to contractors should be similar to that for the project staff, especially reports to key players (like planning architects and general contractors). By entering into contracts, a project company establishes close ties which cannot be loosened without seriously endangering the success of the undertaking. If the right contractors have been selected, there is no need for a reserved attitude but rather a strong demand for early and complete information on the development of relevant project components. If the selection was questionable, restrictive reporting systems will not improve but worsen the contractors' performance.

Reports to the general public should be cautious, consistent, and definite. The general public usually lacks the necessary experience to understand and to evaluate contradictory information. Therefore, it is very risky to disclose information without a reliable basis. The project management of the Apollo Program obviously followed this advice when costs were cautiously estimated at: "...anywhere between $20 and $40 billion." Generally, overoptimisc reporting to the general public does not pay off. It may delay but cannot prevent public questioning. Experience has shown that it is next to impossible to explain the reasons for failures to an inexperienced audience without being blamed for weak performance or being accused of deliberate camouflage tactics. Poor reporting systems may also be the reason for an intensive engagement of the socio-political environment with all the potential problems discussed earlier.

Early feed-back of actual goal achievement to project management and project owners is crucial for MOE success (see Chapter K). Feed-back effects depend not only on collecting data (planned vs. actual performance) but also on their transmission and reception to key project managers. Transmission and reception may be biased by the tendency to repress unfavorable information. This holds true for both transmitters and recipients. The only chance to overcome this shortcoming in reporting is to provide for different sources, different channels, and different recipients.

Our final recommendation refers to the *professionalism of reporting systems*. Project management should not be content with an information system[40] that supplies good news by chance and bad news only in the face of a crisis. It should rather seek to establish a *public relations system* which will provide information on the difficulties of technological innovations as well as the potential benefits for users. Successful public relations for MOEs is more than window-dressing on glossy paper but rather continuous and consistent information on the overall progress of the MOE. The success and failure of projects may depend on the performance of public relations activities.

V.   The Futility of Final Words

Our final topic deals with the time and intensity of project controlling. The basic requirement for project controlling is the *early involvement of all participants*. Controlling in the traditional sense may be useful for routine processes but not for events like MOEs. Project owners and project management should not rely on their formal authority to approve or disapprove because the process of searching for and evaluating information is already prejudging the issue (see Witte's early findings on innovative and complex decision-making processes, 1969, p.493). Early involvement in MOEs is absolutely necessary, as the most crucial decisions for MOE success are decisions in the early phases.

Early involvement includes the engagement of the project management in the formulation of the goal framework, not only for motivational reasons but also to balance authority and responsibility for goal achievement. This engagement helps to press for the early formulation of a complete and balanced goal framework with ranges for the levels of goal achievement (see Chapter G). At the Games in Munich, for instance, project management failed to state its cost goals when the bids for the basic design were invited. After the project management had decided on one of the designs, cost goals had to be adjusted to the design since there was not enough time – and nobody wanted to take the risk – for inviting and evaluating new proposals.

A special type of futility refers to the procedures of *MOE auditing*. Crises are likely to initiate special auditing procedures (as in the cases of the Olympic Games in Munich and the Vienna Hospital). Audits usually cause feverish reactions by the press, eager to pick up topics which will increase their audience and the circulation of their journals. Project management and boards are tied up with audit reports and discussions (often public). They ultimately result in delays or even standstills of other management activities. The effects of such auditing – apart from tying up management capacity – are rather negative because auditing usually starts only after crucial and irreversible decisions have been made. Therefore, traditional auditing procedures are not only inadequate but also likely to cause control overkills. They tend to deal with minor issues instead of key factors, even when MOEs are suffering a crisis. In such a situation, the general public demands

---

[40] For a survey of project management information systems (PMIS) see Harrison 1992, pp.211

immediate action. It has been proven that short-term measures (like establishing controlling or savings committees, setting up new auditing procedures, as well as replacing senior project managers) are often insufficient with regard to their long-term effects and the long-term requirements of MOEs. The Vienna Hospital is an example of how infectious the audit virus can be.

In view of the problems of traditional auditing procedures, a new audit procedure was invented. It is called *concurrent audit* with audit activities running parallel to the MOE process. Experience with this audit procedure has not been very satisfactory so far. The question of how to sufficiently incorporate auditors and controllers into the MOE management system without adding additional bureaucracy is still open.

So far, we believe that the only way to secure the interests of project owners (and selective parts of the public) is by their early involvement in MOEs, the realistic formulation of the initial goal framework, the establishment of a clear management structure of the project company, and the proficient recruitment of project managers. Failure to meet these basic requirements will not be compensated by more auditing and controlling. Audits are a serious indication of distrust and cannot make up for the weak commitment and poor capabilities of project owners and project management.

List of Figures

List of Tables

References

Allgemeines Krankenhaus Wien (2003): Allgemeines Krankenhaus - Universitätskliniken. www.akhwien.at, 03-12-20

Arbeitsgemeinschaft Institut für Tourismuswirtschaft, Hochschule für Wirtschaft HSW, Luzern und Rütter + Partner - concertgroup, Rüschlikon (2002): Wirtschaftliche Bedeutung der Olympischen Winterspiele Berne 2010, Luzern/Rüschlikon, www.itw.ch/pdf/berne2010_bericht_n.pdf, 03/12/20

Archibald, R.D. (1992): Managing High-Technology Programs and Projects. 2nd ed., New York et al.

Armbrust, S. et al (1976): Nutzen der Windenergie. In: Energiequellen für morgen? BMFT (Ed.), Vol. III, Frankfurt

Auf der Maur, N. (1976): The Billion-Dollar Game. Jean Drapeau and the 1976 Olympics, Toronto

Baer, W.S. et al. (1976a): Analysis of Federally Funded Demonstration Projects: Supporting Case Studies. Santa Monica, CA., April 1976, R –1927-DOC

Baer, W.S. et al. (1976b): Analysis of Federally Funded Demonstration Projects: Final Report. Executive Summary, Santa Monica, CA., R-1925/6-Doc

Baker, B.N. et al. (1988): Factors Affecting Project Success. In: Cleland, D.I./King, W.R (Ed.), Project Management Handbook, 2nd ed., New York, 902-919

Baker, B.N. et al. (1988): Project Management in the Public Sector: Success and Failure Patterns Compared to Private Sector Projects. In: Cleland, D.I./King, W.R., Project Management Handbook, 2nd ed., New York, 920-934

Baker, B.N./Wilemon, D.L. (1977): Managing Complex Programs: A Review of Major Research Findings. In: R&D Management Vol. 8, 23-28

Barrie, D.S./Paulson, B.C. Jr. (1992): Professional Construction Management, Including C.M., Design Construct, and General Contracting. 3rd ed., New York et al.

Baumgartner, J.S. (Ed., 1979): Systems Management, Washington D.C.

Bundesrechnungshof (Ed., 1972): Unterrichtung durch den Bundesrechnungshof. Deutscher Bundestag, 7. Wahlperiode, Drucksache 7/8, Sachgebiet 63, Bonn

Bundesrechnungshof (Ed., 1996): Bericht nach § 88 Abs. 2 BHO über den Stand der Vorbereitungsmaßnahmen für die Entscheidung über den Bau der Magnetschwebebahnverbindung Berlin - Hamburg (TRANSRAPID). Frankfurt

Bundestagsdrucksache (1977): Zweite Fortschreibung des Energieprogramms der Bundesregierung (8/1357, Tz 51). Bonn

Catherwood, D.W./Van Kirk, R.L. (1992): The Complete Guide to Special Event Management. Business Insights, Financial Advice, and Successful Strategies from Ernst & Young, Advisors to the Olympics, the Emmy Awards and the PGA Tour. New York et al.

City of Boston/Town of Brookline (2003): Massachusetts Environmental Policy Act. (MEPA) Process, www.muddyriverproject.org/DEIR/fig1-5.pdf, 03-12-20

Cleland, D.I. (1964): Why Project Management. In: Business Horizons, Winter 1964, 81-88

Cleland, D.I./King, W.R. (1988): System Analysis and Project Management. 3rd ed., Auckland et al.

Crompton, J. (1995): Texas A&M University: Economic Impact Analysis of Sports Facilities and Events: Eleven Sources of Misapplication. In: Journal of Sport Management, 14-35

Cyert, R.M./March, J.G. (1992): A Behavioral Theory of the Firm. 2nd ed., Cambridge, Mass./Oxford

Eichberger, W./Schlempp, W. (1977): Randbemerkungen des planenden Architekten. In: Goerke, H. (Ed.), Klinikum Großhadern der Ludwig-Maximilians-Universität München, 61-73

Eisenhardt, K.M.(1989): Building Theories from Case Study Research. In: Academy of Management Review, Special Forum on Theory Building, 14.Jg., No. 4 (October), 532-550

Endres, A. et al. (1988): Bau der großen Windenergieanlage GROWIAN mit einer elektrischen Leistung von 3 MW, Schlussbericht. Hamburg

Fenneberg, G. (1979): Kosten- und Terminabweichungen im Entwicklungsbereich. Eine empirische Analyse, Berlin

Flyvberg, B. et al. (2003): Megaprojects and Risk. An Anatomy of Ambition, Cambridge

Fowler, T.V. (1982): Project Financing. In: Kelley, A.J. (Ed.), New Dimensions of Project Management, Lexington, Mass/Toronto, 97-105

Gaddis, P.O. (1959): The Project Manager. In: Harvard Business Review. May/June, 89-97

Gemünden, H.G. (1990): Erfolgsfaktoren des Projektmanagements. Eine kritische Bestandsaufnahme der empirischen Untersuchungen, in: Projektmanagement, No.1/2, 4-15

Goerke, H. (Ed., 1974): Klinikum Großhadern der Ludwig-Maximilians-Universität München. Festschrift aus Anlaß der I. Teilinbetriebnahme, Munich

Goerke, H. (Ed., 1977): Klinikum Großhadern der Ludwig-Maximilians-Universität München. Festschrift aus Anlaß der II. Teilinbetriebnahme, Munich

Grün, O. (1973): Das Lernverhalten in Entscheidungsprozessen der Unternehmung. Tübingen

Grün, O. (1975a): Beiträge zur Projektorganisation, Iss. 1: Olympische Spätlese – Schwachstellen bei der Projektierung von 15 Großbauten, Vienna (Depot DBW 77-4-4)

Grün, O. (1975b): Beiträge zur Projektorganisation, Iss. 2: Methoden zur empirischen Analyse der Projektorganisation, Vienna (Depot DBW 77-4-5)

Grün, O. (1977): Beiträge zur Projektorganisation, Iss. 3: Kosten und Kostenrechnung in der Projektorganisation, Vienna (Depot DBW 78-3-3)

Grün, O. (1981a,b): "Höhe mal Breite mal Donnerstag" – Zur Problematik von Kostenschätzungen bei Großprojekten der öffentlichen Hand. In: Journal für Betriebswirtschaft, 66–76 (Part I), 148–165 (Part II)

Grün, O. (1983): "Höhe mal Breite mal Donnerstag" – Zur Problematik von Kostenschätzungen der öffentlichen Hand. In: Journal für Betriebswirtschaft, 203–225 (Part III) mit einem Anhang von G. Paar, 226-232, und einem Nachtrag (1984), 50

Grün, O. (1985): Beiträge zur Projektorganisation, Iss. 5: Das Klinikum Großhadern – Projektbiographie und Vergleich mit dem Allgemeinen Krankenhaus Wien (AKH), Vienna (Depot DBW 85-5-1)

Grün, O. (1988): Beiträge zur Projektorganisation, Iss. 6: Die Olympischen Winterspiele 1980 in Lake Placid (USA) – Projektbiographie, Vienna (Depot DBW 88-1-4)

Hall, P. (1980): Great Planning Disasters. Berkeley/Los Angeles

Harrison, F.L. (1992): Advanced Project Management. A Structured Approach, 3rd ed., Hants

Harvard Business School (Ed., 1977): Managing the U.S. Supersonic Transport Program. Boston Mass.

Hauschildt, J. (1977): Zielbildung in innovativen Entscheidungsprozessen: Theoretische Ansätze und empirische Prüfung. Tübingen

Hausner, E. (1986): Empirische Analyse von Großprojekten der öffentlichen Hand am Beispiel der Tauernautobahn-Scheitelstrecke und Internationales Amtssitz- und Konferenzzentrum Wien. Diss., Vienna

Heinen, E. (1983): Betriebswirtschaftliche Kostenlehre. Kostentheorie und Kostenentscheidungen, 6th ed., Wiesbaden

Hirzel, M. (Ed., 2002): Multiprojektmanagement: Strategische und operative Steuerung von Projektportfolios. Frankfurt

Horwitch, M. (1979a): Managing a Colossus. In: The Wharton Magazine, Summer 1979, 34-41

Horwitch, M. (1979b): Designing and Managing Large-Scale, Public-Private Technological Enterprises: A State of the Art Review. In: Technology in Society, Vol. 1, 179-192

Horwitch, M./Prahalad, C.K. (1982): Managing Multi-Organization Enterprises: The Emerging Strategic Frontier. In: Kelley, A.J. (Ed.), New Dimensions of Project Management, Lexington, Mass./Toronto, 17-36

Hoyte, J.S. (1982): Regulatory and Socioeconomic Factors in the Siting and Construction of Major New Facilities. In: Kelley, A.J. (Ed.), New Dimensions of Project Management, Lexington, Mass./Toronto, 37-55

Jeanrenaud, C. (Ed., 1999): The Economic Impact of Sport Events. CIES Université Neuchatel

Kelley, A. J. (1982a): The New Project Environment. In: Kelley, A.J. (Ed.), New Dimensions of Project Management, Lexington/Mass./Toronto, 5-14

Kelley, A. J. (1982b): Project-Management Control: New Needs of Owner-Management. In: Kelley, A.J. (Ed.), New Dimensions of Project Management, Lexington/Mass./Toronto, 121-133

Kerzner, H. (2001): Project Management. A Systems Approach to Planning, Scheduling, and Controlling, 7th ed., New York et al.

Kharbanda, O.P. et al. (1987): Project Cost Control in Action, 2nd ed., Cambridge

Kharbanda, O.P./Stallworthy, E.A. (1983): How to Learn from Project Disasters. True-Life Stories with a Moral for Management. Aldershot, Hants

King, W.R./Cleland, D.B. (1988): Life-Cycle Management. In: Cleland, D.B./King, W.R. (Ed.), Project Management Handbook, 2nd ed., New York, 191-205

Klinikum Großhadern (2003): Zahlen auf einen Blick. www.klinikum.uni-muenchen.de/pdf/Zahlen.pdf, 03-12-20

Kontrollamt der Stadt Wien (Ed., 1980): Gebarungskontrolle. Prüfung des Auftrages und des Vergabevorganges der Planung der Betriebsorganisation für den Neubau des Wiener Allgemeinen Krankenhauses, Vienna

Kontrollamt der Stadt Wien (Ed., 1981): Bauwirtschaftlicher Prüfbericht über den Neubau des Wiener Allgmeinen Krankenhauses. Vienna

Köppl, B.J. (1979): Rüstungsmanagement und Verteidigungsfähigkeit der NATO. Munich

Kotnour, T. (1999): A Learning Framework for Project Management. In: Project Management Journal, Vol. 30, 2, 32-38

Larson, E.W./Gobeli, D.H. (1989): Significance of Project Management Structure on Development Success. In: IEEE 1989, 119-125

Lechler, T. (1997): Erfolgsfaktoren des Projektmanagements. Frankfurt et al.

Lillehammer Olympiske Organisasjonskomité AS (Ed., 1994): De XVII Olympiske Vinterleker Pa Lillehammer. Sluttrapport til Kulturdepartementet, Lillehammer

Magee, J. F. (1982): Management Challenges in the 1980s: What is ahead in Project Management. In: Kelley, A.J. (Ed.), New Dimensions of Project Management, Lexington, Mass/Toronto, 3-4

Malouf, A.H. et al. (1980): Report of the Commission of Inquiry into the Cost of the 21st Olympiad. 4 Vol., ISBN 2-551-03775-1

Martinowsky, A. (1987): Methode und Anwendung der kostenzielorientierten Effizienzanalyse zur Feststellung von Erfolgsfaktoren von Multi-Organization Enterprises (MOEs). Diss., Vienna

McClintock C.D. et al. (1979): Applying the Logic of Sample Surveys to Qualitative Case Studies: The Case Cluster Method. In: Administrative Science Quarterly, Vol. 24, No.4, 612-629

McCullough, D. (1982): The Great Bridge. New York

McEachron, N.B./Teige, P.J. (1977): Constraints on Large-Scale Technological Projects. SRI International (Ed.), Menlo Park, Files No. 77-169, 77-209

Miller, R./Lessard, D. (2000): The Strategic Management of Large Engineering Projects. Shaping Institutions, Risks, and Governance, Cambridge, Mass.

Morris, P.W.G. (1982): Project Organizations: Structures for Managing Change. In: Kelley, A.J. (Ed.), New Dimensions of Project Management, Lexington, Mass./Toronto, 155-172

Morris, P.W.G./Hough, G.H. (1993): The Anatomy of Major Projects. A Study of the Reality of Project Management, Chichester et al.

Murphy, D.C. et al (1974): Determinants of Project Success. School of Management, Boston College, (Ed.), Chestnut Hill, Mass.

Nevison, J. M. (2000): Multi-Project Management: Executing the Details of Project Portfolio (2 Parts), www.oakinc.com/pdf/multiproject.pdf, 2003-12-29

Nicolini, D. et al. (2000): Can Target Costing and Whole Life Costing be Applied in the Construction Industry?: Evidence from Two Case Studies. In: British Journal of Management, Vol. 11, 303-324

Norris, K.P. (1971): The Accuracy of Project Cost and Duration Estimates in Industrial R&D. In: R&D Management 2, 1, 25-36

Official Website of the Olympic Movement, International Olympic Committee (2002): Salt Lake City 2002, Marketingfact file, www.olympic.org

Olympia-Baugesellschaft mbH i.L. (Ed., 1973): Olympia-Bau: Eine Dokumentation der Olympia-Baugesellschaft mbH über ihre Tätigkeit in den Jahren 1967 bis 1973. Munich

Organisationskomitee der XII. Olympischen Winterspiele 1976 (Ed.,1973-1976): XII. Olympische Winterspiele Innsbruck 1976. Bulletins 1-13, Innsbruck

Organisationskomitee für die Spiele der XX. Olympiade München (Ed.): Die Organisation. Vol. 1 (1972a); Die Bauten. Vol. 2 (1972b), Munich

Persson, B. (Ed., 1979): Surviving Failures. Patterns and Cases of Project Mismanagement, Atlantic Highlands/N.J.

Pinto, J.K./Slevin, D.P. (1998): Cricital Success Factors in R&D Projects. In: Pinto, J.K. (Ed.), Project Management Handbook, San Francisco, 379-395

Preuss, H. (1999): Olympische Studien. Ökonomische Implikationen der Ausrichtung Olympischer Spiele von München 1972 bis Atlanta 1996, Auszug aus dem IV und Schlussfolgerungen, Kassel

Pulczynski, J. (1991): Interorganisationales Innovationsmanagement – eine kritische Analyse des Forschungsprojektes GROWIAN. Diss., Kiel

Rechnungshof (Ed., 1980): Bericht des Rechnungshofes über die Durchführung besonderer Akte der Gebarungsüberprüfung betreffend die Betriebsorganisationsplanung für den Neubau des Allkemeinen Krankenhauses in Wien. Vienna

Rechnungshof (Ed., 1989): Bericht über das Ergebnis der Gebarungsprüfung bei der Arbeitsgemeinschaft der Republik Österreich und der Stadt Wien für den Neubau des Allgemeinen Krankenhauses, Universitätsklinikum (ARGE-AKH). Vienna

Rechnungshof (Ed., 1995): Wahrnehmungsbericht des Rechnungshofes. Reihe Bund, Vienna, 23-47

Rechnungshof (Ed., 2003): Wahrnehmungsbericht des Rechnungshofes. Reihe Bund, Vienna, 45-70

Reich, K. (1986): Making it Happen. Peter Ueberroth and the 1984 Olympics, Santa Barbara

Reinhold, H./Scholz I. (1988): Betrieb der großen Windkraftanlage mit einer elektrischen Leistung von 3 MW. Schlussbericht, Hamburg

Ritterbush, S. W. (1982): Assessment and Management of International Project Risk. In: Kelley, A.J. (Ed.), New Dimensions of Project Management, Lexington, Mass./Toronto, 109-119

Rubenstein, A.H. et al. (1976): Factors Influencing Innovation Success at the Project Level. Research Management, Vol.5, 15-20

Rüssel, L.B. (1992): Management des Kostenrisikos von Raumfahrtprojekten. Ein Beitrag zur Beherrschung von Risiken technologisch-komplexer, öffentlich getragener Projekte. Diss., Koblenz

Sayles, L.R./Chandler, M.K. (1971): Managing Large Systems. Organization for the Future, New York

Sayles, L.R./Chandler, M.K. (1982): The Project Manager: Organizational Metronome. In: Tushman, M.L./Moore, W.L (Ed.): Readings in the Management of Innovation, Boston, 488-503

Schröder, H.-H. (1980): Fehler bei der Vorhersage der Aufwendungen für Forschungs- und Entwicklungs- (F&E-) Vorhaben – Ein Erklärungsversuch. In: Zeitschrift für betriebswirtschaftliche Forschung, Vol. 32, 646-668

Schultz, R.L. et al. (1987): Strategy and Tactics in a Process Model of Project Implementation. In: Interfaces, Vol. 17, (3) May-June, 34-46

Seamans, R.C. Jr./Ordway, F.I. (1977): The Apollo Tradition. An Object Lesson for the Management of Large-Scale Technological Endeavors, in: Interdisciplinary Science Reviews, Vol. 2, No. 4, 270-304

Slevin, D.P./Pinto, J.K. (1988): Leadership, Motivation, and the Project Manager. In: Cleland, D.I./King, W.R. (Ed.), Project Management Handbook, 2nd ed., New York, 739-770

Spilling, O. R. (1996): Mega-events als Strategie für regionale Entwicklung: Der Fall der Olympischen Spiele 1994 in Lillehammer. In: Unternehmertum und regionale Entwicklung, 321-343

Steiner, G.A./Ryan, W.G. (1968): Industrial Project Management. New York

Stewart, J.M. (1965): Making Project Management Work. In: Business Horizons, 54-68

Structurae (2003): International Database and Gallery of Structures. www.structurae.de, 03-12-20

Swenson, L.S. et al. (1966): This New Ocean. A History of Project Mercury. NASA (Ed.), Washington, D.C. (The NASA Historical Series)

Sykes, A. (1982): Reducing Neglected Risks on Giant Projects. In: Kelley, A.J. (Ed.), New Dimensions of Project Management, Lexington, Mass./Toronto, 141-151

Teigland, J. (1996): Impacts on Tourism from Mega-Events: The Case of Winter Olympic Games, Vestlandsforsking (Western Norway Research Institute), Norway

Wallack, F. (1960): Die Großglockner-Hochalpenstraße. Die Geschichte ihres Baus, 2nd ed., Vienna

Wheelwright, S.C./Clark, K.B. (1995): Leading Product Development. New York

Wildemann, H. (1982): Kostenprognosen bei Großprojekten. Stuttgart

Wilemon, D.L./Baker, B.N. (1988): Some Major Research Findings Regarding the Human Element in Project Management. In: Cleland, D.I./King, W.R (Ed.), Project Management Handbook, 2nd ed., New York, 847-866

Witte, E. (1968): Phasentheorem und Organisation komplexer Entscheidungsverläufe. In: Zeitschrift für betriebswirtschaftliche Forschung, Vol. 20, 625-647

Witte, E. (1969): Mikroskopie einer unternehmerischen Entscheidung. Bericht aus der empirischen Forschung, in: IBM-Nachrichten, Vol. 19, 490-495

Witte, E. et al. (Ed., 1988): Innovative Entscheidungsprozesse – Die Ergebnisse des Projektes „Columbus", Tübingen

Wübbenhorst, K.L. (1984): Konzept der Lebenszykluskosten. Grüsch

Wyklicky, H./Skopec, M. (Ed., 1984): 200 Jahre Allgemeines Krankenhaus in Wien, Munich

Wynant, L. (1980): Essential Elements of Project Financing. In: Harvard Business Review, May-June, 165-173

Successful Management

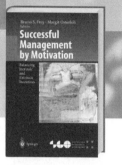

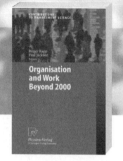